Young Muslim Women in India

This book, based on extensive, original research, details the changing lives of youth living in slum communities (*bustees*) in Kolkata (formerly Calcutta). Using young people's own photos, art and narratives, the book explores how Muslim girls and young women are contributing to, and impacted by, changing youth culture in India. We are invited into the risky world of mixed-sex dance taking place in clandestine spaces in the slums. We join young people on their journeys to find premarital romance and witness their strategic and savvy risk taking when participating in transgressive aspects of consumer culture. The book reveals how social changes in India, including greater education and employment opportunities, as well as the powerful middle-class Muslim reformist community, are impacting youth at the very local level. More than just fantasy we see that *Bollywood* is an important role model which young people consult. By carefully negotiating risks and performing multiple iden-tities inspired by modernity, globalisation and, most of all, Bollywood culture, young people actively participate in a changing India and disrupt dominant discourses about slum youth as poor victims who are excluded from social change.

Kabita Chakraborty is an Assistant Professor in the Children's Studies Program, Department of Humanities, York University, Canada.

ASAA Women in Asia Series

Editor: Louise Edwards (University of New South Wales)and Lenore Lyons (The University of Sydney)

Editorial Board:
Susan Blackburn (Monash University)
Hyaeweol Choi (The Australian National University)
Michele Ford (The University of Sydney)
Trude Jacobsen (Northern Illinois University)
Vera Mackie (University of Wollongong)
Anne McLaren (The University of Melbourne)
Mina Roces (University of New South Wales)
Dina Siddiqi (The City University of New York)
Andrea Whittaker (The University of Queensland)

Mukkuvar Women
Gender, hegemony and capitalist
transformation in a South Indian
fishing community
Kalpana Ram 1991

A World of Difference
Islam and gender hierarchy
in Turkey
Julie Marcus 1992

Purity and Communal Boundaries
Women and social change in a
Bangladeshi village
Santi Rozario 1992

Madonnas and Martyrs
Militarism and violence in
the Philippines
Anne-Marie Hilsdon 1995

Masters and Managers
A study of gender relations in
urban Java
Norma Sullivan 1995

Matriliny and Modernity
Sexual politics and social change in
rural Malaysia
Maila Stivens 1995

Intimate Knowledge
Women and their health in
North-east Thailand
Andrea Whittaker 2000

Women in Asia
Tradition, modernity
and globalisation
*Louise Edwards and
Mina Roces (eds) 2000*

**Violence against Women in
Asian Societies**
Gender inequality and technologies
of violence
*Lenore Manderson and
Linda Rae Bennett (eds) 2003*

Women's Employment in Japan
The experience of part-time workers
Kaye Broadbent 2003

Young Muslim Women in India

Bollywood, identity and changing
youth culture

Kabita Chakraborty

Routledge
Taylor & Francis Group

LONDON AND NEW YORK

First published 2016
by Routledge

2 Park Square, Milton Park, Abingdon, Oxfordshire OX14 4RN
711 Third Avenue, New York, NY 10017

Routledge is an imprint of the Taylor & Francis Group, an informa business

First issued in paperback 2017

British Library Cataloguing in Publication Data
A catalogue record for this book is available from the British Library

Library of Congress Cataloging in Publication Data
Chakraborty, Kabita.
Young muslim women in India/Kabita Chakraborty.
   pages cm. -- (Asaa women in Asia series; 44)
   Includes bibliographical references and index.
      1. Muslim youth--India--Social conditions--21st century. 2. Muslim
women--India--Conduct of life. 3. Poor youth--India--Social conditions--
21st century. 4. Social change--India. I. Title.
   HQ799.8.I4C43 2016
   305.48'6970540905--dc23
               2015014488

ISBN: 978-0-415-56324-6 (hbk)
ISBN: 978-1-138-47699-8 (pbk)

Typeset in Times New Roman
by Taylor & Francis Books

Contents

List of figures

Acknowledgement

I am indebted to the young women of the *bustees* who have allowed me to share their lives, and to include the details of their adventures, heartbreaks and *timepass* in the context of this book. Without their trust and generous participation this book would not be possible. I am also grateful to all the young men, parents, community elders and everyone at the non-governmental organisation for sharing their time and knowledge. As with most academic books, this has been a long drawn out process, and many institutions, editors and peers have been involved. Thank you: Centre for Critical and Cultural Studies and School of Social Work, University of Queensland; the Shastri-Indo Canadian Institute (Canada and India office); Centre for Asia Pacific Social Transformation Studies, the University of Wollongong; the Nossal Institute for Global Health and School of Population Health at the University of Melbourne; the York Centre for Asian Research and Faculty of Liberal Arts and Professional Studies at York University for generously financially supporting various portions of my research, writing and editing processes. Thank you past and present WIA series editors, Lenore Lyons for your patience and understanding especially during challenging times, and Louise Edwards for providing me with encouragement.

The text has grown out of doctoral, postdoctoral and contemporary research, and there are many people involved in that process. A big thank you to my PhD supervisors Harriot Beazley and Graeme Turner for providing me with the most supportive and critical guidance. Harriot in particular, I am so happy to have met you; thank you for being such a great colleague, friend and supervisor. I miss our car rides a lot, much love! I am grateful to the late Judith Ennew who started the ball rolling back in Bangkok. She was a stellar mentor and is greatly missed. In Melbourne: thank you Linda Rae Bennett for supporting my postdoc. Your mentorship, friendship and kindness, and the generosity of your spirit has been overwhelming and I am proud to call you my friend, and thanks for the good times my urban family especially Raphy and Jacques for martial arts and cuddles. In India: thank you to the Shastri Indo-Canadian Institute (Delhi office). In Kolkata I am particularly grateful to my friends Shreya and Salma, Shafkat, Feroz, Sana and Saba. In Canada: to all of my friends, old and new, especially Ruby (B) and Shawn

(Smelly). New colleagues Andrea and Caroline, thanks for important critical discussions about race and class.

Lastly to my family: Tripti, Asok, Roshan, Scott (SLB) and my sister Nibedita (Kathy). Thank you for all your love and support.

Permission

Parts of Chapter 4 have appeared in the following texts, and permission has been granted to reproduce them here. "Unmarried Muslim Youth and Sex Education in the *bustees* of Kolkata". *South Asian History and Culture* 1(2): 268–281; "The Sexual Lives of Muslim Girls in the *bustees* of Kolkata, India". *Sex Education* 10(1): 1–21; "Bollywood as a Role Model: Boyfriends, Dating and Negotiating Romance". In C. Bradford and M. Reimer (eds), *Girls, Texts, Cultures* (pp. 238–263) Wilfred Laurier University Press.

1 Introduction

Introduction

This book provides a detailed account of changing youth culture in the urban slums, or *bustees*, of Kolkata. It specifically explores how young unmarried Muslim women negotiate India's changing social, economic and cultural environments, and reveals the risks they undertake to fulfil transgressive identities and desires within a globalising nation. The book speaks directly to rumours about slum youth and slum life in India, in particular that slums are giant urban disasters and its people a poor, sorry lot (Hutnyk 1996; Moxon 1998). While this rumour about slums and slum life dominates most discussions about Kolkata, particularly in the Minority world, there is another rumour about Kolkata which can be heard throughout India. It is the tale of a magnificent mega-city that is developing at a rapid pace, full of employment, opportunity and riches. This rumour attracts people from around India to find their fortune in the city and creates rapidly changing slum communities and changing youth cultures, ones that mirror social change in India.

While shifts in middle-class life are well documented (cf. Donner 2008; Derne 2008; Ganguly-Scrase and Scrase 2009) the impact that globalisation is having on youth in India, particularly young Muslim women in marginalised communities, is less discussed. Dominant public discourse in India suggests that young Muslim women from the *bustees* are experiencing limited mobility and freedoms in the face of social change. Others point to expanding opportunities for social and economic participation that youth have gained as a result of shifting access to education and employment. This book reveals that while young women have greater access to social freedoms compared with previous generations, they face both pressures and desires to maintain various normative practices. Young women navigate through social change and craft more self-directed lives through calculated risk taking, and by drawing heavily on Bollywood popular culture. The book shows how young women employ Bollywood as a guide, and how popular culture allows young women to write more self-determined life courses, including their own love biographies and consumer identities, particularly during their leisure time. For many young women Bollywood is more than entertainment. It is a frame of reference that is consulted to understand certain identities and lifestyles, it guides them through middle-class arenas, and helps them navigate through social risks in a changing nation.

In the slums, young Muslim women's desire for more self-directed lives represents a challenge to communal ways of life and normative expectations of youth. Many youth who participate in independent romance and who secretly learn mixed-sex dance, for example, negotiate numerous risks. They are at risk of being branded by their peers and community members as snobs, as being 'too modern' or 'bad girls' who are easily (sexually) available. Other members of the community are more supportive of young women's desires, providing them with encouragement. While this book depicts how young women negotiate risks and use Bollywood to write multiple identities and pursue transgressive desires, I will show that individualised acts – finding one's own partner, participating in popular dance and consumption culture – often do not translate into more equal relationships or a more individualised life course as Giddens (1992), Beck (1992) and Beck and Beck-Gernsheim (1995) have suggested. Rather, young women's social position sits firmly within a patriarchal and communal society where young women bargain with patriarchy and manage kinship relationships. Thus this book contributes to our understanding of youth culture and what young people think it means to be a 'modern' young person in India, and explores how young women are responding to, and living within, a globalising India which is changing unevenly. In doing so it contributes to contemporary South Asian Studies, Cultural Studies and the growing discipline of Children and Youth Studies. The book speaks to larger scholarship on the youth bulge in Asia, and in particular it adds to research on changing youth culture in India (Lukose 2009; Jeffrey 2010, 2011; Bansal 2013; Nakassis 2013; Dyson 2014; Balagopalan 2014; Schinder and Titzmann 2015).

Urban slums/*bustees*

The work presented in this book draws on research conducted in two large slums in Kolkata.[1] These *bustees* are over 50 years old and intermixed with a variety of residential statuses, land uses and a socio-economically diverse population. While there are some wealthy families in the slums, the *bustees* are home to a majority poor and migrant Muslim population. The dominant public discourse about these two *bustees* is that they represent a 'conservative Muslim space', and there are many orthodox Islamic political and cultural organisations present here. Although Muslims make up the bulk of the population, there are pockets of lower caste Hindus and Christian communities as well.

In Kolkata, a city of over 15 million, an estimated 30 per cent of the population lives in slums (Sengupta 2010). Across India, slums are commonly evolved from burgeoning population growth, particularly in large urban centres. *Bustees* also house populations that are forced to shift in response to natural disasters, war and events not directly tied to economic disparity such as sporting events like the Commonwealth Games held in 2010 in Delhi. This growing population puts pressure on existing city land and infrastructure, often resulting in urban slum settlements. Slums in Kolkata may be established or non-established communities, and they can be quite diverse. An established slum is usually a row of one-room homes sharing a common wall, often constructed using brick and/or cement (often called *pukka* homes). Paved or semi-paved roads may surround the cluster of homes, and some infrastructure including water taps and public toilet facilities may exist. Established slums often have a recognised history, with many residents living in tenancy settlements. Non-established slums (or *jhupris*) often have a shorter history and sporadic political representation with residents facing threats of eviction. *Jhupris* can evolve into *pukka bustees* over time. In Kolkata *jhupri* communities are often referred to by the State and non-governmental organisations (NGOs) and community-based organisations (CBOs) as 'squatter settlements'. Like many *bustees* throughout India it is common to have both *pukka* homes and *jhupris* alongside each other sharing resources, so the demarcation between established and non-established communities can be blurred.

The *bustees* in which this research is conducted are similar to other slum communities in their ability to attract NGO support and inspire CBO formation. Like many poor urban spaces in India there are numerous NGOs in the *bustees* that manage education, health, religious and other community needs. While there are important and community-based social justice actors filling in service needs and advocating for the disenfranchised, the plethora of NGOs/CBOs in poor communities is yet another way rumours about Kolkata continue to flourish (see Hutnyk 1996). While organisational goals aim to support communities, they can also play a role in creating developmental dependence, as well as support the blanket labelling of communities as 'marginalised' and 'poor', which can be problematic particularly as poverty is read in different ways across India, and indeed in the *bustees* (see Kilby 2011). In this book the work of NGO *Azeem*[2] figures prominently in the lives of youth. We will see how the intersection of contemporary youth culture with NGO programming is particularly important in the lives of youth in the *bustees* of Kolkata. *Azeem* began as a CBO in the *bustees* and has transformed into one of the most well-known NGOs in the area. Established over 15 years ago, one of its goals are to address the 'welfare and wellbeing of girls and young women' in the community (annual report, 2006). Over the years the organisation has been able to obtain both foreign and State funding, and has expanded from a local operation to a multi-site organisation within these very large slums. Education is one of the key focuses of the NGO and it operates more than five non-formal education (NFE) centres.

Many young women who participated in this research eagerly join the various educational and social programmes that the NGO organises, and it is without a doubt that *Azeem* offers opportunities (such as free schooling and employment) that many young women can only undertake with NGO assistance. *Azeem*'s NFE centres operate at flexible times to accommodate students, such as working children, who may not be able to consistently attend school. In the slums *Azeem* provides free NFE classes from primary school up to class five and these attract students up to the age of 20. While some of the early classes attract boys and girls, the NGO supports only young women in further schooling. Young women with academic potential are sponsored by the NGO to attend government high schools (including Central Board of Secondary Education schools, or CBSE), a prestigious feat for many young women in the slums. While *Azeem* itself is secular, it employs some locally well-known and respected Muslim reformers who advocate for greater Muslim economic, political, educational and religious participation in the slums. The CEO of *Azeem* and his son (the Organiser,[3] male 21) for example are two very outspoken supporters of Dr Zakir Naik[4] and his teachings. Dr Naik is an incredibly popular and influential Salafi teacher, who has a particular pull with middle-class communities in these slums (see Swami's 2008 paper for more information). Some of Dr Naik's televised teachings include stamping out 'low class beliefs' like superstitions, poor education practices amongst Muslims, and sympathy for Hindu culture including partaking in Hindu holiday festivals. As Swami notes his anti-Hindu sentiment in particular 'is profoundly attractive to one element of Naik's core audience: the pious petty bourgeoisie in India's inner-city Muslim ghettos, who are hit hard by organised crime' (Swami 2008: 313), which describes very closely the realities in the *bustees*. Reformers who desire social mobility and greater participation of Muslims in secular and religious life in India have strong class and status links in this community. We will see throughout the book how local youth in the slums are often the target audience of reformer proselytising, and how this influences change in youth culture.

The *bustees* in which this research has been conducted are two large slum communities located in an inner-city locale, and they are located side by side. Together these are considered by the State to be very large *bustees*; they occupy an area of roughly 2.5 square kilometres, and local NGOs estimate the combined *bustees* to have a population of over 300,000 people (2014 estimate, *Azeem*). One of the slums has a longer history in the area and is made up of both established one-room slum homes, as well as built-up family homes. Second- and third-generation migrants of middle-class and poor backgrounds can live alongside each other in this community. The second *bustee* is dominated by large and medium-sized industries and recent migrants living in *jhupris*, as well as mixed settlement housing. The established community was settled by migrants after Indian independence and there are also internal Muslim migrants from predominantly Bihar with a long history in this community. Recent migrants that settled in the *jhupris* may have arrived in Kolkata only months or a few years ago, and are usually from within India, particularly Bihar, but also from Muslim districts in West Bengal, especially Murshidabad and Maldah. The *bustees* are characterised by class and status-specific occupations including rubbish and scrap collection, rickshaw pullers, taxi drivers and leather workers. The average monthly income for a young man in 2011 was a little over Rs 4000,[5] and by 2013 I knew some young men earning upwards of Rs 5000 a month, which is considered a very good salary. Families in the *jhupris*, however, may not be working at all, or may be making the transition from rural work to urban work.

The *bustees* are a stronghold of local politics that lean towards socialism; like many communities across West Bengal there is a particularly strong rivalry between the Communist Party India Marxist, CPI (M) and All India Trinamool Congress (AITC). More than just a hotbed of political rivalry, the slums are a known place for political parties to recruit thugs (*goondas*) during elections, while politicians from different parties spend considerable time making promises of newer homes and piped water. The *bustees* are also home to a large and powerful underworld, which has pan-India influence, and house pan-India mafia members. They are currently home to gangs that specialise in power theft, illegal construction and drug distribution, and the community has a growing profile in the trade of small arms. The underworld presence is a normal aspect of everyday life in the slums, and young people I work with are connected to the underworld in different ways. Some young people's own family members are involved in the local mafia, while other young people, particularly young men, may work for local dons. It is through illegal means that many ordinary things get done, from electricity connection to employment, and for many the mafia is a place where one can find gainful employment. The underworld has also impacted the community in more negative ways, including the proliferation of cheap heroin, and over the last decade this has profoundly changed the lives of many young men who have become addicts, particularly in the *jhupri* community. Unlike other mafia strongholds such as *bustees* in Bombay, communal tensions do not (normally) dominate the everyday culture of the slums. This may be a reflection of socialist politics that focus on class issues rather than religious differences (Husain 2005).

Fewer communal tensions does not mean residents are not concerned about the possibility of communal violence. During the 2014 general election which saw the Hindu nationalist Bharatiya Janata Party (BJP) sweep into power, for example, the community was incredibly tense about what a BJP victory would mean at the local level. The *bustees* saw heavy political action at that time to rally support for CPI (M) in particular, using the platform of community safety, housing and economic security. The ghettoisation of the Muslim population in Kolkata, particularly poor Muslims, suggests that residents of various social backgrounds believe in the power and protection of numbers. As Aysha, a 15-year old girl who participated in this research remarked, 'we don't feel that tension because we all stay together and we won't move away'. Religious identity in this community is very important. All of the young people in this research identify as Muslim; although technically they are Sunni Muslims, mostly from the Barelvi and (less so) Deobandi communities

(Hanafi School), many cannot/do not classify themselves along these lines. While participants identified as Muslim, and some understood the differences between Sunni, Shi'a and Sufi schools, I agree with Simpson (2008) that many cannot explain the divisions within Sunni schools, or between Shi'a and Sunni branches. There are important class divisions in school membership, with Deobandi and Salafi Muslims often members of the powerful middle class in the slums, and Barelvi Muslims the bulk of poor *bustee* dwellers. Throughout the book I try to capture what young women think it means to be Muslim, and many of their experiences remind us of Simpson's findings that the lived realities of piety and faith in India can be fluid and include evolving interpretations of textual Islam.

The community in which this research has been conducted is organised spatially around railway tracks, while a large *masjid* is the figurative heart of the community. Stalls selling religious merchandise surrounding the *masjid* intermix with established stores, established homes and hawker stalls peddling a variety of goods from batteries to fresh fruit. In the last decade both hawker stalls and established businesses have faced increasing pressure to leave their valuable inner-city land to make room for larger businesses that have been slowly encroaching into the community.[6] In the established slum, second- and third-generation and more middle-class migrants live near the mosque. The centre of the community has many established residences, shops, smaller mosques and other community sites which are permanent in nature. Some of the more prosperous community members live comfortable middle-class lives with all of its associated consumption and social luxuries. Thus it is important to stress that while poverty and marginality are conditions of slums, Davis reminds us, 'Not all urban poor live in slums, nor are all slum dwellers poor' (Davis 2007: 25). Those in very difficult situations partake in temporary and insecure work with a combined household income of less than Rs. 2000/ month (*Azeem* definition). Most families live in the thousands of one-room *bustee* homes, many sharing at least one wall. Most *pukka* homes are brick structures approximately 15 sq. ft in size and house an average of seven people, usually members of a joint family. They are one-room homes with a small stoop in the front to conduct cooking. Meals are prepared on small portable gas stoves, and most homes do not have a separate kitchen or washroom facility. Water is obtained from public taps placed intermittently around the slum, and toilets and bathing stalls are few and public, free or for cost. At the centre of the single room dwelling is the family bed, which is elevated by bricks to provide for storage space underneath, and also to protect the bed from flooding. Most families in *pukka* homes own one or more wardrobes (*almarih*) in which they store their valuables. A small dresser can also be used as a stand for the family's television set, one of the most important items in the home. Most families in the *pukka* community own a television set.

Jhupri communities are situated close to sewers, large rubbish dumps and rail lines; many of these homes have been constructed with bamboo, tarp and tin. As mentioned, most residents are newly arrived migrants from around West Bengal and Bihar. This community is significantly more marginalised than the established slum, with widespread unemployment and heroin abuse amongst young men more common here than in the adjacent slum. There are established homes in the area, and these homes may have access to infra-structure including public water taps, toilets and bathing facilities. Electricity lines in *jhupri* communities are usually hooked up illegally, and few families have television sets. Families who do not have their own television sets gain viewing access through public viewings in political, religious or NGO centres, or in individual homes.

Television in the *Bustees*

Television brings the world outside the slums directly into the homes of youth. Of particular importance, it is through television that young women in the *bustees* participate in Bollywood culture. The hyper-exposure of Bolly-wood culture through television programming has directly impacted youth culture in the slums. For young women Bollywood culture is more than films, it also includes different television and music media. Bollywood literacy is an essential part of everyday youth discourse and discussing popular shows and films, singing to the latest Bollywood songs, and playing games like 'guess the song' is a way friendship groups socialise and form close bonds. Bollywood culture has proven to be an important learning tool in matters related to sex, love, fashion and technology for youth in India, and following Dwyer, in the slums:

> [Bollywood] is a better guide to the realities of modern India than other, more scholarly work ... films are an unparalleled guide to the thoughts, aspirations and attitudes of the hundreds of millions of members of the emergent middle-classes ... this does not mean that film reflects Indian society; rather that it shows us how life should or could be. The images of wealthy lifestyles, of the extended family, of beautiful people, where everything is gorgeous, traditional and functions under a religious atmosphere is modern India as it should be; these are its aspirations.
>
> (Dwyer 2010: 381)

Television plays an imperative role in facilitating young people's relationship with Bollywood, while viewing films in the cinema hall is not frequent for the obvious reasons of cost and limited mobility. The television set is of particular importance to families. It is a source of entertainment, a symbol of wealth and a revered 'modern' feature of the home. It is kept in pristine condition and treated with a great deal of care; it is almost always covered with a spe-cial cloth or plastic guard, and those families that can afford to do so place the set within its own unit that can be closed. The position of the television set is generally up high, to protect it from the curious hands of small children, and to maximise viewing positions from around the home. Multiple sets are rare and homes generally have only one small or medium-sized remote-controlled unit. When I began fieldwork in 2005 both coloured and black and white televisions were available, and by 2014 only coloured units were purchased. Some families also have a unit with DVD and VHS capacity. In addition, a majority of the homes that I worked in had cable television, either legal or illegal connections, which further widened viewing choices.

Families who have video or DVD capacity often use this technology to watch films. Pirated disks are bought, rented or passed throughout the neighbourhood amongst friendship circles. A pirated DVD/VCD of a popular film showing currently in the theatres can be purchased for as little as Rs. 20 on the streets, compared with a single movie ticket, which can cost upwards of Rs. 150. TVs allow the entire family to watch a film together, facilitating family time and making the film enjoyable since everyone can comment on the entertainment together. Commenting on media is an important aspect of viewing, thus if the television is on, it is being watched and is not usually used for background noise in the home.

The viewing habits of families differ from home to home, but generally the set is not on in the morning because family members are busy preparing for work, household or schooling obligations. After the children and workers of the home leave for their respective tasks, women, elders and non-schoolgoing children may watch some selective programmes throughout the day while performing household duties or while having lunch. Though there are viewing opportunities elsewhere, men in general do not watch much television during the day. Depending on the location of their school, young people may return home after school and watch television while they eat or rest. This time might be limited if young people have to do their homework or ready themselves for tuition classes. Family viewing by all occurs late in the evening, during dinnertime, and on the weekends. The watching of a particular television programme, usually a Hindi-language drama, is a ritual of the entire family (see also Munshi 2010). Young women spend a considerable amount of their leisure time within the home watching television. Most young women state that daily serial dramas, reality shows and Bollywood films are their favourite types of shows, and through these they learn about the world around them. This is particularly the case for young women whose public mobilities are heavily monitored by members of the community.

A changing India

The Bollywood popular culture that young women crave to watch is itself a product of economic liberalisation and a globalising India. Much has been written about various changes in television media post 1991 liberalisation of the Indian economy (for example Kohli-Kandhekar 2010; Butcher 2003; Kumar 2006; Mankekar 1999; Mazzarella 2003; Rajagopal 2001). Although cable television in India can be traced back to the early 1990s, transnational television really arrived in India with the launch of StarTV in 1991 and ZeeTV in 1992.[7] These satellite networks offered 24-hour access to Bollywood films, music, award shows, serials and sitcoms, news and sports. These hyper-entertainment networks display glamour, music, song and dance in stylised formats unlike anything ever seen on the national television station Door-Darshan. StarTV and ZeeTV exemplify the success of cultural hybridisation – a melding of different cultural elements that combine, for example, the music and melodrama of Bollywood, stylised Hollywood reality programming and Hong Kong martial arts.

The importance of television in India can be seen in the recent 2011 census, which shows almost 50 per cent of the total population owning a television set, compared with 30 per cent in the 2001 census (GOI 2011). Similarly the privatisation of national radio in 1993 altered the mediascape for many. Popular Bollywood music, talk show programmes and advice shows are given considerable air time, an immense change from post-Independence radio. Like television, radio is accessed by millions of Indians in rural and urban communities.[8] The liberalisation of media in India has meant an enormous expansion of cultural knowledge amongst young people across India in both urban and rural areas, and sites of contemporary youth culture now include players such as Radio Mirchi, MTV India and Colors (Viacom), some of which have less than a 20-year history in India.

For the average Indian, privatised entertainment conglomerates like Star have brought a hyper-exposure of Bollywood culture into their everyday lives.[9] 'Bollywood' is the colossal Hindi–Urdu language cinema industry of India. The term is a melange of the words 'Bombay', where the industry is based, and 'Hollywood', the American film capital. Bollywood is also called popular Hindi cinema, *masala* cinema or simply 'film' or 'picture' in India.[10] The cultural influence of this Bombay-based 'Epico-Mythico-Tragico-Comico-Super-Sexy-High-Masala-Art' (Rushdie 1995: 148–149) percolates into almost every aspect of the entertainment spectrum in India, from television and radio to advertising, traditional theatre and music. Thus within this book when I speak of Bollywood culture I refer not only to popular film, but also to its presence in the entire entertainment industry (see Rajadhyaksha 2003). It is Bollywood cinema, however, that is the most globally important cultural phenomenon in India, and the statistics tell the tale of its success and influence: Bollywood cinema is viewed by an average of 11 million people each day in India – Mumbai has produced up to 900 films per year and Bollywood culture is distributed to over 100 countries around the world. This has led Das Gupta (cited in Mishra 2002) to proclaim: 'cinemas are the temples of modern India'. In the course of its century-long history, Bollywood cinema has steadily retold the myths, folk tales and legends of India through the modern medium of motion pictures. Bollywood cinema has changed tremendously in the last 20 years, and this has been an important area of scholarship (for example Ganti 2012; Dickey 1993; Dudrah 2012, 2006; Banaji 2006a; Derne 2000; Kazmi 1998). While in the past films were based on the 'epics and myths of the country (India)' (Das Gupta in Chakravarty 1993: 125), films are now highly influenced by upwardly mobile urban Indians and the diasporic or non-resident Indian (NRI) communities in (predominantly) North America and the UK.[11]

This change in direction, observers argue, challenges the production of 'Indian' within Bollywood films. Malhotra and Alagh (2004: 19) show that wealthy middle-class Hindus and diasporic Indian communities find a prominent place in the production of 'Indian' in contemporary Bollywood culture:

> Consequently, certain minorities like Muslims and Christians find themselves excluded and increasingly erased from this terrain ... [in addition] particular socio-political and economic trends: (*Hindutva* [Hindu national movement], global capital flows and regressive gender politics) further marginalise and often erase the experiences of religious minorities and the poor who do not fit this constructed norm.

Urban Indian middle-class sensibilities present in the media are very influential in shaping young people's understanding of modernity. Scholars argue that values like individualisation, consumption and nuclear family structures are contributing to a changing 'youth culture' in India (Banaji 2005, 2006a, 2006b; Lukose 2009). These changes have resulted in scholars arguing that Bollywood post-liberalisation is a globalised culture where 'the representational politics of the male star in particular is central to a re-imagining of a distinct middle-class India for global consumption' (Ciecko 2001). Deshpande (2005) suggests that the modern Bollywood hero is urban, Hindu, rich (at least middle class), and conformist in social attitudes. Our hero consumes at a global level, making product placement in Bollywood an important display that is directly related to middle-class consumption aspirations (Uberoi 2006; Kripalani 2007; Wilkinson-Weber 2011). Another important feature of a globalised Bollywood is the prominence of NRIs within the films, with entire movies being devoted to their lives (see for example *My Name is Khan* 2010). More recently we have seen upwardly mobile upper-class Indian youth participating in high levels of travel and consumption across India (for example *Yeh Jawaani Hai Deewani* 2013; *2 States* 2014).

Newly merged female characters also mirror change in India, as Bollywood actress Shabana Azmi comments:

> Although there's been a change (in Hindi cinema), I think there is a lot of confusion about who this new woman should be. Society accepts that there is a new woman, but does not know how much freedom this woman should have before she threatens the very fabric of our society. So unless society can come to terms with who this new woman is, our heroine will continue to be clouded in what is good or what is bad, because a heroine, a heroine or hero, is somebody who is a personification of the morality and aspirations of the society.
>
> (Ganti 2004: 190)

Viewing Bollywood/Bollywood viewers

We know very little about how a globalising Bollywood impacts non-elite Indians, particularly young women. In his notes towards an agenda for the next generation of film theorists in India, Ashis Nandy (2003: 79) expresses discomfort that there are few empirically grounded research studies of the Indian film audience and their diverse interpretations of Indian films. He argues that most writings on the subject of popular Hindi cinema are weighed down by Western ways of dissecting film that disturbingly imprint ideological purposefulness on such cinema. Using the example of the Bollywood 'super hit' *Border* (1997), Nandy shows how this film depicting an India-Pakistan conflict became controversial amongst expatriate Pakistani and Indian news-papers in the UK. The diasporic media labelled the film xenophobic, as it portrayed the Muslim Pakistanis in a negative light. However Nandy found that ordinary Pakistanis living in the UK did not take the entire film at face value, stating that they knew what to discount or ignore in Bombay cinema. Nandy (2003: 80) argues that the audiences 'have their way of interpreting or criticising it (while) film theorists have poor access to their subjectivities'. His call for more ethnographic studies on the Bollywood film audience, especially in India, is an acknowledgment of a significant gap in academic understanding of Indians' everyday interpretations of, and interactions with, Bollywood.

The ethnography of young Bollywood viewers in India is uneven. Though there has been ample written about the Indian diaspora's relationship with popular Hindi/Urdu cinema there have been few studies focusing on how Bollywood impacts the everyday lives of youth. Rao (2007: 19, also 2010) contends that most modern Bollywood films cater to an audience that are mostly 'the upper-middle-class diasporic and urban communities whose tastes, values, desires and consumption are reflected and re-energised by these films'. Rao's work in North India represents a conceptual shift in the popular argument that Bollywood has long spoken to the lower and working classes, which Derne (2000, 2005, 2008) has discussed in detail. An analysis of the superhits of the 1970s and 1980s exemplifies how the 'angry young man' – personified by the incomparable Amitabh Bachchan – enacted the frustrations of everyday Indians and was a reaction to the political and economic climate of India at the time (see Nandy 1998; Kazmi 1998). As a poor person struggling in the dog-eat-dog world of inequality and corruption, the angry young man resists exploitation and stands up for all that is good. Indian liberalisation significantly altered the socio-political and economic face of the country and its cinema. This shift can be seen with the rise of the new middle-class, brand-savvy, highly mobile and technologically proficient 'Hinglish' (a mixture of Hindi/English) speaking hero (see Deshpande 2005: 7; Mazumdar 2000).

If cinema is a window into how India is coming to terms with its own 'modernity', as Rachel Dwyer (2010) has argued, studying the Bollywood audience is studying the way Indians are viewing, consuming, negotiating and coming to terms with modernity in their everyday lives. As Nandy (1998: 7) eloquently states, 'studying popular film is studying Indian modernity at its rawest, its crudities laid bare by the fate of traditions in contemporary life and arts'. The few studies on the experiences of the globalised Bollywood audience in India have shown that relationships with popular culture are varied and contextual.

Studies of the Bollywood audience in India reveal a complex relationship. Derne's (2000, 2005, 2008) work on non-elite males in North India shows that young men have increasing access to global media, including English films, pornographic films and Western television serials. Despite this access and the growing proclamations (or moral panics) that cultural globalisation is robbing youth of its 'Indian values' Derne shows that young men are firmly attached to social structures that favour them. These include arranged marriages, joint family systems and traditional gender arrangements. This is not to say that men are not influenced by cultural globalisation – rather, Derne argues, they pick and choose cultural productions that are meaningful in their lives. These choices are often grounded in a patriarchy, which can prop up male violence and the viewing of women as objects of male pleasure. Thus contemporary media can 'reinforce ways that local popular culture supports male dominance' (Derne 2005: 41).

Rao's (2007: 18) study of non-elite Hindi film audiences in Punjab shows that while viewers find contemporary popular culture 'entertaining', films that have social, political or moral messages and some connection to their lives are the most appealing. Participants in Rao's study are quick to condemn the new 'international' flavour of music video styled 'item numbers' within films. As one female respondent claims, 'I avoid films where I know there are item numbers. That way I know I can go to the film with my brother and not feel embarrassed' (in Rao 2007: 17). Non-elite audiences in Rao's work disapprove of the overt sexualisation depicted on screen, and prefer films with 'good messages', or regional (in this case Punjabi) cinema that portrays lifestyles that speak to their culture. Further, audiences found themselves detached from 'the dreamworld of Bollywood and were less and less likely to consume them in the future' (Rao 2007: 19).

In contrast, Banaji (2005, 2006a, 2006b) found that young middle-class youth in Bombay (and London) view Bollywood films as sources of knowledge which can influence their life choices. She is careful to show that the times and places of viewing are important in understanding the effects of Bollywood on their everyday lives:

> [I]n the more pressured and public arena of cinema halls, young people whom I spoke to were less likely to take the themes of films seriously, or to engage with the possibility that their own behaviours and views were connected to the films they watched, although they were frequently willing *to impute to others* the seeming stigma of having been 'made' to do something by a film scene or narrative.
>
> (Emphasis in original, Banaji 2006a: 26)

Meanwhile, writer Sukethu Mehta's (2004, New York Times Online) personal relationship with Bollywood reveals a wholehearted consumption of the media:

> Why do I love Bollywood movies? To an Indian, that's like asking why we love our mothers; we don't have a choice. We were born of them. ... (they) have made me who I am. They shape the way I conduct my love affairs or think about religion or treat my elders.

Mehta's love and reliance on Bollywood culture to understand his place in India, his relationships and appropriate behaviours aligns closely with young women's experience with popular culture in the slums. For youth in the *bustees* Bollywood popular culture is an important 'expert' in their lives and is eagerly consulted and greatly valued as an educator. Beck (1992) argues that in a globalising world, traditional sources of knowledge, such as community elders, are often unable to keep up with a changing society, allowing new experts and new sources of knowledge to emerge. These experts can challenge the norms and values of society. In the slums we see young women turn to Bollywood when making more self-directed choices and pursuing individualised lifestyles, particularly in their leisure time.

This book shows that Bollywood is an important role model in the everyday lives of young Muslim women. It allows young women to dream big, and plan for a life that is different from that of their parents' generation, and in this way Bollywood moves beyond fantasy. Here it is useful to draw on Appadurai who has argued:

> Whatever the force of social change, a case could be made that social life was largely inertial, that traditions provided a relatively finite set of possible lives, and that fantasy and imagination were residual practices, confined to special persons or domains, restricted to special moments or places. In general, imagination and fantasy were antidotes to the finitude of social experience. In the past two decades, as the deterritorialization of persons, images, and ideas has taken on new force, this weight has imperceptibly shifted.
>
> (Appadurai 1996: 53)

Moving beyond fantasy or *timepass* the book shows how Bollywood is an expert in the lives of youth. We also see how young women using Bollywood to navigate through a changing nation do not always wish to overtly defy the normative structures of *bustee* society. Rather, many choose to transgressively use Bollywood in a private geography, and these spaces have their own political systems, morals, values and hierarchies. I illustrate that transgressive Bollywood-inspired identities and desires are able to flourish in these spaces, thus young people discerningly and selectively use popular culture in their lives.

Working with young women

I have an over 11-year relationship with the community in which this research has been conducted. I first started working in these slums in 2003 as a consultant with an international NGO. I developed a good connection with the NGO *Azeem* at this time, and began research on contemporary youth culture and Bollywood in 2004. This book represents 20 months of fieldwork drawn over nine years – a year was spent in the field in 2005 and 2006, and shorter research visits between 2007 and 2014. Ongoing connection with 30 young women and 25 young men, all between the ages of 14 to 24, was also facilitated by emails, phone conversations, text messages and social media. These represent consistent participants and not participants I have limited contact with (that number is obviously much larger). During this period of time I saw youth graduate from school, enter paid work and become parents. Although the book focuses on the lives of young unmarried women in the *bustees*, their life trajectories are present throughout and this means that the voices and experiences of young men and adults are also present. In its entirety the book draws on the experiences, opinions and visions of young Muslim women in slums that are rapidly changing. It describes a youth culture which values negotiating social risks to live out particular challenging desires and identities, and maps how young women navigate through a changing nation. It highlights the role of Bollywood in helping make these journeys and a running theme throughout the book is how young women negotiate their relationship with normative religious, gender and class discourses in order to participate in a 'cool' Indian and global youth culture. It also presents how class and status divisions are created between peers, in particular between peers who attempt to live more (self-perceived) modern lives and those who do not.

Young people's experiences presented here add to growing scholarship around what it means to be a 'modern' youth in India (for example Jeffrey 2010; Lukose 2009; Nakassis 2013). The book argues that the dominant discourses of being a modern young person in India – having a love marriage, or participation in 'modern' youth culture – do not always define modernity for youth in the slums.

The methodological framework for this study is grounded in a children's rights framework which understands that young people have the right to participate and express their opinions freely, and the right to freedom of expression including the right to seek, receive and impart information and ideas (Ennew 2010; Beazley *et al.* 2009), and informed consent throughout the process. The rights-based framework to research with young people lends itself to participatory and qualitative methods of data collection. The importance of the right of participants to express themselves using their own verbal, creative and cultural literacies is strongly supported by the UNCRC, especially Article 12 'children's right to participation' and Article 13 'children's right to expression'. Thus the research actively seeks youth participation, and highlights their own expressions by using participatory methods of voice, art, words, images and movement (I have discussed this elsewhere: Chakraborty 2009, see also James, Jenks and Prout 1998; Prout 2005; Punch 2002; Beazley *et al.* 2011), and formulate their own methods of expression (see also Chakraborty *et al.* 2012).

The rights-based approach to research lends itself to multiple participatory methods, informed consent and outcome strategies aimed at youth collaboration and capacity building. Young people worked with me to formulate questions and points of discussion, and decided in consultation on methods to use. I also worked with local youth at *Azeem* to put together sexual health workshops ('girls classes'), film screenings, fieldtrips and library activities. The variety of tools used by young people in this research includes: art, interviews, participant observation, yoga, Bollywood films, popular culture text, photography and focus group discussions. For example using a combination of yoga and drawing, young people envision their future careers and paths toward that career.

Stylistically, throughout the book I move fluidly between terms such as 'girl', 'boy', 'girlhood', 'boyhood', 'young woman', 'young man' and 'youth'. There is reasoning behind this; the United Nations Convention on the Rights of the Child (UNCRC 1989), which India has ratified, defines 'children' as all human beings less than 18 years old. The National Youth Policy of India defines 'youth' as those aged 15 to 29 years (NYP 2014). These overlapping definitions point to confusion regarding, legally, when childhood ends and adulthood begins. These age-centred definitions, however, do not adequately capture the cultural understanding of children and youth, and as I show in the next chapter, transitions between childhood, youth and adulthood are slippery. The fact that I use the terms 'girl', 'boy', 'girlhood', 'boyhood', 'young woman', 'young man' and 'youth' interchangeably throughout this book is a reflection of the ambiguity of what it means to be a young person in India today. Importantly, throughout the book I favour the term 'young women' to describe girls' post-pubescent lives. I do this to gender the term 'youth', but also to reflect how young people I work with see themselves – not as *baccha* (child). I have deliberately not used the terms 'teen', 'adolescent' and 'adolescence' as these are linked strongly to the Western developmental models of childhood like G. Stanley Hall's 'storm and stress' and Eurocentric ideas of the angst-ridden teen, which do not fit well within the cultural context of the *bustees*. Indeed the book demonstrates the need to disrupt the dominant Western models of childhood and youth to include more lived experiences of youth, and youth culture, in the Majority world.

Qualitative and participatory methods have been ongoing in my fieldwork since 2005. Many formal and informal interviews, focus group discussions, art and yoga activities have been conducted over the years. Throughout the book I draw on this rich collection of material, with quotes, photographic images and drawings peppering the text. I have tried to be clear of timelines to show changing viewpoints or contexts over time, and while some large transcripts have been date-marked, many smaller quotes from young people have not, and I have done this to streamline the text. All quotes are derived from Hindi/ Urdu/Bengali translation which I am responsible for (including mistakes). I have tried to use Indian English phrases in translations, but this was not always possible, in which case I used direct translations. Terms used within the book including 'poor', 'modern', 'traditional' and 'backwards' are terms young people use themselves in the context of their own lives and experiences. I have tried to unpack what young people mean by these, and in doing so, I describe a changing youth culture and changes in status at a very local level.

Another stylistic note is young people's ages. I have used the ages where I first met young people; for some I describe parts of their life story over years, others I have not. I have tried to make this clear. What is present in the book are viewpoints of select young people with whom I have worked, and should not be read as an all-encompassing reality of the youth experience in the *bustees*. Rather I have tried to make clear differences between individual youth, and how these differences shape their perceptions of class and status within the slums.

Chapter overview

I review the normative expectations of Muslim femininities in Chapter 2, and this exploration reveals young women's understanding of an idealised Muslim girlhood. Through discussing the 'good girl', young women also share what actions they perceive challenge this ideal. In the chapter we get a sense of the expected and accepted morals, values and behaviours of female youth in the slums and the risks that young women negotiate in order to live out more challenging aspects of their identities.

In Chapter 3 I show how young women who choose to learn and perform Bollywood mixed-sex dance challenge the hegemonic culture of the *bustees*. I demonstrate that the dance identity develops in 'third spaces' and confronts young women's understanding of Islam, acceptable premarital mixed-sex interactions and different class and status constructions. I describe how dance is made possible through calculated negotiations of risk, as well as by 'kinship complicity' (Bennett 2005a) – both private and public supporters of one's dance identity.

In Chapter 4 I explore how young women look to Bollywood to guide them in romantic relationships. I detail how they strategically negotiate risks in order to engage in heterosexual dating, love and sexual encounters. I provide a comprehensive description of individualised love, detailing the dating, romance and breaking up processes that young people experience. Self-chosen love is a risky venture, and young women have to manage both internal risks that challenge their identity, and external risks from society. I demonstrate that young people's pursuit of love can be an attempt to gain safety in their marriage. Some young women may be trying to shift class and status positions through marriage, however overall love-matches exist in a patriarchy that is steadfast.

In Chapter 5 I describe young people's Bollywood-inspired consumption practices. Consumption is shown to be much more than purchases of products and services; rather it is seen as a means of self-expression and an important tool in identity formation. I show how education and employment are related to the consumption of Bollywood-inspired clothing and food. It is clear that for many, consumption participation can transgress the social norms of the *bustees*. I discuss how consumption allows young women to participate in middle-class arenas, but how these tools also represent an obstacle in young women's participation in a globalising India.

In the last chapter I provide some concluding thoughts on young women's participation in youth culture in a globalising India, and the role of Bollywood culture in the everyday lives of young women in the rapidly changing *bustees*. I point to how research with young women in the slums adds to contemporary theories on risk and individualisation, and how studying young women's lived experiences provides an alternative to the dominant rumours about their lives.

Notes

1 According to UNHABITAT a 'slum' is a relative concept, with too many local variations and complexities to permit a single universally applicable definition. What is agreed upon is that 'slums, like poverty and secure tenure, are multi-dimensional in nature. Some of the characteristics of slums, such as access to physical services or density, can be clearly defined, and others, such as social capital, cannot' (UNHABITAT 2003: 11). Kundu (2003) also describes the complexity of defining slum communities in Kolkata.

2 All participant names and identifying markers of the community have been changed to ensure anonymity.

3 I will refer to the current youth organiser of *Azeem*, and the son of the CEO of the organisation, as 'the Organiser'. I will refer to the daughter of the CEO and the choreographer of the Azeem cultural show as 'the Choreographer'.

4 Dr Naik is a Mumbai-based Islamic scholar and televangelist. In India he is best known for being a popular and controversial Islamic speaker, and the founder of Peace TV, an Islamic cable television channel. Peace TV is widely available on cable television in many parts of the world, and DVDs and YouTube videos of Dr Naik's lectures are widely available. Most of these lectures are in a mix of English and Urdu, thus attracting literate middle-class Muslim viewers in the *bustees*. Dr Naik preaches on a variety of topics, many advocating greater Muslim participation in education and religion. He has become well known for gendering piety, particularly around issues of women's clothing and public mobilities. His comments on women's modest dress, on terrorism, on Islam's relationship with other religions, and on Shi'a/Sunni differences have caused protest in many countries around the world including in India. He is in India one of the most well-known Muslim reformers to emerge in recent years, and his target audience is a well-educated and mobile one.

5 At the time of writing $1USD= Rs 60.

6 While new and larger retail businesses coming into the periphery of the slums hold the prospect of new work opportunities, most of the established retail sectors hire fluent English speakers to hold coveted higher income positions. Local community members were in demand for other positions in upmarket businesses close to the slums, including cleaning and cooking positions.

7 See Butcher 2003; Dudrah 2002, 2005, 2006, 2012; Fernandes 2000a; Ninan 1995. For example in Mumbai the three most popular radio stations have approximately 9 million daily listeners above the age of 12 (ILT 2004).

8 For a detailed understanding of these processes and detailed history and contextual analysis of Bollywood in India and the Diaspora see Dwyer 2000; Mehta and Pandhairpande 2011; Raheja and Kotari 2004; Mishra 2002; Ciecko 2001; Ganti 2004; Desai 2004; Kazmi 1998; Dasgupta 1996; Dwyer and Patel 2002; Malhotra and Alagh 2004; Punathambekar 2005; Bhattacharya 2004; Srinivas 2005; Gopinath 2000, 2005; Vasudevan 2000.

9 In addition, as a verb, when something is inspired by Bollywood it can be referred to as *filmi* or *masala* in India.

10 NRIs are citizens of India or foreign citizens of Indian origin who have left India and reside abroad.

11 The technical meaning of a 'blockbuster' or 'superhit' film in India is a film that made more than one *crore* (Rs. 10 million) in each state where it was released.

2 The good Muslim girl

Introduction

The lives of youth in a globalising India, their relationships, transgressions and social and cultural negotiations, are complex, and studying this complexity in the field can be difficult. In the *bustees* one of the main challenges to understanding the experiences of Muslim youth, girls in particular, are the pressures and expectations that young women should (and must) behave in a particular way, especially in public. In the slums a young woman is expected by her family and community to be a 'good Muslim girl'. The rules of the 'good girl' are not uniform. Rather the state, society and individuals are constantly writing and re-writing their rules of behaviour and performance. Within the slums there is more than one way to be 'good'. Variables such as class, caste and culture are too complex to allow for a narrow idea of an ideal girl. Moreover for young Muslim women, religious identity does not create a singular experience or expectation of a Muslim femininity or a Muslim girl-hood, as local and personal interpretations of Islam are diverse throughout India, and indeed the world. Rules are underlined by normative expectations of femininity in India and these intersect with, amongst other things, religious practice and local contexts.

A fundamental aspect of the good girl is public perception – it is very important in the *bustees* to publicly maintain a particular image of being good. For many families the public reputation of being good is just as important as doing good. The consequence of not following the rules and developing a poor public reputation can be violent. Physical and verbal violence by families and communities are common ways to deal with challenges to normative gender rules and poor public reputation. The importance of representation in the slums means that as an outsider it is very difficult to gain the trust of young women. To add to this complexity is my own position as a non-resident Indian (NRI) from a caste Hindu background – to say I am an outsider is a grand understatement. Throughout the process of research I have tried through trust-building exercises, through listening, taking young people's experiences seriously, providing support with practical issues and maintaining confidentiality, to build trust with young people and the community. More than particular exercises, trust was cemented through my over 11-year relationship with the field which occurred in person, on the phone and online. While rapport building and trust is central to my research practice, and can represent a challenge, being an outsider in this community also has great advantages. As an NRI it is taken for granted I am an expert in sexuality, for example, and this saw young people approaching me to discuss these matters. I have described throughout the text my own reflexive under-standing of issues where it is important to the context, but have generally centred on young people's own opinions and experiences.

Honour, seclusion and protection

The lived experiences of young Muslim women in the *bustees* is an important area of study because little is known about how youth in urban poor com-munities are responding to social, political and economic shifts occurring in the nation. This paucity of research is related to both the positionality of Muslim youth in India as minorities, the cultural expectations of *purdah* (separation of the sexes) and *izzat* (honour), and the perception of 'slum youth' in global discourse. Nieuwenhuys (2009) correctly argues that there are a plethora of studies on issues-based experiences of children and young people in India. She argues that the dominant work on child labourers and street children has done 'little to undo the colonial imagination of India as a country lacking a proper notion of childhood' (Nieuwenhuys 2009: 148). Adding to Nieuwenhuys, I show now the behaviour and consumption patterns of youth challenge the dominant discourse about what it means to be a 'poor Indian child' and provide context on how childhood is constructed at a local level.

In contrast to the representations of the 'lost' or 'lacking' poor South Asian child – a prominent critique in Nieuwenhuys' thesis – is the reality that both girls and boys in the *bustees* are well loved and valued members of the household. I state this explicitly to disrupt the dominant discourse in India and globally of 'slum youth' as neglected members of the household. While there is a very real problem of son-preference within the slums, there is growing discussion in *bustees* about the importance of daughters. Some of this discussion is tied to the value of young women as caregivers:

> We are seeing in these *bustees* that many are saying daughters are better, they care for parents and family, boys are caught up in their own desires ... you don't see the sad reactions to birth of girls like before, it is celebrated like boy births are celebrated, as long as the family has not too many girls.
>
> (NGO employee, female)

Celebrating the birth of girl children by community members needs to be understood within the context of a patriarchal society – girls contribute significantly to unpaid labour in the home, and they are expected to, and do, take on caregiving roles of children, elderly and the ill. Thus while they might not have the same status as boys who are breadwinners, girls in the slums are often seen as responsible, and are well loved. But they also face discrimination, which is discussed often *through* discourses of love and honour. The expectations of girl children are different than boy children and the status and reputation of 'good girls' is tied to larger issues of sexuality, risk and patriarchal power. For example in the slums the notion of *izzat* (honour) frequently drives young women's actions. *Izzat* places considerable emphasis on young women as the guardians of family integrity. In the *bustees* 'saving face', 'shaming the family', 'protecting honour', 'good reputation', 'good family' and 'good girl/boy' are some of the common expressions of *izzat* which intersect everyday discourses. Although honour is a concern for the entire family, across India it is young women's actions which are highly scrutinised using the discourse of honour. Moreover scholars have also shown that knowledge of *izzat* is recognised as inherent so young women cannot claim they did not know their dishonourable actions were inappropriate.[1]

In the *bustees* threats to young women's honour can take many forms including socialising with the opposite sex in public; being seen as disobedient and not family-oriented; having a strong public identity; and wearing inappropriate/immodest clothing. Research also reveals similar concerns of honour in different communities across India. Still's (2011) work on Hindu girls' education in India, for example, describes parental concerns about young women meeting young men at school. She shows how families can withdraw girls from schooling to prevent the dishonour of girls socialising with boys, or from becoming highly independent during schooling.

Throughout India concern over *izzat* can lend itself to a preoccupation with young women's virginity before marriage, her socialising opportunities and her public behaviour.[2] Concerns over *izzat* in the slums can include the practice of *purdah*. *Purdah* is the separation between males and females which in the past in India was practised in both Hindu and Muslim communities.[3] In contemporary West Bengal it is particularly practised in ghettoised Muslim communities, and usually by post-puberty young people and adults. Feldman and McCarthy (1983: 949) define *purdah* in the context of Muslim Bangladeshi women as:

> [A] pattern of exchange between the sexes. The pattern includes an internalised acceptance, by both men and women, of the social subordination of women *vis-a-vis* elder male and female family relations and non-family social exchanges ... this represents a culturally and historically specific form of the social control of women.

In the *bustees purdah* is enforced by many members of the community, and can include rules around behaviour, physical space and dress, including the *burqa*.[4] In families where *purdah* is practised men and women try to maintain separation of the sexes in public and private spaces. In public spaces women use back alleyways (*goli* or *galiyan*) and the *bustees* have a maze of back alleys connecting homes, shops and toilet/water facilities, as Layla (female, 20) shows in her photo.

In private spaces *purdah* may also be practised by women and men occupying different rooms in a home. This is not always possible in a one-room *bustee* home and in these homes men tend to congregate in public spaces like streets or tea stalls, making the home a predominantly female space, especially in the daytime. The interpretation of *purdah* in this community means that an initial view of the space looks like there are only men in the slums: men do the grocery shopping; they operate rickshaws and fix cars; and they hang about drinking tea and playing card games. Young children who do not practise *purdah*, are also everywhere in the public areas playing and conducting errands. Young women rarely 'hang out' in public, but can be seen walking to and from destinations (like school) and collecting water. In contrast the *golis* are buzzing with activity: there are girls playing, gossiping, washing clothes and cooking. Because modest covering (especially the *burqa* and *niquab*) allows young women in the public space to maintain *purdah*, young women often don some covering when they are visible.

The relationship between seclusion, *izzat* and patriarchy has been discussed by scholars throughout South Asia and many argue that concerns over *izzat* and social exclusion decrease young women's ability to participate in many aspects of public culture (Amin 1997). Moreover in her analysis of what it

Figure 2.1 'This is one *goli*' (Layla, female 20)

means to be a Muslim woman in Kolkata, Roohi (2007: 1) argues that Muslim women are not 'stakeholders' in a globalising West Bengal:

> [L]arge sections of Muslim population in India in general and West Bengal in particular, are found living at the margins and are often completely excluded in the government's plan of actions such as quality education and jobs.

One cannot doubt that Muslims in India certainly are excluded from participating in many aspects of the nation. There are over 170 million Muslims in India, and while the experiences of Muslims are rich, varied and diverse, the Muslim community, particularly the poor community, is ghettoised in Kolkata. According to the 2006 Sachar Report on Muslims in India, a disproportionate percentage of the Muslim population does not live in permanent housing structures or *pukka* homes made of bricks and cement (2006: 146). Muslims across India have limited access to water, electricity and cooking fuel. Their public participation especially in civil services, is also comparably poor to the majority Hindu population, but also compared to other minority groups including the Sikh community. In the state of West Bengal, for example, Muslims make up over 30 per cent of the population but constitute less than 10 per cent of the employees among the state's largest employers, the KMC (Kolkata Municipal Corporation) and Kolkata Police (Roohi 2007). What is more telling is that of the more than one million Muslims living in Kolkata, 80 per cent live in *bustee* communities (Sachar Report 2006). Roohi (2007: 2) further argues that Muslim women in contemporary Kolkata are:

> Doubly marginalised by virtue of being what is referred to as 'minorities within minorities', the women here lack agency to take part in any community discourse, – often being subsumed by the increasingly strengthening clutches of religious discourses set out by men of the community. Quoting the *Qu'ran* selectively, providing no scope for deliberation, intellectual discourse or *ijtihad*, a very conservative, subjugating and suppressive argument is built by the men of the community to keep the women away from the 'public' into the 'private' sphere.

I do not wish to detract from Roohi's observations of the inequality and injustice faced by Muslims, particularly youth, in the *bustees* of Kolkata – as this book will show, she is painfully correct at times. I do, however, wish to complicate this by reviewing how young Muslim women are, *through* the private sphere, challenging the dominant constructions and expectations of their lives and finding ways to fulfil personal transgressive desires in different public spaces. In fact it is in their manipulation of the 'the good Muslim girl' – that they are expected to be respectful, unaware, modest and submissive – that young Muslim women in this research win time and space to pursue multiple identities and transgressive desires. They blend transgressive identities with normative expectations of femininity to live out their desires in highly monitored spaces, and participate in a changing Indian and global youth culture in ways they see fit.

Children and youth/girls and young women

The good Muslim girl in the *bustees* is someone who is understood to publicly practise and observe the rules of a normative femininity. These rules are varied. As an unmarried girl, rules support: young women as homebodies who avoid interactions with the opposite sex; who are chaste and modest; who attend some schooling; who help with domestic chores and home-based work; and who submit to an arranged marriage. When a young woman challenges these expectations she risks being stigmatised as a 'bad' girl. This label affects her and her family's *izzat* and scholars have described similar expectations of dis/honour across India.[5]

In the field discussions of girlhood revolve around what it means to be a 'good girl'. Girlhood is difficult to define as it is understood to be both an age range and a social construct. As an age range the period of girlhood can take place within the categories of both 'childhood' (0–18, UNCRC 1989) and 'youth' (15–29, NYP 2014), as understood by policy. As discussed in the introduction, the overlapping definitions of child and youth according to international and Indian policies point to confusion regarding the end of childhood and the beginning of adulthood, or the end of 'child' and the beginning of 'youth'. The interchangeability of the terms 'girl', 'young woman' and 'youth' are a reflection of this liminality.[6]

The social expectations of the 'good girl' are bound by experiences of girlhood and expectations of marriage. Muslim girlhoods in the *bustees* take place when females are single. Girlhood in the *bustees* usually comes to an end when a young woman gets married, whether she marries at 16 or at 26. As pre-pubescent beings, girls in the *bustees* are expected to go to school, to play with friends and to help with chores around the home. During this time families 'tolerate' children playing loudly, support school-going and extra-curricular activities, and allow girls to experiment with clothing and accessories. These freedoms are considered to be temporary, and often wane when girls reach puberty. Puberty is a very important milestone in this community, particularly for girls, and we can loosely base the beginning of the youth period as aligning with puberty. In the *bustees* puberty signifies a move closer to marriage, and marriage is usually when girlhood and the youth period comes to an end. Biology, however, is not the sole determinant of transitions towards youth or adulthood, and I will show how extended education, employment and consumption possibilities, are challenging girlhood and the youth period, and shifting transitions to adulthood. To distinguish girls from youth I favour the term 'young women' to describe their pubescent lives, and to gender the term 'youth', but also to reflect how young women see themselves – not as children, but not quite adult either.

Like many cities and towns across India, the *bustees* are undergoing significant social, political and cultural changes. Many of these changes have impacted the normative gendered expectations of young women and youth culture in general. For example there has been growing acceptance in the *bustees* that 'good girls' complete higher levels of schooling, and a majority of young women in this research have completed class 10, or secondary school, representing a marked difference in schooling participation in one generation. There has been increase in support for young women's education participation in public schools, a growing culture of non-formal education (NFE), and greater availability of private schools, tuition classes and tutors (Jeffrey, Jeffery and Jeffery 2004, 2005; Akhtar and Narula 2010; Jeffrey 2010). Other changes in the slums include evidence that romantic love and self-determined relationships are more frequent than a generation ago, and evidence exists that young women from different class backgrounds are participating in the public world of work. Depending on the context, these actions can either conform to, or disrupt notions of a 'good girl' – and as I show, it is not uncommon for one's romantic biography or working identity to be considered both 'good' and 'bad'. Indeed, similar changes have been reported throughout India.[7]

While the desire to participate in different avenues of a changing India, is strong, including participating in public work and tertiary education, young Muslim women in the *bustees* face considerable pressure to conform and behave in standardised ways that may not allow for independent romance or public employment. Although there is leeway to bend the rules of *purdah* in the slums, overtly transgressing acceptable behaviour of the 'good girl' can pose risk. In the *bustees* young women may experience physical and verbal violence, and be withdrawn from school when transgressing normative expectations. Other scholars have shown that young women across India also face similar experiences of risks when transgressing norms.[8] Researchers in Muslim communities around the world show young people transgress normative constructions of being 'good' in various ways and for various reasons including for love, pleasure and artistic expression.[9] Similarly young women in the slums pick and choose when and where to transgress the normative expectations of the 'good Muslim girl'.

'The good Muslim girl'

While individual experiences of girlhood will inevitably differ, young women describe a similar understanding of the normative constructions of girlhood in the slums. To understand what it means to be a 'good Muslim girl' young women participated in PhotoVoice activities where they took photos and edited and captioned images.[10]

I have written about using PhotoVoice in my research elsewhere (Chakraborty 2009). It is important to be critical of PhotoVoice within research, particularly with children. Within Children and Youth Studies there has been immense interest in visual methods. Like some adults, it is true some children and young people have varied literacy and verbal skills. Visual methods such as drawing and photos are particularly relevant with children who perhaps struggle with reading and writing, or are in the process of learning these skills. However, the way PhotoVoice is often presented within the discipline, as a method that children will be immediately attracted to because it is rooted in technology and seems fun, needs critique. The success of PhotoVoice in this community exists because of access and space; *purdah* culture means many spaces are off limits and as an adult, in particular as a caste-Hindu Canadian, I am not privy to certain spaces, nor do I feel comfortable working with young people in certain contexts – I discuss later about feeling uncomfortable joining young people on romantic dates, for example. Real-time visual images best explain or help to understand young people's lives in these private spaces, but many young people are equally if not more comfortable with informal interviews, focus groups and art. The success of PhotoVoice in this project also exists because it allows young people to share and discuss their printed photos and create photobooks, which they really enjoy. Through methods training they also develop a reputation in the community as 'expert' photographers. In a tech-savvy world where photos are increasingly created and consumed as digital images, young people's expertise and skill in film camera operation, and as owners of their own photo album with printed photos, provides them with important cultural capital, particularly amongst their peers.

Young people own the images that are present in this book, and many (not all) young women desired their images, real names and community location to be truthful and visible. However, since many young people reveal transgressive experiences, I have removed all identifying markers. This was a challenging decision, and is another aspect of visual methods, and PhotoVoice in particular, which needs critique, especially in research underpinned by children's rights. The importance of protecting anonymity and the best interests of the child are especially (but not always) rooted in Western-academic ethics processes, and this can present a conflict with young people's right to participate in research the way they see fit. In my own discussions with young people they stressed that the community are not attracted to academic publications that have come out of the research because they are drawn to community-centred documents and events that we have organised. Here I draw on Deacon's work on youth sexuality in South Africa, where she found categorising her participants as vulnerable, and vulnerability: 'did not always resonate with those which the participants locate for themselves' (2014: 264). I do not delve into this debate in this book (I have discussed children and ethics processes elsewhere: Chakraborty *et al.* 2012). Of course the history of unethical research with children influences (and rightfully so) these ethics processes and conceptualisation of vulnerability; however, the endpoint reinforces that the adult researcher makes final decisions on what is 'ethical'. In this case that means I made the final decision to block all identifying markers and use pseudonyms in this book, in spite of children's wishes, to respond to the potential of risk.

PhotoVoice is but one of the many visual methods that add to a repertoire of qualitative and participatory methods which I have used to understand young people's lives. Images are presented in this book to add to young people's expressions, and where young people themselves felt visual images help clarify their experiences. In this text I present young people's own images, particularly around the ideological construction of the 'good Muslim girl'. These activities were conducted between 2005 and 2014 and it is important to note that images of the good girl have not changed during this time (although discourses about being good have). All of young people's photos and discussions reveal a strong undercurrent of responsibility, duty and honour. With their photographs young women participated in one-to-one interviews, focus group discussions, peer-to-peer interviews and photobook creation. Fiza (female, 19) for example, describes in her photo (Figure 2.2) how the good Muslim girl is bound by her duties to her family. Fiza believes 'the good girl lives in a joint family and she will do anything for her family'.[11]

Fiza is from a large joint family in the established *bustees*. With her siblings, parents, grandparents and an unmarried aunt, Fiza's 14-member family provides her with a sense of closeness and familiarity; 'I don't think I'll ever be able to sleep alone' she once confessed to me when I told her about my recent experience in a hotel outside of the city. Although Fiza is very close to her family, at times she found the lack of privacy in her home to be difficult.

Figure 2.2 'The good girl lives in a joint family' (Fiza, female 19)

Practising Islam with sincerity and commitment is another way young women felt a good girl behaves. Asking young women what this means, Layla (20) offered that it meant to read the *Qu'ran* with serenity and sincerity. While Layla tried very hard to read the text as often as she could, she explained that most young women have difficulty understanding what they have read. 'Everyone reads in Arabic, as most of us have done, but its meanings are not that clear because it is Arabic and not Urdu'. While it is difficult for women to understand the meaning of *Qu'ranic* text, the physical act of both reading and praying, and the respect people have for the text, is an important aspect of being a good Muslim girl, as Mumtaz (female, 15) describes of her photo (Figure 2.3), 'the good girl takes *namaz* [prayer] five times a day'.

The photo shows Mumtaz's brother and his friends at their Islamic school (*madrasa*) inside the mosque (*masjid*). Interestingly, women are not allowed inside the *masjid* in the *bustees*. Mumtaz describes how she was able to take a photo of a *madrasa* in the mosque by manipulating the good girl, 'I was crying, saying that my brother was sick and didn't want him to go to school on his own and wanted me to walk him to the gate'. As we will see in the next three chapters, by manipulating the normative constructions of the good daughter, sister and schoolgirl, young women gain access to spaces and identities that are generally off-limits. Mumtaz, by her own admission, came from a very conservative family from a *jhupri* located at the periphery of the established slum. Both her brothers are unemployed, and there were rumours in the community that they are both heroin addicts. One of the most significant social changes to occur over the years has been the exponential rise of

Figure 2.3 'A good girl prays five times a day' (Mumtaz, female 15)

the availability of cheap and poor quality heroin (or 'brown sugar') in the *bustees*. This availability has affected the slums in different ways, with both increased profits for many drug dealers, as well as more male addicts from poor backgrounds. As I will show in the book, the number of prospective boys suitable for marriage has decreased as a result of this epidemic, but this did not stop young women from pursuing romantic relationships with local boys.

For many young women puberty amplifies their duties in the home. Many of these duties test or prepare them as future wives and mothers. Zafreen (female, 17) for example explains 'the good girl studies very hard and she hits her siblings if they are not studying either' (see Figure 2.4). Learning and enforcing discipline is a skill Zafreen felt would benefit her own siblings so 'they take studies seriously'. They also contribute to her performance of a good girl who is learning mothering skills of discipline and sternness.

Zafreen is from a comparatively wealthy family in the established *bustees*. Her small six-person family has two working members, her father and older brother. With two younger brothers left to certainly contribute financially, Zafreen enjoyed luxuries such as two pairs of eyeglasses and daily pocket money from her family. Her perceived higher status and her calculated attempts to maintain friendships with similar status girls did not win her many friends with the bulk of participants in this research. During focus group discussion she found most girls ignored her.

Many photographs reveal young women conducting activities that relate closely to marriage and motherhood. In her analysis of a photo taken of her

Figure 2.4 'You study hard, and can hit your siblings too, this earns respect' (Zafreen, female 17)

older sister (Figure 2.5), Layla (20) articulates the normative construction of a good girl is to have control over all food preparation and serving.

Layla explains that in her house her oldest sister is in charge of all meals. In Layla's family her sister developed a reputation for being a good cook, which Layla is at times envious of. In many families it is girls and women that are responsible for preparing meals, with the main cooks often the last to eat. Boys and young men, in contrast, are often responsible for the public marketing since *purdah* rules deem these larger public spaces male space (although older married women can be seen marketing at times). Young women eating last can ensure that the breadwinners, usually the fathers and sons, are fed first, but also reaffirms the cook's position as a self-sacrificing and respected controller of meals (see also Donner 2008 in middle-class Kolkata).

By her own admission Layla came from a poor home and she describes herself as a 'strict Muslim'. After the death of her mother in 2003 Layla began to read the *Qur'an* regularly and found tremendous comfort in her faith. She is one of only a handful of young women who took the full covering *burqa* on a regular basis including at work and at shopping centres (as opposed to the long robe (*niquab*) and hair scarf (*hijab*) in daily life, or using the *burqa* only in the streets). Mobility restrictions are also a concern that develop in earnest post-puberty (see Lamb 2000 in Hindu rural West Bengal),

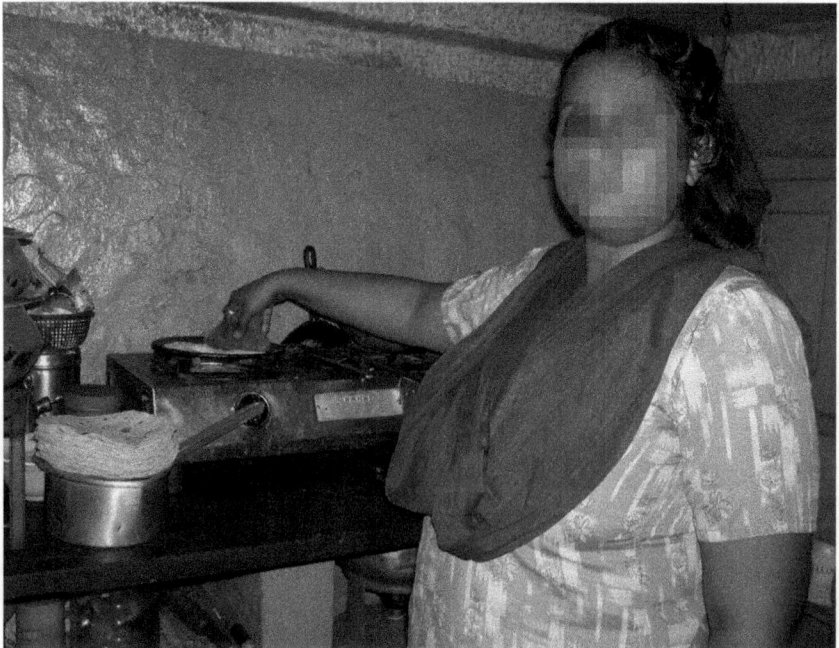

Figure 2.5 'The good girl prepares all the meals, and always eats last' (Photo of her older sister by Layla, female 20)

and Layla's taking of the *burqa* allowed her to practise *purdah* and remain modest in public places. This public modesty allowed her to maintain paid public employment and work with a variety of people including boys and men – something many of her non-*burqa*-wearing peers could not do. As I show the *burqa* is an important tool in young women's lives, with many young women choosing to manipulate the *burqa* to live out alternative identities.

Clothing is a critical marker of young women's public identities in the slums. Clothing choices are tied to the arrival of puberty for many girls. Often what is lost at puberty is the 'innocence' of being a young girl – physically the 'innocence' of girlhood wanes as young women's bodies begin to develop. Young women in this research recall how abruptly their dresses and skirts went from being acceptable home and street-wear, to absolutely unacceptable in both private and public. They expressed sadness as they remembered how their favourite frocks, trousers and shorts were decisively passed down to their younger siblings shortly after bodily development which occurred after the onset of menstruation. The onset of puberty is understood by Shazana (female, 15) as a time when 'tomboy' activities make way for more 'feminine' pursuits. She explains of her photo of Layla's younger sister (Figure 2.6) that 'a good girl covers her body' and takes pride in her modest appearance.

Shazana implies that 'good girls' are feminine, and she constructs this femininity through dress sense, behaviour, family duty and physical movements. Femininity is understood in opposition to masculinity, thus 'good girls' are everything 'good boys' are not. Best friends since small children, Shazana and Aysha (female, 15) are two of the most exuberant young women that I knew in the *bustees*. Both from strict households – Shazana from the *jhupri* and Aysha from a *pukka* home – they constructed elaborate schemes to win opportunities to participate in various activities including wearing sexy Western clothes in public shopping malls, actions with serious implications to one's *izzat*.

Concerns about developing bodies are one of the reasons why young women have restricted mobility in the *bustees*. Puberty alters mobility for all girls. Young women expressed annoyance, for example, when explaining the burden of sometimes carrying water back to their homes to bathe in private (see also Jeejeebhoy 1995), or waiting patiently in the home for siblings to bring water. The public water taps, once the site for meeting friends and partaking in gossip and play, became a short stopover in their everyday lives post-puberty. Wet bodies in public laneways drew attention to a young woman's developing breasts, which is both dangerous and dishonourable. If water collection continued to be a daily chore, young women seldom stayed for long periods to chat. More often the duty of water collection gets passed down to younger siblings or older married women, further decreasing young women's public mobility.

The heightened discourse of *izzat* is something young women in this research understood to be a consequence of being of poor socio-economic status which creates a particular kind of conservative neighbourhood that

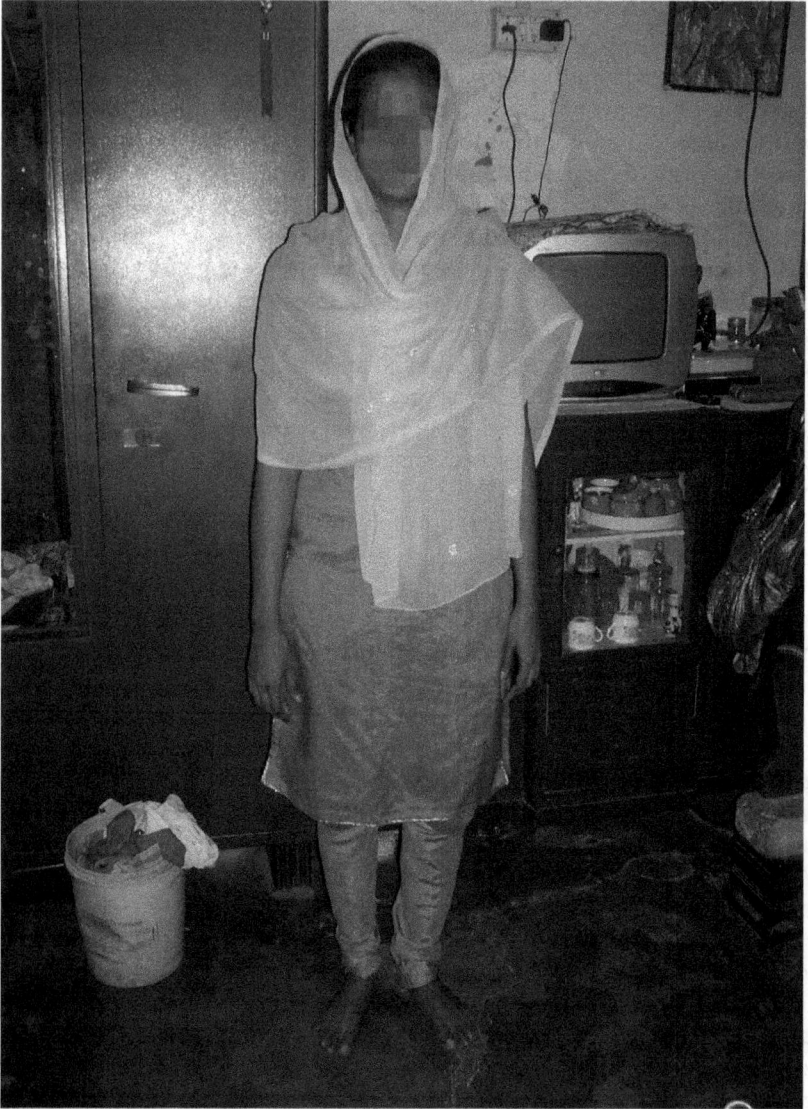

Figure 2.6 'A good girl covers up her body' (Photo of Layla's sister, by Shazana, female 15)

young people express as '*kharab para*' or '*kharab maahaul*' (living in a 'bad neighbourhood'). Many young women felt that middle-class Muslim girls from 'good neighbourhoods' did not experience similar heavily monitored mobility or restrictions on their clothing or their social relationships (see Mehra *et al*. 2000). For some young women the burden of the bad neighbourhood also influences the practice of *purdah* in the slums, while for others *purdah* was an expression of faith. For many young women *purdah* and patriarchy are inseparable. For Parveena (female, 18) the *burqa* protects a young woman's modesty in public (see Figure 2.7)

Parveena felt the garment showcases one's 'strict Muslim' identity and that young men who view her should not be interested in her. Both *purdah* and the use of the *burqa/niquab* is one of the key ways girlhoods in the *bustees* differ from other girlhoods, including other Muslim youth, in India. The way *purdah* is interpreted in the community also keeps young women from working in public, and this restricts their already limited work opportunities, which is something Parveena was very critical about, 'these rules should allow you to work outside, but instead even with *burqa* you cannot work outside'. Parveena is one of the most economically deprived young women in this research. Her mother, a widow, works 12 hours a day in the home to provide for Parveena and her younger sister. At times Parveena helps her mother cut shoe soles to bring home extra income. Parveena's limited mobility did not stop her from contributing to her household, and she often obtained gifts from her boyfriend to help the family. This activity was looked upon with suspicion by some of her peers.

Although independent premarital romance and love marriages are on the rise in this community, for many speaking to similar age boys not related to the family in public can hamper one's *izzat*. Public knowledge and display of premarital romance is looked upon with negativity, particularly if young women are in relationships with the 'wrong' sort of boy: local, poor and un/der employed. Given that *most* young women end up in relationships

Figure 2.7 'A "good girl" wearing the *burqa*' (Parveena, female 18)

with poor local men, slander and possibilities of violence often initially greet those whose relationships become public before marriage. Developing romantic relationships certainly is not considered to be the proper behaviour of good girls, as Aliah (female, 16) describes (Figure 2.8).

In discussing this photo, Aliah explains that the love of a boy is not worth hurting one's family. 'I have seen mothers cry because of their daughters. A boyfriend is not worth that – I will trust the choice of my parents and *inshallah* I will have a good future.' Aliah has faith in her parents and God that her future arranged marriage will be successful. She did not want to leave such an important decision to herself and felt that young people have a moral obligation to marry a partner of their parent's choice.[12] Aliah is viewed by her peers as well-to-do because she lives in a flat with her family. In actuality she struggles economically as her father is the only earning member of the family. Rent for their flat is on par with rent of a one-room *pukka* home. The perception of Aliah's wealth is due to her living quarters – her home is on the second floor of what was once one of the only three-storey buildings in the *bustees*. When I first met Aliah in 2005 she was the envy of her friends because of her sophisticated home. During the course of research many government-tenanted *bustees* were demolished to make room for high-rise living. The period between 2011 and 2014 saw rapid construction in the community, with almost every square metre of free land in the *bustees*, including old garbage dumps and sewage canals, being paved over to make way for residences, many of which are multi-levelled, a reflection of the population pressures in the heart of the city. Aliah is aware of her perceived reputation of being well off, but

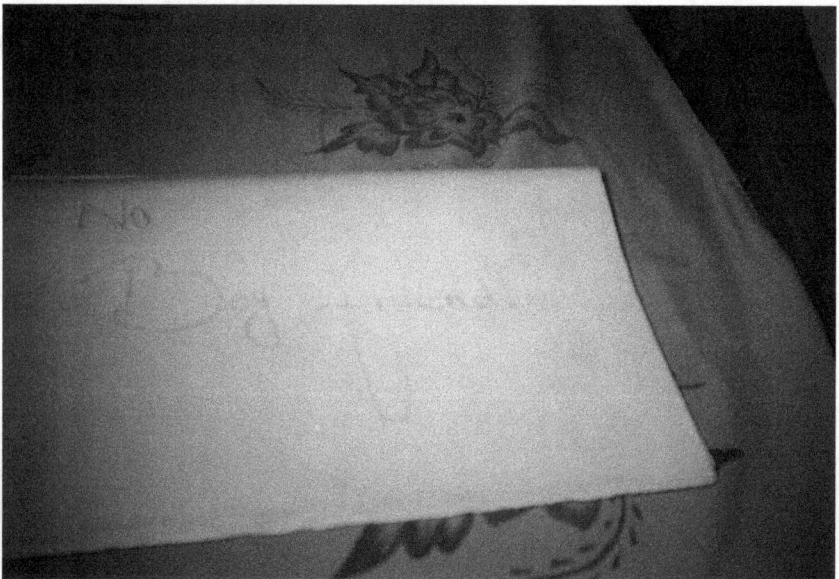

Figure 2.8 'A good girl does not have a boyfriend' (Aliah, female 16)

she is personally not keen on high-rise living. She told me that ground-level *bustee* homes are often larger, and young women can have access to spaces around the home without supervision, including courtyards and laneways. When I first met Aliah she could not conceive of having a romantic relationship and avoided interactions with boys in all capacities. In 2011 she was happily, and secretly, pursuing a relationship with a local Christian boy. Her thoughts on romance changed over time, particularly as she gained access to public space and started co-educational college. During school travel she met her current partner and confessed to me in 2013 that she was even thinking of eloping with him.

When it came to developing a relationship with the opposite sex, a good girl relegates this task to her family, as Aysha explains, 'after she has fulfilled her school and household duties, the good girl will trust her life to her parents and marry (*shaadi*) the boy of their choice. She will never desire the love from him before that.' The good girl, thus, is heterosexual, and maintains heteronormativity in the slums.

A 'good Muslim' girlhood in the *bustees*, then, is socially constructed as a linear process. As young children, girls are expected to enjoy a carefree childhood. Puberty entails changing expectations regarding their behaviour, duties and freedoms. Finally marriage ushers young women into womanhood, effectively ending girlhood. While this is the dominant model of girlhood young people are very critical of this linear expectation. For many young women I spoke with there is room to challenge the normative constructions of girlhood, especially in leisure times; young people create time and space to play with different fashions, participate in mixed-sex dance, join higher levels of schooling and even public paid employment. This book shows how a globalising India makes room for many to transgress ideal girlhoods. We also see shifts to discourses of the ideal girlhood to include extending schooling and paid public employment, which is creating a new youth culture in the slums. I also map the various levels of support for such shifts. This support comes from a number of sources including peers, family members, community leaders and Bollywood popular culture.

Bollywood and identity in the *bustees*

Private and public debate about a 'rapidly modernising' India often converges in the discursive production of youth culture as the site of conflict. The recent implementation of learning yoga in secondary schools as a way to challenge the felt Westernisation of the sex education curriculum is an example of the state trying to manage threats to 'Indian culture' (see Chakraborty 2010b). Youth in such policy endeavours are seen as a body in need of protection, in spite of youth demonstrations that sex education from reputable sources is desperately needed. Youth as a site of conflict is a message that Bollywood takes up in earnest. The well-educated, well-travelled young (usually) Hindu middle-class protagonist negotiating his/her 'Western' inspired lifestyle, duty

Figure 2.9 'A good girl gets an arranged marriage' (Photo of Aysha's friend by Aysha, female 15)

to country, and various 'Indian' inspired values, is a tale that can be seen on screen numerous times, particularly in Bollywood films of the 1990s and early 2000s. Explicit in these productions is a self-aware and anti-colonial nationalism, where 'the Indian' writes his/her identity though participation in an imagined occident and orient. This anti-colonial nationalism, Lukose (2005: 917) argues, has 'created homologous dichotomies such as Indian/Western …

private/public, tradition/modernity … in order to produce a nationalist identity that could be seen as separate from and superior to Western domination'. In Bollywood this predictably sees a 'good Indian' trying to participate in premarital dating without the sex, consumption without the greed, and importantly, embody Indianness through the institution of 'the Indian family' (see Uberoi 1998; Chakrabarty 2002). We see throughout this book young people drawing on these Eastern/Western and other dichotomies presented in Bollywood when taking risks and adopting transgressive identities.

The 1990 and early 2000 Bollywood productions are the most popular and the preferred viewing choice for young people. Pirated copies of these films are the most purchased at local shops, and these are also the films that tend to be shown on television. Over the last five years, however, Bollywood has become very different in its story telling. While the typical 1990s style 'family film' (and remakes of the 1980s 'actions films') still exist, there are a lot more regular depictions of young people enjoying premarital sex, living together before marriage, alcohol and partying (for example *Aashiqui 2* [2013]). As we will see, not all young people embrace these new (liberal) depictions of sex, partying and mobility at all times; rather they pick and choose when viewing and modelling this behaviour is appropriate in their lives.

Young women in the *bustees* turn to contemporary Bollywood culture for inspiration in their everyday lives, but more than just as a vehicle for fantasy and entertainment, globalising Bollywood entertainment represents to Muslim youth a national popular culture. In fact, it is through their rejection of regional (especially Bengali) popular culture that youth in the *bustees* write their identity as young Muslims. Young people articulated to me on countless occasions that they did not identify with the dominant Bengali youth culture of West Bengal. Asking Golu (male, 23) if he watched any Bengali television serials, he responds, 'are you kidding? I hate it, I'd rather turn off the TV and watch nothing than watch a Bengali serial. Ask anyone here they'll say the same … it's so boring and slow'. While for Layla (20), Bollywood 'is the best *timepass* [time passing activity] because it's *bindaas* [cool]'. For young people Bengali culture belongs to the 'local/traditional/oriental India' (Saldanha 2002), and this culture has distinct social, class and religious links. Hollywood is also not at all on the radar of young people in the *bustees*, and this is in contrast with upper-class youth culture in Kolkata where Hollywood, Western pop music and video games factor significantly in their leisure time.

Young Muslim people's identification with Bollywood as their own national popular culture meant positioning themselves within a Hindi–Urdu-speaking pan-India (North India, in particular). This India is well represented and in some cases dominates film, television and radio programming in Kolkata. The Hindi–Urdu dominance of Bollywood helps to reinforce young people's belief that Muslims are powerful in the entertainment industry, 'you see all the big names, Salman Khan, Shah Rukh Khan, Amir Khan … they are all the big draws, they have (the industry) in their hands' (the Organiser, 21). The Organiser explains that Muslims may represent a minority in the nation, but many young people perceive that Muslims dominate the areas that matter, including the entertainment industry and the city of Kolkata itself. 'Kolkata you can't say is a Bengali city … at least the core of the city is pure Muslim' (Heera, 20). Popular cultural dominance in particular is viewed with great pride by young people in the *bustees* who described Hindi–Urdu language programming as far superior – especially in its stylistic production, music and promotion – to any other popular culture in India. Claiming Bollywood as their own is also another way many young people respond to the discrimination, exclusion and persistent poverty which exists in *jhupri* communities in particular. Young people are not under the illusion that Muslim dominance in Bollywood translates into their real lives. Layla (20) argues that young Muslims' awareness of exclusion outside of the Kolkata-Muslim world keeps them insular, 'for us then it means to stay in the *bustees*, stay in the city-proper where we can just learn Urdu, not have to go outside to bigger schools to get Bengali'. Bengali language skills in the slums, thus, are an indicator of high mobility and educational support; however speakers of Hindi/Urdu/Bengali will notice that young people use a mix of all three languages in their communication throughout the text.

Bollywood's connection to the Urdu language is important. The knowledge of Urdu is considered a key feature of Muslim identity in North India and is understood to be a distinct 'Muslim' language across the nation. The importance of Urdu as a Muslim language is significant in the Bihari-dominated slums whence this book draws its material, as it separates this community from Bengali-speaking Muslims in the area. But it is not solely the Urdu language that makes Bollywood a popular choice for youth – it is the *bindaas* factor attributed to the music, fashion, choreography and production which meant that by claiming Bollywood culture as their own young people align themselves with a dynamic, modern, oxidant India.

Bollywood as a cultural production, however, can and does exclude Muslims. Scholars have explored how the experiences and identities of minorities including (and especially) Muslims can be (and are) unfairly stereotyped or completely excluded from the cultural construction of 'the Indian' in popular culture.[13] But the audiences are also skilled readers of popular culture, and have their own analysis and interpretations of stereotypes and exclusions, which can be complex and shifting.

When discussing the dominant representations of Muslims in popular culture, young people in the *bustees* are flippant about stereotypes. They often do not take on board these representations, 'so they are showing the [Muslim] guy as a terrorist, so? That's not me … and there are bad people in every community, they show other bad people too in the films' (Layla, 20). For Layla films and serials are entertainment that aim to engross a large audience, and should not be unpacked 'too much'. Aysha (15) further reflects that stereotypes of the 'Muslim terrorist' are socio-historically specific and thus she understands why films typecast terrorists too in such a way: 'I think after [September 11 and Kargil and the Mumbai bombings] people were very uneasy about terrorists and so in the films they are showing how we face such problems and the way to combat them'. Aysha contends that films cinematically depict current events which entangle Muslims including India-Pakistan tensions and post-9/11 tensions, and that films give the audience examples of ways to counteract negative forces in society. Moreover, both Layla and Aysha did not see themselves in many of the negative Muslim stereotypes present in popular culture because they assume 'most of the Muslim bad ones are Pakistani, not Indian like us' (Aysha, 15). Rather, they understood that these stereotypes were examples of 'real bad guys' that exist in every community, but in particular outside of India. Young people in this research are hyper-nationalistic, and even more specifically, are very proud Kolkattans. The threats they do feel as Muslim minorities are articulated most violently through central government politics, and thus for many young people, 'I will never leave Kolkata, I never can, I can't see a life outside this city' (Rena, female, 17). Young people see Muslims at the root of this city's success, culture and future, and in this way the Muslim-terrorist-from-Pakistan trope in Bollywood, rings especially distant.

While all of the young people in this community agree that the stereotype of the Muslim terrorist or *goonda* (thug) is a dominant image, they selectively engage with Bollywood culture as an entertainment and teaching tool. More than just *timepass*, Bollywood culture proves to be an important educational tool and although Bollywood and the worlds it conjures are far removed from the realities of the *bustees*, young Muslim women look to Bollywood and pick and choose messages of dance, consumption, love and fashion to inspire them. Bollywood is an important role model particularly in the face of changing social norms where normative resources and traditional knowledge keepers are inept or fading in importance.

Notes

1 See Gill and Brah 2014; Abbas 2011; Oza 2001, 2006; Rajan, Dhanraj and Lalita 2011 for more information about *izzat* in the Indian context.
2 See other examples including Jejeebhoy and Sathar's (2001) exploration of Muslim women's autonomy in India and Pakistan.
3 See other examples in Bangladesh such as Amin 1997; Rozario 1992, 2006 and Kabeer 1994.
4 I use the spelling *burqa* throughout this text, keeping with Amin's (1997) work in Bangladesh.
5 For other examples see Sodhi and Verma 2003; Alexander *et al.* 2006; Still 2011.
6 I discuss the conflation of youth/child/adult in other places (Chakraborty 2010a, 2010b, 2012a, 2012b).
7 See Kapur (2010) and Patel's (2010) work on women employed in call centres in India. The experience of love and romance amongst Indian youth is also a burgeoning field of investigation (Donner 2008; Mody 2008; Grover 2009, 2010; Netting 2010).
8 Mody (2006, 2008) has shown how some young women are disowned by their families when seeking individualised romantic love in Delhi. Kapur (2010) discusses how young women who divorce are viewed as sexually accessible and available to all men. Maslak and Singhal (2008) demonstrate how young women

who pursue their desire for college can be burdened by the possibility of being branded 'unmarriageable' in the future.

9 In different parts of the Muslim world Bennett (2005a, 2005b), Beazley (2002, 2008) and Schielke (2009) talk about transgressions to obtain personal pleasures, while Abraham (2010) discusses artistic expression – animation culture – as a site of transgression.

10 I have discussed my methodology elsewhere (Chakraborty 2009). See also Wang and Burris (1997) for the history of PhotoVoice.

11 Research was conducted in Urdu/Hindi/Bengali. I have translated the voices of participants using, where possible, localised English words and expressions.

12 High-profile cases, including the death of Rizwanur Rahman, a young Muslim young man who was thought to have been murdered after secretly eloping with a wealthy young Hindu woman (see Hindustan Times 2007), help reinforce the safety of arranged marriages, and the moral obligation of youth to submit to them.

13 See for example Malhotra and Alagh 2004; Desai 2004; Dudrah 2006; Kaur 2002; Mishra 2002; Desai, Dudrah and Rai 2005; Akhtar and Narula 2010.

3   Bollywood dancing in the *bustees*

Introduction

On a warm night in December 2004 local non-governmental organisation (NGO) *Azeem* staged its first ever 'professional' cultural show, complete with an experienced choreographer, a large rented auditorium and professional lighting. Cultural shows are standard practice for schools, NGOs and other organisations across India. It is an event that showcases the cultural learnings and/or talents of the community. *Azeem's* performance was far from a small-time local show; it comprised 40 performers, an audience of over 900 people, and important dignitaries (VIPs) including local politicians. When I first started fieldwork in 2005 the show was discussed with great pride. Local youth who worked at *Azeem* expressed pride that hundreds of local *bustee* residents and VIP guests were able to sit in plush red velvet seats to watch children, youth and some NGO staff recite poetry, perform folk and Bollywood-style dance in same-sex groups, and sing love songs. The biggest source of excitement was the last event of the evening, which the audience knew was going to be different, because when the curtain lifted on the stage there were a handful of young men *and* two young women. According to local youth the group danced with fervour – a choreographed Bollywood routine complete with gyrating pelvises, thrusting bodices and sequin crop-tops. It was with great excitement that youth described how mixed-sex Bollywood dance had found its way into the real lives of Muslim youth in the *bustees*. The show ignited the possibility of public mixed-sex Bollywood dance being incorporated into youth cultural practices and thus when I entered the field in 2005 local youth were waiting in anticipation for their call to participate in a similar event the following year.[1]

Song and dance sequences, arguably the most distinguishing feature of popular Indian cinema, have always had an important role in films. They move a plot forward and offer timely interruptions in addition to providing the audience with entertainment. Popular film dance can also denote a cultural specificity. Tamil cinema, for example, can draw heavily on indigenous *Bharata Natyam* dance culture. Indeed cinema dance plays an important role in identity building, where learning particular dance styles can be a way to write and perform one's cultural identity, particularly in the Indian diaspora.[2]

In recent years song-and-dance numbers in Bollywood cinema have taken on an identity of their own resulting in films incorporating stage-managed 'autonomous' song-and-dance sequences in its filmic design (Mishra 2002: 2). The autonomous music-video sequence, along with the growing use of 'item numbers' – song-and-dance productions performed by guest star(s) – is a piece of entertainment conveniently ready for screening in various spaces including the plethora of music video television shows in India (see also Nijhawan 2009). The popularity of music videos with a distinct life for television audiences allows Indians, including youth in the *bustees*, to have access to hundreds of song-and-dance clips a day on channels like MTV India, without having to watch hundreds of full-length movies. This type of access, uncommon a generation ago, is an important part of youth culture and a quotidian part of young women's lives in the *bustees*.

The viewing of Bollywood dance and song on television in the slums is generally enjoyable for all members of the family, but the comfort and viewing pleasure of the family audience is dependent on the level of provocativeness of the entertainment. With the family in one room, raunchy dance sequences like Rakhi Sawant's item number in *Krazzy 4* (2008) results in the channel being swiftly changed. In contrast, with similar aged peers, provocative dance is joyfully viewed by young people. Young women in the *bustees* greatly enjoy the gyrating (*jhatka/matka*) and sexualised styles of Bollywood dance, especially item numbers. Although some young women express their distaste towards these numbers in public, most love to view, comment and discuss these dances with close friends.

In homes across the slums there are many young women who copy sexy dance moves like Malaika Arora's famous hip swivel in *Dabangg* (2010). Conversations with parents and elders reveal that the community is tolerant of young women mimicking Bollywood dance in the privacy of their own homes, and in front of only same-sex family members if the dance moves are provocative. Although I have observed elders reprimanding youngsters dancing during television programmes, it is often due to the distracting nature of the activity.

In the *bustees* it is inappropriate for young women to dance (especially provocatively) in public, and Morcom (2013) has discussed in detail the reception of women dancing in India in different communities. Mixed-sex dancing is particularly risky and can be met with slander and possible violence by one's family and community. Both young women who danced with young men in the first *Azeem* show, however, did not face any harm. One participant, the Choreographer (female, 23), was omitted from negative gossip by locals because according to young people she was a middle-class woman from a prominent family, 'she is not like us, she comes from a higher place' (Shazana, 15). In fact, she was the daughter of *Azeem*'s CEO and sister of the organiser, and young people were correct in their observations. The other young woman Raya (16) was from a family that publicly supported her choices, 'her family is strong, they don't even listen to what anyone says they just go their own way' (Shazana). Participants argued that it is local young women from 'traditional families' with little family support that are affected by taunts and gossip, and for them public Bollywood dancing is overwhelmingly risky.

Bollywood dance does not exist without its partnering song. In the *bustees* popular Bollywood music can be heard at various decibels playing from televisions and radios in shops, in homes and in vehicles at almost any time of the day. Young Muslim women listen to Bollywood music through television and radio for *timepass*, that is for fun and to pass time as a hobby, while performing chores and doing housework. In schools young women also sing songs in same-sex environments, and play *filmi* music games including 'guess the song'. Singing in public places by young women (other than girl children), however, is rare in the slums. Singing out loud is particularly unacceptable because it draws attention to oneself, and drawing attention to one's presence, particularly through provocative Bollywood lyrics, is unacceptable. Singing in public is also a well-known technique used by female sex workers in the area to gain the interest of prospective clients. In the *bustees* a young woman's public relationship with music and dance, like all of her other public relationships, is intertwined with concerns of *izzat* and the public reputation of herself and her family. Thus the desire to learn and perform publicly mixed-sex Bollywood dance in *Azeem's* cultural show is very risky for young women.

Discos and class

Most young women in the slums believe that the freedom to participate in Bollywood song and dance culture in public is reserved for upper-class youth. Saldanha's (2002) work on dance in youth culture in Bangalore depicts upper-class youth participating in dance cultures in various spaces including at parties, nightclubs and in cars. He shows that public dance culture in large Indian cities is a way for upper-class youth to perform their higher-class status and make connections with a global youth culture in the face of an India that is changing, but is predominantly rural and poor. Youth in the *bustees* of Kolkata have little access to these avenues of dance culture. They view at a distance the lives of upper-class peers through weekly re-caps of disco events and parties in the 'page two' gossip columns of newspapers, and on local news reports.

During my fieldwork I had opportunities to go to nightclubs (or *discs* – an abbreviation of the term disco) on the weekend. These opportunities allowed me to interact with many upper-class and elite members of Kolkata society from all cultural and religious backgrounds. Many of these participants viewed their class status and dominance in the *disc* scene as interrelated. As a Canadian of Indian and caste Hindu background, young people in the *bustees* also viewed my *disc*-going as normative non-resident Indian (NRI) behaviour.

In fact when I did not go to the nightclubs young people expressed concern, asking if I was unwell on the weekend. When I did go to the *discs* I was overwhelmed with requests to describe these events when back in the *bustees*. Young women brought out the current page two columns to ask me about events they had read. This re-cap was enjoyed by all, especially if I reported the 'bad behaviour' or interesting clothing choices of local celebrities. Importantly, these meetings reinforced my foreign (*ferengi*) status and the mobility freedoms of upper-class young women like myself, while making room for *bustee* youth to learn and gossip about public Bollywood dance culture and gain knowledge about upper classes, vicariously. The *disc* scene is different to the organised dance and Bollywood (aerobics) classes that take place in different parts of the country, which Morcom has discussed. For young women in the *bustees*, *discs* are much more youth-centred thus more cool than the 'bored housewife' organised class (Morcom 2013: 128).

In contrast to the rarity of females dancing in public, amongst young men Bollywood dancing can be viewed in certain public spaces in the *bustees*, especially during festivals or at *baraats* (wedding reception party). Most young women I worked with felt that these young men were *goondas* (thugs) or *bekar* (losers), usually rowdy 'low class boys who are up to no good' (Shazana, 15). Shazana suggests that poor boys mark their low status reputation through public dance. In contrast public dancing that occurs in nightclubs is seen as a high class act performed by elite youth who have freedoms of socialising, mobility and greater social awareness; 'people from good neighbourhoods can dance together like that [at *discs*], they don't think of it negatively' (Shazana).

Another venue where men and boys can be seen dancing publicly is at the cinema hall. Often mimicking the moves on screen, this dancing may be encouraged by other men, who cheer them on (see also Srinivas 2002). The cinema hall, particularly in poorer neighbourhoods and especially on the weekdays, is a male-dominated space, one where dominant masculinities including overtly sexualised dancing with peers is performed (see Derne 2000). Other spaces where public dancing and singing amongst youth can occur in the *bustees* include manual work places, where young men tune in to small radios or portable music players. Singing and moving to the music is a crucial way to pass the working day for some jobs, including auto-rickshaw driving and manual labour. A good example of the latter is at construction sites where workers sing songs to a particular beat to follow the rhythm of labour. The ritual of using song to engage in work such as digging wells or farming can be observed throughout India and is a commonly accepted form of public singing by ordinary people.

In the slums young men also use song as a means of 'eve-teasing', roughly translated as the public sexual harassment of women. Acts of 'eve-teasing' range from sexually explicit comments and catcalls, pulling or grabbing young women, to sexual molestation in public areas. Bollywood songs play an important role in this harassment, as common 'eve-teasing' involves serenading a young woman with a film song. A young man may burst into song when he sees a young woman passing by, singing a provocative song to express his desire. The song choices for these occasions often convey lust and may be specific to the situation – a young woman walking down the street with a handkerchief (*rumal*) in her hand may be serenaded with a rendition of '*mera pant bhi sexy*' where the lyrics mention how the hero's own *rumal* is more than practical, '*ye rumal bhi sexy!*' (my handkerchief is sexy). Different to the *badnam* (literally bad name or reputation) that occurs when young women sing in public, 'eve-teasing' is a way young men perform their heterosexuality in public, and single youth may find eve-teasing acts have limited support in the community. While recent campaigns in India have tried to decrease this harassment, 'eve-teasing' is still used throughout the *bustees* to reaffirm male heterosexual desire and dominance of public space (see the growing literature of eve-teasing including Gosh 2011; Phadke, Khan and Ranade 2011; Ramasubramanian and Oliver 2003). The tricky intersections between eve-teasing, harassment and flirting makes it difficult for many young women and young men to clearly read whether the teasing is harmless flirting, if young women like the boy in question or if they are afraid.

Bollywood participation and local Islam

While young men and women participate and perform Bollywood dance in different ways in the *bustees*, the position of song and dance in local Islam is not very clear. Some Muslim elders in the community believe that men and women should never dance together, and others have different rulings. A popular understanding is that dance is permissible privately between married couples and within same-sex environments. Some Islamic interpretations view mixed-sex dancing, especially in public, as *haram* (forbidden), 'Men and women dancing together is absolutely *haram* in all cases, except when a wife dances in front of her husband. The reason behind this prohibition is that with mixed dancing bodily contact is close and improper sexual desires are aroused' (Salamah 2007: online).

Religious differences regarding what constitutes acceptable forms of dance and music vary considerably across India. There is no homogenous form of Islamic artistic production and appreciation, nor is there blanket intolerance of dance and music in Islam, evidenced by well-known artistic cultures present throughout India including *qawwali, baul* and *kathak* cultures. Moreover popular Muslim singers and Bollywood actors reaffirm young women's understanding that it is their socio-economic position expressed through '*kharab para*' (bad/low class neighbourhood) that prevents young women from publicly participating in Bollywood dance and song culture in the *bustees*. We will see later on that it is not just their *kharab para* that prevents dance, but young people's own understanding of boundaries between childhood and adulthood.

Azeem's cultural show thus was a unique event to learn and practise provocative mixed-sex Bollywood dance routines. To participate in this event, systematic and organised risk taking at a group and individual level was necessary. Young women practised mixed-sex Bollywood dancing in an isolated geography, a rehearsal space located on the roof of a home. Dance in this 'third space' (Bhabha 1994, 1996) allowed young women to emulate *filmi* identities and desires that are saturated in a middle-class globalised youth culture which values individualisation and conspicuous consumption, and these intersect with local norms. The pursuit of dance in third spaces is not separate from the cultural constructions of dominant girlhoods, traditional gender and class roles and normative religious identity, and this chapter describes how young women negotiate multiple identities and desires when learning mixed-sex Bollywood dance. The accounts presented show how the success of a unique youth culture in this third space is a result of calculated risk taking and various levels of public and private support.

Supporting a Bollywood show

Azeem's first professional cultural show in 2004 was the beginning of the organisation's extravagant quasi-annual cultural programmes (there have been four staged since 2004, with funding being the biggest obstacle to organisation). The NGO itself started off as a small, one-room two-staff member organisation. Over the years they have been able to attract funding from the Indian government as well as foreign funding. The founder of *Azeem*, 'the CEO', is a well-known community leader and with well-known political connections. His family has resided in the area for two generations and its members have the reputation of being able to overcome adversity. Within a single generation the CEO was able to secure stable well-paying employment, set up his own NGO and attract large amounts of foreign funding. The CEO's elevation from a regular *bustee* resident to a middle-class elite, provides encouragement to young people who dream of making such leaps themselves. The CEO and his family (including his children, the Organiser, male 21 and the Choreographer, female 23) also have a reputation of being 'moderate Muslims' and passionate advocates for poor Muslims. In my conversations with the CEO he spoke of his ambition to lift Muslim slum dwellers out of poverty through societal recognition of their human rights, and he articulated strongly that he saw Islam and universal discourse about human and children's rights as compatible.

The dance show was one way Muslim youth could participate in something that challenged the public perception of their lives. The show first came to fruition after the NGO received funds from a foreign organisation interested in sponsoring 'cultural events'. According to the donor, the money was gifted to allow 'poor children one day to live out their dreams' (foreign donor representative, 2005). At the time *Azeem*'s CEO felt the event would 'celebrate the lives of the young people, which gives a chance for these hopeless children to have some light in their lives'. Verma (2002: 150) argues that NGOs and their funders are a new class of middlemen who speak on behalf of the poor. Some organisational visions are often underpinned by ideologies of a 'helpless' poor population in need of rescuing, even when using the rhetoric of human rights, which Bernal and Grewal (2014) have detailed. Indian human rights activists like P.K. Das have strongly critiqued the work of many NGOs, arguing they:

> ... subvert, dis-inform and de-idealise people so as to keep them away from class struggles. They adopt and propagate the practice of begging favours on sympathetic and humane grounds, rather than making the oppressed conscious of their rights ... their effort is constantly to divert people's attention from the larger political evils of imperialism to merely local issues.
>
> (P.K. Das cited in Davis 2007: 78)

While *Azeem* does at times buy into discourses of 'the helpless poor', cultural shows provided opportunity for youth to participate in Bollywood dance. Indeed without *Azeem*'s persistence of giving youth a chance to learn dance and have fun, such daring shows would not have been organised. Thus while *Azeem* may redirect attention away from issues of imperialism, neoliberalism, and promote stereotypes about poor Muslims 'in need of aid', at a very local level they are providing spaces for youth to realise desires and live out identities, albeit in a neocolonial and paternal way.

The second show in 2005–2006 clearly highlighted the NGO's growing status in the slums. This extravagant event allowed the community to witness the organisation's new-found foreign partnerships. In conceiving the show the Organiser felt immense pressure to create something spectacular:

> (We need to) make the show better than last year. Last year was just the beginning, this year we have to make it bigger and better. We want people to demand tickets and talk about the event for years to come.
>
> (The Organiser, male 21)

To ensure success, preparations for the show began well over six months in advance. Sign-up sheets were sent to several non-formal education centres. The idea of the show was well received by the female students, with over 40 young women signing up. During the sign-up process there was a flutter of activity as young women anticipated participating in the show. They described to me later that the atmosphere was electric. Young women were hugging each other in excitement. If going by the previous year's show, participation meant an opportunity to learn to dance, to meet boys and dance with them, to perform publicly, to meet new friends and live dangerously. Each element represented an important step towards participating in an India that they saw on their television screens. However not all young women signed up for the show, many because they did not want to disobey their parents: 'Yes I wanted to learn dance, but we are not allowed to publicly perform' (Sana, 16).

The Organiser was employed as the Youth and Cultural Coordinator of *Azeem* and he felt considerable pressure to pull off a grand show. Together with his sister, the Choreographer, the new programme was set to include a mixed-sex dance component and same-sex dance component. While the Choreographer did not have a formal role in the NGO, she was the choreographer for the previous year's show. She also had professional dance experience, having taken professional dance classes in the city. As ambitious, educated, upwardly mobile Muslim youth, the Organiser and Choreographer had developed a highly discussed reputation amongst *bustee* youth for having high-class aspirations and modern subjectivities. The siblings believed in their father's passions for sharing their middle-class privileges of education and social knowledge with the poor. Their generosity and willingness to share their time, their belongings (including Western clothes and make-up) and their family home during rehearsals is undeniable. In their own way the Organiser and the Choreographer were actively contributing to what they deemed 'social reform' for local Muslim youth *through* Bollywood popular culture literacy.

> We are giving a chance to these girls that they only see on the screens, and this will impact their lives ... in the future they can say "we danced on stage"; not everyone can say the same thing.
>
> (The Organiser, 21)

The Organiser was also involved in a romantic relationship with a young woman from the *bustee* that he also saw as a benefit to the community, 'if she marries a high class guy like me, it moves her family up too'. Romance is an important way young upwardly mobile and self-identifying 'modern' young women write their modern identities, as we see in the next chapter.

For most young women the Choreographer and Organiser represent contemporary youth in a globalising India. Their lives are on a par with the young people they view on screen, and thus very different to *bustee* girls, 'she (the Choreographer) is different from us, she is from a good family so she can go to *discs* and wear Western clothes' (Mirza, 17). Although they both came from the *bustees*, to Mirza the Choreographer was from 'a good family' because of her middle-class status. Her middle-class reputation was reinforced by access to an English medium school, Western clothes and comprehensive dance knowledge. According to young women it is the Choreographer's middle-classness that allows her to participate in a modern youth culture with little threat to her *izzat*. Like my *disc*-going participation, knowledge of modern arenas of youth culture was expected of her. For young women the Choreographer's Bollywood consumption practices 'become an index of the presence and reach of globalisation' (Lukose 2005: 915), and her identity as a modern young person was often tested by young Muslim women through Bollywood and consumption literacy.

Nach Baliye

While popular references to a global youth culture such as college-going and travelling seemed to be outside the reach of the average *bustee* girl, young women in the slums use the freedoms they have to create their own youth culture using Bollywood references. The *Azeem* show was one of these freedoms. Every show comprised of a dance (*nach*), drama (*natak*) and song (*gana*) component. The format of the show was developed by the show's Organising Committee which was composed of the Choreographer, the Organiser and three young employees from *Azeem*. Participants came from the various NFE centres *Azeem* operated. An elementary school NFE was responsible for the drama component and a centre with secondary school children was drafted for the singing aspect of the show. The dance portion of the show was split into two categories, a performance category with several girls-only groups, and a competitive programme for mixed-sex couples. Female participants for the girls-only group and the mixed-sex group were drawn from several secondary school NFE centres.

Of all the planned programmes, the mixed-sex competitive dance was the most exciting and challenging for young women. From the onset participants and the Organising Committee expressed that public knowledge of the event had to be contained in order to keep young people safe. Access to rehearsal space was restricted and guests invited to the final show would be hand-picked. The mixed-sex dance competition drew on dances from the latest Bollywood videos and was a take on the popular television series *Nach Baliye*. In September 2005, Star One launched *Nach Baliye*, a televised dance competition similar to the global 'Dancing with the Stars' series. *Nach Baliye* was a live celebrity dance-off where couples, generally actors from the small screen, undergo Bollywood dance training with well-known choreographers before facing other contestants in a competition. Spread over several weeks, the show saw one couple being voted off each week by a panel of judges from the entertainment industry. The show was a phenomenal success:

> *Nach Baliye* has been a universal super hit. Not only has it captured the imagination of Mumbai, Delhi and the metros, it has cut through into smaller towns … this is one show that has broken the barriers of mass and class.
>
> (Star India Vice President of Marketing Ajay Vidyasagar in Bijoy 2005)[3]

The programme was a hit in the *bustees*, as Shirzad (female, 16) explains 'when it initially was airing you couldn't find a single person in the *bustee*'. The dance reality show market has since grown with shows like *India's Dancing Superstar, Boogie Woogie, Dance India Dance* and *Dance India Dance Li'l Masters* (with only child participants), stirring the imagination of young people in the slums as they feature ordinary and sometimes *bustee*-dwelling youth living out their dance dreams on television. The reality dance concept has also made the crossover into Bollywood film (*Rab Ne Bana De Jodi* 2008) and television (*Sasural Simar Ka; Dil Dosti Dance*). The popularity of these reality shows made the dance competition format a contemporary inclusion in the *Azeem* programme. For many, dancing on the *Azeem* stage 'is like being a celebrity ... (like) people ... from good neighbourhoods' (Shirzad). It gave them the chance to live like stars and practise class fantasies, similar to both David (2010) and Dudrah's (2008) research in the Indian dance diaspora.

Learning dance was not the only reason to join the programme; there were other freedoms that were equally compelling:

> We were obviously excited to join *Nach Baliye* for many reasons, so we can learn how to Bollywood dance, and spend fun time with our friends ... for many of us it was because we knew that boys would be there, and we were scared and excited because of this. It was a chance to meet and talk and hang out with boys, a chance we rarely get. So for a lot of girls, whether they admit it or not, this was definitely a factor in their decision making.
>
> (Aysha, 15)

The opportunity to dance, meet young men and develop romantic relation-ships that may lead to marriage, had a significant impact on the young women. As Parveena (18) explained, 'at the sign up time maybe we didn't want to find a boyfriend, but once we started dancing all the girls did'.

Young women also looked forward to spending more time with their friends: 'why do it without your friends, it's too boring' (Tania, 16). In fact all of the young women signed up with their friends, knowing that rehearsals would allow them to spend more time together. In the *bustees* same-sex friends enabled young women to participate in mixed-sex dance. Young women travelled with friends to the rehearsals, and friends also provided moral support by cheering on one's dance progress. Young women's agency and desire to dance is rooted in friendship and same-sex support networks.

While recruiting young women involved a simple process of sending out sign-up sheets to NFEs, a wide call for male participants was not made. The Choreographer and the Organiser only recruited male participants by con-tacting known members of the community. Other young men were subse-quently recruited through positive recommendations (snowballing). From the onset there were concerns over how to recruit young men in order to 'keep away boys who had bad intentions' (NGO employee). Informal interviews and character checks by the *Nach Baliye* committee helped identify young men who were 'serious about dancing and of good character'. Aware of the potential risks associated with mixed-sex interactions, the organisers were looking for young men who were 'respectable' and 'committed to dancing'.

Of particular concern was ensuring the privacy of the young women, 'you can't just open up the *bustee* and say, "come on everyone who wants to do dancing, come". That's not how it works here' (the Choreographer, 23). However the Choreographer was also aware that young women were desperate to dance with boys:

> I know that most girls in the all-girl group are upset that they can't dance with the boys, but what to do? There are not enough boys to dance with this time around. I said to them they will have to wait until next year when hopefully we have more good boys to dance.
>
> (The Choreographer, 23)

The Choreographer felt that by denying young women a place in the *Nach Baliye* rehearsals she was restricting their already limited scope to meet 'decent' young men. This was a dilemma for her as there were only a handful of trustworthy young men known, and these boys were often personal contacts, and some were not local. We had several discussions about how to pair up the limited number of male dancers, and how she had to regretfully tell many young women they did not make it to the mixed-sex programme. During these conversations the Choreographer's middle-class positioning became quite clear, 'you know for some of these girls, the next man they will be this close with is their husbands, *becharis*'. The Choreographer is sympathetic that many of these 'unfortunate darlings' (*becharis*) are from homes where mixed-sex interactions are viewed as suspect, unlike her socially progressive friends and relatives who view mixed-sex (but non-sexualised) interactions as 'normal'. Through her ability to separate friendship from attraction, non-sexualised mixed-sex interactions were a sign of the Choreographer's own 'progressive' attitudes and middle-class status.

The Choreographer was in the powerful position of picking and choosing dancers, and she made executive decisions regarding who could participate in *Nach Baliye*. While young men had to be known, trustworthy and of noteworthy character, her criteria for female dancers were also very clear, 'I can't take the risk and choose everyone, I choose only the most committed, mature girls who will come to all the rehearsals'. She avoided at all costs girls from perceived 'very conservative families', not only because of fear of family disapproval or the consequences of getting caught, but also because these young women had less opportunity to attend rehearsals. 'They have more to negotiate at home to get out (to the rehearsals), I know they won't be consistent.' So the Choreographer also filtered participants on the anticipated amount of risk-taking she felt young women would have to take and successfully manage. Discussing dance selection with the Choreographer it was obvious that she viewed her commitment to the rehearsals and investment in the show as a social service. This social reform was underpinned by a self-conscious modern outlook – to modernise these *bechari* slum girls through cultural literacy and mixed-sex interaction.

Because of space and participant restrictions, many young women who signed up to dance were not admitted to *Nach Baliye*. This disappointed a great number of hopeful dancers including Sakina (female, 16):

> Last year I was in the all-girl group, it was boring because it was for babies. This year I said to (the Choreographer) I won't do the show unless I get to be in the *Nach Baliye* contest with the boys. But there was not enough room for me.
>
> (Sakina, 16)

The importance of mixed-sex interaction in her development from a girl to a woman was important to Sakina. Her comments reveal that although learning Bollywood dance is a keen goal for many young women, it was the *mixed-sex* dance that they really wanted to experience. Mixed-sex dance is viewed as 'proper' Bollywood style dancing. In contrast same-sex dancing is less exciting and seen as a compensatory style.

After much deliberation the Choreographer chose 13 young women and 13 young men between the ages of 15 and 21 to participate in the *Nach Baliye* competition. Most of the boys were working in manual labour jobs in and around the slum. The young women were all school going from similar social and class positions. Of course all young women are not alike and participation in the dance event and a growing Bollywood literacy magnified the fissures between more self-identifying 'modern' young dancers and their 'traditional' peers.

The Choreographer placed the 13 couples into partnerships. She paired the teams based on height and although this method was practical, it left many young men and women of dissimilar height who were initially romantically interested in each other quite disappointed. The Choreographer vowed to teach all of the young people who signed up to dance, but from the onset she recognised this would be a difficult task and enlisted the help of two dance 'captains', a male dance captain to supervise the young men, and a female dance captain to supervise the young women.

The captains, both veterans of the previous year's show, were regarded as being the best male and female dancers. The captains had non-traditional backgrounds – Roy (male, 18) was living in an orphanage and Raya's (female, 16) dance participation was supported by her entire family. Both had greater opportunities to practise dance and thus were perceived to be technically skilled dancers. The captains were chosen on the sole basis of their dance abilities. Roy had a reputation as a strong, flexible dancer and very fast learner. The female captain, Raya, was the only young woman in the group with any mixed-sex dance experience, and her style was considered to be technically superior. She had the reputation of being a tomboy and, apart from the Choreographer, was the only young woman in the *bustee* whom I knew of who had parental support from her entire family to participate in mixed-sex dance in public. The role of the captains was to keep the Choreographer informed of any issues that arose in their teams, help teach dance routines and resolve conflict.

A Western show

I first arrived at rehearsals in August 2005, and rehearsals at this time were going on for a little over a month. I was warmly welcomed by all the young people. I initially presumed I gained access to the rehearsal space because of the art and female education workshops I was hosting in the slums. The young women in the workshops invited me to the rehearsals, and after obtaining permission from the NGO, I began attending all of the rehearsals. On my first day I observed that the dance style being taught was character-istically *filmi*: young men and women were dancing together to popular Hindi songs using Bollywood-style dance moves with close physical contact and many sexually suggestive actions including gyrating pelvises, mock kissing and suggestive hand placement. I was shocked. Because of the public perfor-mances of the 'good girl' I had only known girls to be generally modest and often reserved. Suddenly watching young people grind up on each other without as much as an inkling that such organised and provocative steps were secretly being learnt really did surprise me. And at the time I very much doubted that a Bollywood programme like this could *ever* be publicly staged in the slums.

Although I saw the dance routines as typically *filmi,* the Choreographer and the performers saw the dance style as 'Western' and that *Nach Baliye* would be 'a Western show'. Moreover the Choreographer and the young women described the type of dance that took place in Bollywood films to be 'Western dance'. As Aysha explained:

> Western dance to me means the way that modern people dance in the *discs* in the West ... this type of dance is also done here in India in the *discs.* In real life these people are from good families and live in good neighbourhoods. It's also done in the films.
>
> (Aysha, 15)

Youth in the slums felt that Western dance was performed on screen in Bolly-wood films and in various Bollywood-inspired live-stage/television shows. It was also performed by youth in Western nations, and occurred in modern Indian society amongst upper-class people, those from 'good families and good neighbourhoods'. Thus there is a conflation between Indian youth culture and global youth culture, and this has been reported in youth cultures elsewhere (see for example Beazley in Indonesia 2002, 2003). It was not performed by *bustee* youth because of class and status restrictions and conservative attitudes. The Choreographer's dance inspiration came from Bollywood cinema. In the *bustees* Bollywood dance had a distant relationship to Indian dance; 'Indian dance' was the traditional folk and classical dance viewed on public television and at various cultural shows. 'Bollywood dance' was modern Indian dance, with some traditional familiarity, but not a lot. These findings relate to Rao's (2010) and Morcom's (2013) ethnographic work in India, where the local audience wanted some cultural familiarity with Bollywood, but that these familiar aspects of culture should intersect with global brands and perceived Western culture.

Like Nandy suggests, viewing Bollywood culture allows youth to study 'Indian modernity at its rawest' (Nandy 1998: 7). Young people's equation that upper-class Indian youth lived similar lives to foreign youth in the West is supported by Nandy's (2007) controversial essay which argues that many Indians 'are convinced that their future lies in being exactly like Europe and North America', and that Indian nationalism is fuelled by, amongst other things, a sense of inferiority and the need to play catch-up to a modern (imagined) West. This means for youth in the slums there is a conflation between Western culture and Bollywood culture, and Western youth and middle/upper-class Indian youth. The expectation that modern Western youth lived their lives like Bollywood stars in films obviously affected young people's expectations and assumptions of me as well. As a caste Hindu Canadian it was assumed that I participated regularly and fluently in the Western culture that they viewed in Bollywood films. I was expected to know about the latest fashions, technology and, importantly in this case, dance; *this* was the reason why I was able to gain access to the rehearsal space.

When I first arrived at the rehearsal I was immediately asked by young people and the Choreographer to dance the way 'Westerners in Canada dance in a *disc*', so they could get some ideas to improve their performance, 'and make sure we have it right' (the Choreographer). When I mustered up the best moves I could possibly coordinate without making a fool of myself (or so I thought) the young people looked at each other, puzzled, and exclaimed, 'that's not Western dance … this is Western dance!' and proceeded to dance very coordinated *filmi* moves. 'Kabita*di*, you don't know Western dance?!' they exclaimed in shock. Initially everyone was excited to have me provide dancing advice, but they were disappointed when they realised I could not dance in a Bollywood style. My cultural authenticity as a hip Westerner was diminished after this incident, but luckily regained through my nightclub excursions! My Western cultural competence was also tested in participants' homes. At one home watching an unmemorable Bollywood film with a female participant and her family, the leading actress with a very short dress on, exited a car. The participant's brother commented knowingly to the room, 'this is the kind of clothes you get to wear back home, don't you *didi*.' Contemporary Bollywood culture shows a fetishised view of the West. One of the most confronting is thin, white women interacting with often Indian male characters in different ways, usually as backup dancers. Within the last 10 years we see that Bollywood film production, award shows and reality television are including more female, thin and young Caucasian actors/dancers, whose presence is rooted in patriarchal Indian culture. Young people felt they understood my life in Canada and often knowingly discussed with their friends how I and my beautiful, thin, white female friends who also wear very short dresses, must go out to parties every weekend. For many young people living in the *bustees* popular culture 'is the slum's point of view of Indian politics and society and, for that matter, the world' (Nandy 1998: 2). This popular culture fuels the slum's imagination of the 'West', the geography of which extends from countries across the seas *and* to the upper and middle classes within India.

Kaur (2002: 206) argues that popular Hindi cinema reveals 'long-held images of the West and the eventual making of a celluloid Occident'. These stereotypes, drawing on discourses of 'moral bankruptcy', are necessary to define an 'authentic' India as different from the West. It constructs an Indian nationalism in a globalising India, as able and willing to play by the rules of democracy, economic reform and consumption, but on their own terms – with moral advantage. Concurrently, construction of a morally bankrupt occident defines and reiterates an orient through equally simplistic and problematic stereotypes. To create a Western show, young people drew liberally on the stereotypes found in films. In addition to dance choreography, suggestive dancing with the opposite sex was also an important element in creating a proper Western dance performance. However, rather than jump wholeheartedly into sexually provocative mixed-sex dance, the young women cautiously approached their partners, uncomfortably practised dance with them, and quickly fell back into the safety of their girlfriends when not practising. Rather than lose themselves in moral bankruptcy, their initial discomfort with mixed-sex dance can be read as an anchor to their 'Indianess'.

In addition to mixed-sex interactions, the organising committee and dance participants also felt that sound and lights were important considerations when creating a Western show:

> This is going to be a Western show, not some *para* (local) show. The music has to be loud, we are going to hire speakers and it will carry the show at 120 decibels, have you experienced this? … It has to be something that is mind-blowing, so it must be very loud … We are going to have a laser light show – it's going to be something they haven't even experienced before.
>
> (The Coordinator, 21)

Azeem was keen to support the authentic creation of a Western show as a 'modern' spectacle highlighting its prowess in the competitive world of poverty-based NGOs. Of particular importance was to impress the foreign dignitaries who planned on attending the event. 'The [*Nach Baliye*] dance moves must be Western so that the [foreign] Ambassador just goes crazy for it … We will have tights with crop tops, and it must be of very bright colours, with lots of glitter' (the Choreographer, 21). The Choreographer believed that colourful pants and sparkly tops would help the dancers look authentically

Western, giving the impression that the NGO had succeeded in helping the poor towards a Western/Bollywood cultural competency. Interestingly it is these criteria – glitter, lots of colour, coordinated dancing to loud music – that are read as the 'Indian' cultural features of Bollywood in the West.

The conspicuous consumption of dress, technology and dance during *Nach Baliye* cannot be separated from discourses of a globalising nation. Lukose (2005: 917) argues that discussions of consumption in a post-colonial India are 'marked by debates about Westernisation, tradition, and modernity that emerge out of colonial modernity and are newly reconfigured under new conditions of globalisation'. The show gave young people a chance to embody and perform, albeit temporarily, modern Western and Indian middle/upper-class identities. They did this through the consumption of particular arts, artefacts and values. However, the performance of a modern identity in the rehearsal space was uneven and riddled with contrary and conflicting beliefs of nationalism, femininity and acceptable Islamic practice. Through their participation in *Nach Baliye* young women embarked on a journey of identity negotiation which highlights their modern subjectivities, their agency as consumers, and these mirror the gendered, social and religious tensions of participating in a changing India.

Geographies of performance

The rehearsals took place on the roof of the home of the Choreographer and the Organiser. The dance space began on an open roof but in the early stages of rehearsals neighbours complained about the noise levels. Some young *goondas* (local members of the underworld) also began congregating on the roofs of surrounding buildings in order to observe the dancers. As a result of these intrusions, the NGO paid to erect a *purdah* (a curtain) that encompassed the entire space (save one wall for ventilation) to shield the dancers from public view. This *purdah* created a relatively isolated geography; more-over, the space was located on the rooftop of a three-storey building, one of the highest in the *bustees*. This sense of isolation was an important factor in the strengthening of individual and group dance identity as Shirzad recalls:

> I remember the day the *purdah* went up, we were all so relieved! It was terrible in the beginning without it, with all the *goondas* watching … yes I was afraid they were going to disturb us and that would be trouble for us. But the *Azeem* brought the *purdah*, and we knew we were safe.
>
> (Shirzad, 16)

Although the mixed-sex dancing was more risky for young women, Shirzad remembers that the entire group expressed anxiety over being spied upon. The participants did not enjoy being watched by members of their own community, particularly when the participants and the viewers were on the same side of a culture with certain gender expectations. Shirzad's comments remind us that mixed-sex dance transgresses the accepted gender norms for both men and women, and reiterates that young men are expected to perform by the rules of a normative masculinity, which includes monitoring and disciplining the behaviours of young women in the community.

When I arrived the rehearsals were limited to just two days a week, but as the date for the performance got closer practices became more frequent. One month before the show, the young people were meeting up to six days a week. Rehearsals lasted up to five hours a day during the late afternoon hours after school and during tuition times. Rehearsals consisted of the Choreographer teaching dance moves to individual mixed-sex couples in the centre of the roof. Along the periphery the elected dance captains would consult groups who were waiting for further instruction. Each couple had a different dance routine since they would compete against each other, but all couples tried to observe and support their peers. For most of the performers a majority of the rehearsal time was spent watching couples train, or practising dance moves with their partner. The other times were spent talking, playing games, gossiping and having snacks. Younger women participating in the same-sex dance portion of the *Azeem* show were also occasionally present on the roof, often practising their dance routines shyly in a corner.

Since the rehearsals took place on the roof, access to the space was restricted and controlled. It was restricted from the ground level by the owner of the home (the CEO of *Azeem*) and his older friends who gathered at the bottom of the flat for *adda* (chatting) during the early evening. Access was also controlled on the upper level by the Choreographer and other members of the dance group, who kept the top floor door locked. Privacy was further enforced because of elevation – people on street level rarely looked up to the roof of a three-storey building. Finally the *purdah* enclosed the space to prevent dance identities from being revealed to the greater public. These measures created a sense of privacy and safety for young women who found ways to attend rehearsals. This sense of isolation was an important factor in forging a 'third space' for young people to socialise and create a new youth group.

In his essay on the 'third space' Homi Bhabha (1994) describes a space where colonial and local identities intersect. He argues that in this space a hybrid identity emerges, making room for the creation of a new group identity, an identity which is performative and one that interrupts normative understandings of culture and identity. There were times on the roof where it looked like young people created a unique social group, one which challenged the norms and values of the slum. Membership of the group required knowledge and performance of popular Bollywood dance, as well as access to the space. There were new hierarchies, code of ethics and styles of belonging and this youth social group was unlike those found elsewhere in the *bustees.*

One way it looked like a new youth identity was emerging on the roof was through the development of different gendered hierarchies. At the top of the male group was the best dancer. According to young people on the roof the male dance captain Roy (18), was very flexible and strong and all the participants looked up to his impressive dance skills, which they understood to be 'just like the heroes' (Javed, male, 20) of Bollywood film. In the *bustees*, in contrast, this boy ranked very low on the social scale as he was short, not handsome, 'too dark', poorly educated, and a recent convert to Christianity.[4] At the top of the hierarchy of the female group was the prettiest girl, Tazeema (15). She was not the best dancer, but was admired for her attractiveness and her good figure that was highlighted by the Western clothes she wore on the roof. Outside of the roof, although still considered beautiful, Tazeema had the reputation of being bossy and dominating with an abrasive personality. Some young women including Layla and the Choreographer also felt Tazeema was not very bright, failing class nine twice and unable to do simple maths. While on the roof the social currency revealed a political system which valued dance and aesthetics, isolation did not undo normative gender expectations.

Initially on the roof both young men and women followed the rules of *purdah*, with distinct female-only and male-only spaces. Young women created their own space behind a staircase. It was a space where young women moved freely and were visibly more confident. When the young women had to leave this space they would sit together and were initially very shy. Only when the Choreographer asked the participants to practise their dance routines as 'couples' did young people mix together in the central space of the roof. Aysha (15) recalls, 'the girls didn't automatically go to the boys group, or hang out too much with the boys at first. Then slowly, as we developed friendships, all the groups got mixed up.'

As the rehearsals progressed, gender separation became less pronounced and young people began to mingle freely, reflecting a level of familiarity and growing friendships between dancers. Some young women disclosed to me that they initially felt shy and afraid to mix with the opposite sex. Others stated that this was the first time they were interacting with young men outside of their family. I later found out that many young women were initially lying about inexperience with young men. Many have had boyfriends and experience intimacy with their boyfriends. Thus even when participating in mixed-sex interactions, young women continued at times to perform the 'good girl' with me and with their peers to protect their reputations, and to stay true to some of their beliefs.

Dance supporters, private

Many female dancers were aware that their families would not approve of their participation in the *Nach Baliye* rehearsals. Their biggest concern was their family's reaction to close physical contact with boys. What was not a great concern for young women and many of their parents, as subsequent interviews revealed, was the public aspect of dancing:

> When I heard that there was going to be dancing ... I went home and told (my daughter) to immediately go to the tuition centre and sign up. I

wanted her to make something for herself by dancing on the stage ... this would be an experience of a lifetime for her, and she will be able to make a name for herself.

(Tazeema's father)

To my surprise, most parents were unanimous in their approval of the *Azeem* show. Tazeema's father, for example, felt that dancing on a stage would provide his daughter with important cultural capital including dance skills and public performance experience. While he gave his support to Tazeema to attend the rehearsals a few days a week, Tazeema did not inform him that she was actually on the roof daily. Tazeema's father was also unaware that Tazeema was in fact learning *mixed-sex dance*, something he would not have given approval for, as Shirzad's mother explains:

I think most parents would see this as a matter of pride that their daughter has done something good, was able to learn her moves the best and then was selected to dance on stage in front of a distinguished audience ... yes of course this is only pride if she is dancing with girls, not with boys!

(Shirzad's mother)

Shirzad's mother felt that getting 'chosen' to dance validated her daughter's creative abilities and many parents I spoke with were supportive of their children dancing Bollywood dance, complete with some thrusting pelvises and racy lyrics. Support was given provided dance occurred in same-sex groups and was not overtly provocative. In the *bustees*, then, it was mixed-sex interaction that made *Nach Baliye* a risky event, not the dance moves *per se*. However, as I will show, even some aspects of mixed-sex dance were acceptable and some young women did have private support from female elders.

Only one performer who participated in *Nach Baliye* was able to be honest with both her mother and father about dancing with boys. Raya, the female dance captain, had a very supportive family who encouraged her to be the best dancer she could be:

We want our daughter to be happy and we also want to encourage her talent. We can't doubt she is a great dancer, everyone tells us and this is a matter of pride for us.

(Raya's father)

Raya's father believed that his daughter had a God-given talent and he was proud of the accolades she received for her dance, especially after the first *Azeem* show. However, Raya's father was the only adult male, outside of the *Azeem* staff, to know about and fully support the mixed-sex dance rehearsals. According to Raya's father, mixed-sex dance was not *haram*:

> It's not *haram* ... it is just dance, we know she is not doing anything wrong. And this is the style, and if she can do it to the best of her ability, who knows maybe she can make something of herself.
>
> (Raya's father)

In Raya's father's opinion, dancing was not morally wrong. He viewed it as a talent which his daughter was blessed with and he keenly supported her involvement in the hope that she could use these skills to secure future career opportunities. Shows like *Dance India Dance L'il Masters*, and films such as *Slum Dog Millionaire* (2008) show the possibility of slum youth's entry into the entertainment industry. This has given rise to the possibilities of Bollywood-inspired careers for many in the slums. Indeed in 2011 I became aware of a new talent agency opening in the slums. The owners hoped to specialise in nurturing the dance, song, modelling and acting dreams of youth in these *bustees*. While the agency is a sign of Bollywood-inspired careers, according to Raya's father, supporting his daughter was at times difficult in the slums, 'Of course there are some people here who don't agree, but they are not educated, this is not a good *bustee*. To me it doesn't matter what they say'. Raya's father felt that the lower-class status of the *bustee* dwellers prevented them from accepting his daughter's dancing, and this positions him as a higher status resident. He also insinuates that she would be accepted with greater encouragement within upper socio-economic Muslim communities.

While Raya's family was exceptional with their full-fledged support, other dancers had female adult supporters, usually a mother or an aunt who encouraged young women's mixed-sex participation. Dance support by older male family members in positions of control/authority was scarce. Some younger brothers and cousins, however, lent their jeans and t-shirts to young women to wear during the rehearsals. These younger men looked up to their older relatives with great admiration, commenting that their female relatives were 'experts in dance'. Of course male dancers on the roof were also supporters of dance, but they did not have siblings dancing on the roof. In the *bustees* a dominant masculinity values power over women's movements and behaviours and the reputation of a man can be tied to his ability to control female relatives' actions (see Rajan, Dhanraj and Lalita 2011 in Gujarat). Many young women felt that the lack of support from their older brothers and fathers was to be expected. Shirzad (16) explains, 'boys are more concerned with *izzat*, while we knew that we were doing nothing wrong'. Her view that boys are concerned with *izzat* reflects an understanding that men are enforcers of *izzat*. But as we will see, young women also played their part in monitoring other young women, especially through gossip. During the initial stages of dance, however, female peers supported one another.

Disclosing dance activities to certain peers and adults was very strategic. An adult supporter can help young women gain freedom to attend rehearsals, and many young women stated that their mothers could pacify angry family members (usually a father or older brother) if they were home late from rehearsal by explaining that they were late with tuition. Deception or bending the truth is a common way for young people to participate in dance culture, which is something Bansal (2013) and Saldanha (2002) found in research with upper-class youth in India as well.

In the *bustees* few adult females actively discussed what their daughters were doing on the roof. In general, most mothers and aunts did not want to gossip about the rehearsal process, instead they erred on the side of caution:

> I preferred not to know the details of what was happening during the rehearsals because the more I knew, the more problems it was for me if we got caught. I would be seen as a supporter ... I mean I am, but it's a safer position to not know the details, to plead ignorance.
>
> (Shazana's mother)

Older women felt that their position of ignorance was the safest strategy for both them and the dancers, as this position allowed them to protect the participant if she was caught. In the *bustees* an ignorant mother could protect her daughter because she was in the dark and not accepting of her daughter's 'immoral' actions. By maintaining a position of greater virtue than her daughter, a mother's authority of guardianship would be taken more seriously. If she were aware of explicit details she herself would not be seen as virtuous, and would be a poor defendant of her daughter. Some women also expressed a real fear of verbal and physical violence if they were caught with knowledge of their daughter's activities. They negotiated these risks because they felt *Nach Baliye* was a once-in-a-lifetime opportunity:

> I support my daughter here because I know this is her only chance to do something like this ... after this what? After marriage her life will become (pauses, laughs) she will be a woman not a girl, she can't dance around then. I want her to take advantage of this and let her live out her dream because it is probably the only time she can make something of herself like this.
>
> (Reena's mother)

In supporting their daughters, adult females often reflected on missed opportunities in their own lives, while recognising the unique nature of this opportunity. Many adults expressed regret at not having had a chance to dance in their youth, and how such an event would have been a cherished memory. Further they understood the limitations placed on girls in the slums, especially after marriage. Reena's mother also reveals another avenue for support – by maintaining her unmarried daughter's status as a girl-child. Implying that only children can make mistakes without being severely reprimanded gave participants some leeway to recover from damage to *izzat*, as post-*Nach Baliye* discourses will reveal.

Shirzad's mother explained to me that supporting her daughter's rehearsals was dependent on Shirzad's ability to keep an honourable face in the community through ongoing educational success and undertaking household duties: 'her dancing should not spoil our *izzat*'. For adult women, then, private support was a temporary position taken so young women could 'live out a dream'. When *Nach Baliye* was over, young women were expected to return to the realities of the *bustee*:

> She can dance, of course. But does this not mean she is not going to marry a good boy of our choice, or do her duty as a daughter? This is just dancing, an exciting event to experience, that is all.
>
> (Parveena's mother)

Here Parveena's mother is clear that *Nach Baliye* was an opportunity for children to have fun, and her support was not intended to resist societal norms of 'the responsible adult'. Giving her daughter support *as a child* made room for Parveena to live out some risky desires, but the deal was that Parveena would have to compromise and accept that dance was just temporary fun. This allows for transgressive identities to be supported in one's youth period and not adulthood. As I will show in the next chapter, however, young women were not satisfied with temporarily fulfilling their desires as children. Many tried to create for themselves more permanent realities as they transitioned into adulthood, through love marriages for example, and this caused prolonged conflict and risk.

Dance supporters, public

The public supporters of the *Nach Baliye* performance were the *Nach Baliye* Organising Committee and the *Azeem* executive committee, which comprised several members of the NGO including the CEO. The event was also publicly supported by a foreign funding agency; it was *Azeem*, however, that rallied financial support from the community and provided vocal backing for the staging of *Nach Baliye*.[5] Funding for the show was sought from local businesses, a foreign embassy and NGO and State supporters. When seeking funding for the event, organisers explained the purpose of the show was to showcase the talents of young people. 'Cultural shows' are an important activity for all NGOs, schools and self-help organisations in Kolkata, and local businesses regularly receive funding requests to hold such shows. The content of shows is seen to be fairly standard: traditional Indian dance, a few songs and/or poems, and a skit. Over the last ten years 'girls only' and 'boys only' Bollywood dances have found their way into some shows, but in my experience a Bollywood-type performance involving mixed-sex couples performing sexually suggestive moves has never previously been staged in these large *bustees*. It could be assumed with great certainty that funding would not have been obtained from local sources if the content of *Nach Baliye* had been known.

Support for the programme revealed a generational divide in understandings of social reform and (self-perceived) 'modernity' in the slums. On the ground it was clear that most of *Azeem*'s employees were unaware of the plan to stage the mixed-sex *Nach Baliye*. The Organising Committee kept the revelation of this act a tightly guarded secret, as they did the previous year. Like the previous year the NGO publicly stated that the contents of the show were a secret to increase anticipation for the show. Those who joined the Organising Committee were the younger members of the NGO, aged between 20 and 24. Some of them were local youth employed at the NGO, and some were more middle-class youth. The 'youth' factor of the committee certainly influenced the drive and staging of the *Nach Baliye* show. Their expectations of what constituted an entertaining cultural show were significantly different from those held by adult employees. The young committee members were much more intent on challenging many social norms in the *bustees*. For example, committee members' support of young women's independent love choices, participation in paid work and further schooling, continued beyond *Nach Baliye*. These young employees organised social outings to theme parks and tourist attractions to encourage the development of mixed-sex friendships. Members were keen on 'keeping the momentum of fun' after the show was staged. Some committee members understood their facilitation of mixed-sex activity after *Nach Baliye* as a way to transform traditional gender norms in the *bustee*, by 'allowing girls and boys to mix more frequently' (committee member, male).

As I will show in the next two chapters, these young NGO members also supported young people's dating and romantic lives, and their participation in middle-class consumption outside of the *bustee*. The committee members tried to encourage other adult NGO workers to join the Organising Committee and to come to the rehearsals to see the progress of the show. However, none of the other employees attended rehearsals, mostly because the meetings were after work and they were not paid extra to join the Organising Committee. Many had families and other responsibilities, so joining the committee was not a priority for them. The spirit of volunteerism and social justice was unique to younger members of the NGO possibly because they had fewer family responsibilities, but also because they were keenly involved in social change for youth at a local level. This spirit is something that has had a revolutionary impact on public discussions about gender equality and safety in India (see The Blank Noise Project, http://blog.blanknoise.org/2007/09/interventions-and-techniques.html, Phadke *et al.* 2011). Thus, not surprisingly, it was younger employees who joined the Organising Committee.

Those who knew about the scope of the programme did not dispute the details. The committee members knew that the show was risky, but they were all adamant that the young people wanted to perform Bollywood choreography, and they wished to support this desire.

This is not Canada where you can dance in public everyday with whomever you want. There will probably be no other opportunity for these girls to do such a dance. I mean once they get married, that will be it. So that is why we support them to do this, to give them one night to remember in their lives ... soon though I see that it will change, with more jobs and more culture in the *bustees*, it will change.

(Committee member, female)

This committee member's understanding of Western dancing opportunities is highly influenced by Bollywood popular culture. She believes that in Western and upper-class Indian spaces mixed-sex dancing opportunities are abundant. She hopes that with less poverty and more opportunities the slums will also have mixed-sex dance spaces. In contrast many older members of the NGO did not support mixed-sex dance. The importance of, and possibilities in, Bollywood for young people is an important division between adult and youth cultures in the slums. I discuss later that after the staging of the *Azeem* show there were many older members of the NGO who think mixed-sex Bollywood dancing does not have a place in the community.

Dance and risk

Since premarital provocative mixed-sex dancing is *haram*, participating in the rehearsals involved great deception on the part of young women. They had to find the time to leave their homes to practise and had to constantly monitor their actions and behaviours in public to ensure that their socialising and dancing was not discovered. Young women understood that revelation of their activities embodied considerable risks such as physical and verbal violence and damage to *izzat* – these were external risks. There were also internal risks to negotiate, such as their personal relationship with Islam, and their feelings of guilt. The NGO was equally at risk; they could lose government funding if the programme caused strife in the slums. Understanding the risks that various parties needed to take in order for the show to proceed, I anticipated that the format would be disbanded before the public show. I was wrong.

It was obvious to all concerned that young women's participation would involve considerable negotiation of risk from the onset. Aysha explains, however, that risks and risk taking are familiar aspects of a young woman's life, a consequence of living in a *bustee* society where women's mobility is highly monitored:

Once they said we can sign up for the dance I knew that this is something I wanted to do and I could find a way to do it ... I would obviously have to lie and cover my tracks, but this is not new to any of us girls. When we want to go a friend's house, or shopping after school, we find a way not to be chaperoned or followed by our brothers. We go to a friend's house and say that extra tuition classes will be held there and that her father will escort me home or something … (*Nach Baliye*) is not the first time we are going to do something we are not allowed, but it is the first time for most of us to learn dancing the proper way.

(Aysha, 15)

Aysha explains that traditional gender mobilities in the slums required young women to be chaperoned, but revealed that young women already had strategies of transgression in place, and that these were successful in the past. Hanging out at shopping centres is one transgressive activity that many young women experience through tried and tested excuses such as 'extra tuition work' or 'busy organising something at school'.

Although initially young women felt that they could rely on their tested strategies to participate, the sheer scale of the event – with hours of rehearsals six days a week – required young people to invest more time and energy into their approaches. To win the freedom to meet on the roof, young women manipulated the 'good school girl' image. To do this young women discussed school work and practised their homework at home in front of their family, went to school in the morning on time, and helped siblings study. Presenting a keen school girl identity encouraged parents to continue to allow young women to go to school and many young women cut classes to dance. Schooling in the slums is a privilege and it is not unusual for parents to suddenly withdraw girls from school to contribute to household duties, or to punish them.

Participation in *Nach Baliye* also saw group risk taking and group manipulation of the 'good school girl'. Specifically young people conjured up schemes where they would explain their need to go to tuition class earlier due to excessive schoolwork. If they were escorted to tuition they would make their way into the tuition masters centre, but not pay the tutor, or negotiate with the escort. If supportive young men were responsible for escorting young women they would turn a blind eye. These young men tended to be younger relatives, and it was not uncommon for younger male cousins to visit their 'cool' older cousins on the roof. Weeks before the public show rehearsals were increased, thus cutting school, another tried and tested strategy, made attendance possible.

While at the rehearsal space young women also organised younger siblings or cousins to go to different participants' homes and claim a heightened concern for academics, such as 'she is so busy at the moment with her maths that she forgot her ruler'. Adult supporters also propped up this 'good school girl' performance, giving young women time and space for 'extra tuition classes', making excuses in the home for their absence, and support with chores.

Risk taking, however, did not dissipate once on the roof. During the initial rehearsals some young women revealed to their dance captain that the dance moves were very physical and made them uncomfortable. They also expressed some initial apprehension with some provocative dance moves. When first discussing these concerns young women suggested that their discomfort was a reaction to their modest upbringing and they were not used to such contact. Further discussions, however, revealed that one of the strongest barriers preventing young women's initial mixed-sex interaction was the fear of being labelled 'promiscuous' if they began close physical contact with young men soon after their first meetings. Analysing young women's anxieties over their initial mixed-sex interaction reveals a complex negotiation of risk, and struggles between normative values and personal ambitions. Initial discussions showed a concern for their *izzat*:

> We were scared and shy. Most of us have never talked to boys outside of our family. And we don't want the community to think we are loose, because we have to live there, and this would shame our parents.
>
> (Shazana, 15)

As Shazana explains, revelation of her activities could come from someone on the roof itself, so the risks of slander and betrayal by one's peers was a possibility. But she and her peers shared corporate risks – if they wanted the rehearsals to succeed, they would have to support each other's risk taking.

A bigger concern was how other young men on the roof would view young women, and the possibility that the young men they were dancing with would see them as promiscuous. This concern was important for a variety of reasons; if young women developed a reputation for being 'sexually easy' this could result in unwanted attention and possibly harm them off the roof. Acquiring the label 'too accessible' would also tarnish their image as a good potential girlfriend or wife. Indian women who visibly transgress dominant gender norms offend the status quo and are often stigmatised and ostracised to the point where it can diminish good marriage proposals.

Navigating through risks

Rather than remove themselves from the dancing arena, young women acquired selective identities which allowed them to learn risqué dancing. For example, snack time on the roof was quite a spectacle, with *Nach Baliye* young women bossing around their often younger non-*Nach Baliye* peers to serve food. Young women also reprimanded their peers for serving incorrectly. Early on young men sat down during snack time, some pouring drinks for others, but young women often took charge of the food preparations and serving, leaving young men waiting to be served. Policing and adopting traditional divisions of labour became a way for young women to win space at the top of the 'good girl' hierarchy.

Another way to perform as the good girl was to strictly observe the *azan*[6] as a good Muslim should do. I do not wish to suggest that young women did not regularly observe *azan*, but on the roof they used exaggerated movements to cover themselves. When *azan* was about to start they would remind their peers that prayer time was near, and when the call was first made some would franticly run to a nearby clothes line on the roof to cover themselves with hanging laundry, or with their *dupatta*. Reminding someone that *azan* is near is highly inappropriate as taking *namaz*[7] is understood to be very personal in this community. These performances of piety on the roof were extreme, and can be read as a way young women tried to negate their *haram* transgressions by showing other young men and women that in spite of their activities, they were decent Muslim girls. Exaggerated food serving and praying gestures can be read as a way to neutralise their risqué behaviour on the roof.

Concurrently, many young women presented what they felt to be a more Bollywood-inspired identity. They did this by performing the role of a dance expert and vocalising their acceptance of close physical dance steps, even after expressing discomfort. For example, Raya (16) said of the photo taken of her 'you need to dance that close to be a dancing expert' (Figure 3.1).

Raya demonstrated a high level of dance intimacy on the roof. In her routine Raya and her partner were never more than 12 inches apart during the entire act. For young people much of the time on the roof was spent articulating their knowledge of dance capital that included memorisation of both dance routines and song lyrics. Young women were proud of their ability to watch a dance scene from a film or television or by the choreographer, and pick up the moves quickly. Many boasted of this skill, as Mumtaz (15) explains, 'it doesn't take me long to learn these dance moves because I am familiar with this style, I just had to see (the movie clip) a few times and I can do it easily now'. Mumtaz and her partner Roy (18) performed to the catchy

Figure 3.1 'You need to dance that close to be a dancing expert' (Raya, female 16. Photo taken by Fiza, female 19)

song '*Yeh Dil Tumpe Aagaya*' from the film *Aitraaz* (2004). Like the film characters Priyanka Chopra and Akshay Kumar, Mumtaz and Roy begin their dance with some coordinated arm and hip shakes, followed by hand-holding and close sexually suggestive moves, all the while singing along with the song. Several times during the song Roy moved in to kiss her and she swayed from side to side in his arms, trying to avoid him. At one point in the dance he grabbed her by the waist and lifted her up, spinning together, before placing her on the floor. The routine ended with a spectacular move, him grabbing her hands while she lay on the floor, and swinging her through his legs and up and around his shoulder. Such athletic and physical moves were at the time the most popular way to execute Bollywood dancing, and the Choreographer made sure each routine had physical and athletic steps.

Mumtaz felt she was conversant in modern dance. She explained that she viewed the *Aitraaz* dance number only a handful of times before mastering the dance moves. Unlike her non-dancing peers, her experience gave her valuable cultural capital which many other young women in the *bustees* longed to have. Young women on the roof saw their participation contribute to their 'modern' status in the slums as Shirzad (16) explains, 'yeah, I think now people will see me as a dancing expert. It is something not everyone can achieve.' While their upper-class peers, including the Choreographer, may have access to this culture at dance classes and *discs*, the roof was *bustee* youths' dance class and *disc*, and allowed for them to participate in a 'modern/occidental' global India that they viewed on screen.

Importantly dancing was not just a cool skill they were taught. As dancing experts, their identities were seen as an intrinsic part of their being. Aysha (15) explains that '[when on the roof] dancing is a part of who we are and now doing this we become whole people'. For all young women dancing is a part of their identity that has always been within them, they just never had the chance to express it. Bollywood dance on the roof, thus, allowed them to come close to their imagined 'complete' self (Beck 1992).

Fulfilling their dance identities, however, was complicated by their other social learnings and was not separate from the norms and values of the slums. Young women on the roof found themselves privileging one identity, the good girl, at certain times, and also privileging another, Bollywood dancer, at other times. Hybrid identities emerged on the roof for most young women and men, making the space an important 'third space' (Bhabha 1994).

Meri Marzi

Throughout *Nach Baliye* young women reconciled the conflict between normative social expectations, religious rules and mixed-sex dance, and this proved to be difficult for many:

> The parents have the right to tell Muslims girls they should not dance with boys … (but) I know I wasn't doing anything wrong, I was just

dancing. If they did (pull me out) I would be devastated, and it would really hurt. That being said, if they thought it was for the best then I would understand. They have to live in our *para* (neighbourhood) also, they need to look after my best interest. But I got away with it – that makes me feel relieved. I met my boyfriend here and I feel lucky to have been able to do this. I don't think *Allah* can punish me for finding love, because *Allah* is all about love. Maybe the dancing part is not good, but I pulled off a great feat.

(Aysha, 15)

Aysha explains how many young women on the roof question how Islam can accommodate dance, and at times struggles with finding answers from traditional securities such as religious faith. As Fiza explains:

It is not like I will ask the *Mullah* [religious leader] (if I can dance). We all know he will say no.

(Fiza, 19)

Here Fiza questions how traditional experts often cannot support, or keep up, with Bollywood-inspired lifestyles and desires. Young people's understanding of Islam with its rules against male and female premarital interaction made it difficult for most of the female dance participants to find religious acceptability in their dance identities. Young women tried to come to terms with their choice to dance by adopting an attitude of *meri marzi*, literally 'my choice/my desire'. The attitude of *meri marzi* roughly translates to 'it is my choice' or 'I'll do what I want'. *Meri marzi* allowed young women to negotiate their actions by highlighting their own agency in making a choice that they would face consequences for. This strategy was full of contradictions. These contradictions are best evident when Parveena tried to explain the position of dance in Islam:

Dance is a creative art, and dancing doesn't mean you are a bad person and I know that *Allah* knows that … Islam might not approve of this dance, but in my heart I know that I am doing nothing wrong … at the end of the day it is my own choice, *meri marzi*. Islam isn't going to feed my little sister … I might be a bad Muslim for doing this with boys but this is my choice.

(Parveena, 18)

Parveena sways between *haram* dance, her desire to dance, a lack of faith, Allah's forgiveness and the understanding that choosing to dance made a girl a 'bad Muslim'. She is adamant that dancing with boys is not wrong, but at the same time acknowledges that she might be a bad Muslim for dancing with boys. She is sometimes annoyed with the community, suggesting that conservative interpretations of Islam do little for the community, but also believes she has agency to fulfil any of her desires. Another contradiction is that while she hopes her dancing mistakes will be forgiven, she is confident that Allah knows she is not doing anything wrong.

Meri marzi is certainly not a perfect strategy, but it is one that allowed young women the freedom to make their own choices and choose to learn mixed-sex dance. We see that when using *meri marzi* young women continue to value the opinions of their family and communities. For many young women this practice of adjustment is an appropriate way to live more 'modern' lives, 'if we adjust this way, like keeping the dance a secret but still learning, then we get to have both sides, the dance and keeping the face (of our family) … We can do dance this way, it doesn't have to be totally [like the West]' (Parveena, 18).

Rather than rebel and give up family support to learn dance (which Parveena perceives Westerners to do) she adjusts her participation. *Meri marzi* is not risk free. The risks of choosing to participate in *Nach Baliye* were clear when two fathers discovered that their daughters were actually dancing with boys on the top of a roof. Both of the fathers were absolutely furious about this 'corruption of our girls', and both came to the NGO to express their rage. One of the dancers was promptly pulled out of school the next day, reinforcing the notion in the *bustees* that schooling is a privilege and not a right for young women. Not attending school limits opportunities for unacceptable socialisation and sends out a clear message of discipline. Reducing public mobility also prevents further damage to *izzat* by reducing association with other 'bad' youth, as one father explains:

> We cannot accept that girls should publicly dance with other boys … we take them out of school to teach them a lesson. This way they stay at home and won't have any outside influences.
>
> (Shira's father)

Protection of *izzat* was a major concern of both parents; as a result neither family overtly chastised their daughters or the NGO in public. Rather they quietly removed their children from the space and neither was allowed to return. This reprimand can also be read as a way fathers supported girls – they quietly accepted the girl had a transgressive experience which was punished by removal, and not punished by permanently ending childhood by arranging her marriage. The young women who were caught were devastated at having to exit the programme. As Shira (16) said to me a few days after her exit, 'I thought that this time I was going to fulfil my dream, but now my dream has been destroyed.' The other participant was not removed from school and she spoke to the Choreographer the next day hoping to be let back into the programme. She vowed to 'cover her tracks better', but the Choreographer did not trust her ability to do so. She knew that the girl's parents were strict and it was 'going to be hard for her' to continue. However, she admired her persistence:

This shows how much they love this participation, what being here on the roof means to them. If they got caught they would be beaten, pulled out of school, even married off. But it is a risk they are willing to take, so they ask me if they can come back.

(The Choreographer)

Rather than discourage the remainder of the female participants from continuing to dance, these incidents forced many of the young women to organise even more elaborate schemes so that they could continue to meet for rehearsals:

After we found out about it we became very strict about making sure that we would not get caught. We would coordinate with other girls so that it would seem that they were at the tutorial together ... Occasionally during rehearsal one girl would go to her house to give the impression that other girls were there.

(Shirzad, 16)

The risks of participation were further highlighted when one participant was caught by her family and abused. Fifteen-year-old Mumtaz was caught by her brother who informed her parents of her *haram* activities. She was beaten on a number of occasions by him with her parents', and especially mother's encouragement, reminding us that not all older women support mixed-sex dance. Her beatings continued for weeks, yet she managed to return to the roof. On many occasions she came to rehearsals with a black eye. Mumtaz explained that her brother and parents were livid she was behaving immorally, and her brother was very angry that his own male friends were secretly enjoying dancing with his sister. In order to return to the roof Mumtaz explained she employed a 'good Muslim girl' identity at home and in public so that she would be able to return to the roof. 'After the first beating I told my family I wouldn't go again. Then I helped with all the chores ... I looked after my little brothers and sisters. After a few weeks my brother then stopped escorting me, and once that happened, bam! I was back' (Mumtaz, 15).

Violence also helps a family re-establish a veneer of control over girl children (see also Gill and Brah 2014), while escorting also helps to maintain and reinforce patriarchy:

I was caught and my brother called me *randi* (whore) and beat me very badly. My mom said he should have punched me more. I told (my family) that I will not come (to rehearsal) any more ... After school my brother walks me to the tuition centre, but I did not pay my fees so when I go inside, I wait for the session to start and the Sir does not expect me to stay. I then run to (the space for rehearsal) using the *goli/galiyan* [narrow back laneways of the slum], quickly change, and then rehearse. When I am done I change back and go home using the main road.

(Mumtaz, 15)

To win dance time Mumtaz performed the act of a 'good daughter' aligning with the social and gender expectations of the community. She completed household chores including the caretaking of younger siblings; she did not talk back and was very quiet in the house. As Aysha (15) explains, on the streets and in other public places, young women performed this way 'so that people around us would never suspect "that girl is dancing with boys and has a boyfriend"; instead they will look at you and say, "what a good girl, look how decent she is"'. Knowing her brother could not escort her full-time due to work obligations, Mumtaz patiently waited for her full-time escort to be lifted. Once it was, Mumtaz immediately returned to the third space. She understood that if she got caught again her punishment would probably be worse. The Organising Committee was very aware of this violence, and was supportive of her return to the roof. The Choreographer allowed her return because she felt some members of her family were moderate, and suspected that although Mumtaz did not reveal it, she obtained support from her aunt. More than just Mumtaz's eagerness to dance, she needed to have multiple levels of support to return to the roof.

Paradoxically, many of the young women expressed the view that their parents should actively prevent mixed-sex dancing. Reena (15) explains, 'what the parents did (to Mumtaz) was the right thing to do; Muslim girls should not dance with boys'. At the same time, the young women who were not caught were relieved that their families had not discovered their own transgressions.

The roof, thus, was a space where multiple and intersecting identities were engaged in, and these were highly influenced by Bollywood, contemporary youth culture, social and religious norms and gender relations. We see on the roof young women picking and choosing when and where to show off their dance knowledge and their domestic skills. We get a glimpse of the strategies they use to justify their choices. Intrinsic to their participation in dance culture was calculated group risk taking. Rather than negotiate desires on their own, they teamed up with dancing peers to cumulatively live out risky aspects of their identity. This team effort nurtured a collective identity of their group being examples of 'modern' youth in the *bustees*.

The public performance

Over 900 people packed a large prestigious auditorium almost a year to the day after the first *Azeem* show. The audience included 200 VIP guests comprising local Members of Parliament (MLA), a foreign ambassador to India, dozens of public sector officers and academics from India and Australia who were all seated at the front stage area. On the top balcony hundreds of friends and family, dressed in their best clothes, took in the sights and sounds of the event. The show, as in the previous year, consisted of multiple acts; a small play on the plight of working children had audiences (unintentionally) laughing at the awkward lines of delivery. Employees from the NGO formed a singing group and performed their best rendition of classical (and out of tune) *Rabindra Sangeet* songs. The same-sex dance performers had the audience clapping and singing to popular songs.

When the *Nach Baliye* competition was first announced the reaction was exuberant, and at times frenzied. The audience cheered at the sweaty bodies performing their sexy, clumsy, brilliant and awkward dance routines (see Figure 3.2). Male and female audience members catcalled and screamed with every introduction to a *Nach Baliye* act, and an NGO member later reported that two small children had soiled the seats of the auditorium because they did not want to leave the staging of the show to use the toilet. True to competition format, the foreign ambassador and his partner were given the task of judging the competition and awarding a prize to the winning dance couple.

Each time a *Nach Baliye* act took stage I noticed that the invited foreign ambassador and his partner uncomfortably shrank into their seats as young people confidently performed pelvic thrusts and gyrated to the music. Beside them, the local MLA clapped in earnest, his eyes wide at the titillating view of young girls and boys in sequin outfits.

Though most of the audience members were ecstatic some of my nightclub-going peers whom I had invited were less enthusiastic, with one commenting 'God you can really tell it's *bustee* kids dancing, it's just so gaudy (*ghatiya*)'. In their comments, these acquaintances reveal ownership of a youth dance culture many upper-class youth in India see as their own. While the dances look very similar to college shows or *sangeet* (wedding party) entertainment, to upper-class youth *bustee* kids do not have the refined qualities of Bollywood dance which they can nurture at different venues, including *discs*. This claim over ownership is complicated by the increased availability of Hollywood films, Indie Bollywood films (like *Gangs of Wasseypur* 2012), Western music, popular English (and Western) websites and digital gaming culture, which has upper-class youth including these in their lives, leaving 'traditional' Bollywood consumption as indicators of middle- and lower-class youth culture (this is a new phenomenon and needs greater investigation).

Upon completion of the night's events the VIP judges were asked to come onto the stage to present their award for the 'best *Nach Baliye*' dance. The judges both eagerly approached me on their way to the stage, presumably because I had been introduced to them as 'a Canadian researcher' earlier in the evening. The Ambassador asked me with confusion and wide-eyed bemusement, 'so what did you think about the programme?' It was clear from both of their facial expressions and tone that they assumed I was just as shocked as they were at the vulgarity of the dances. Rather than respond I asked them what they thought of the competition. The Ambassador, dumbfounded, responded, 'I was expecting Indian classical dance'. His partner interjected and confessed, 'We don't know how to judge this'. I understood their reactions to the overtly sexual dance moves, as I too was shocked when I first saw young women on the roof. I also understood that they were unaware of all the negotiating young people undertook to participate. I offered some

Figure 3.2 Pelvic thrusts in action on the night of the show (FZ male, 23)

unconvincing words of support of their judging skills and watched them choose a fairly average routine as the winning dance of *Nach Baliye*.

The winning couple, Tazeema (15) and her partner Waqar (17) were both ecstatic. Upon being crowned, they met their fellow *Nach Baliye* performers backstage and they all hugged and laughed and wept, hoping the night would never end:

> This was the greatest experience of my life! I danced on stage and won the *Nach Baliye* contest with my love (boyfriend); we both have come so far. I know that next year it is going to be harder to participate because now my father knows the kind of dance I was doing, but I don't care. I'm willing to take all the risks to do it again … I will never forget this time in my life!
>
> (Tazeema, 15)

Beyond *Nach Baliye*

After the event the word was out; the NGO declared the show to be a great success, with coverage appearing in most daily newspapers. The Organiser triumphantly came to the NGO's office on Monday with clippings from several newspapers reporting on a 'large cultural show for the poor'. He was very pleased. However, in the office he and the committee were met with a backlash. Some of the irritation had to do with the communities' expectations of an 'authentically Indian' cultural programme. The foreign NGO who had contributed financially to *Nach Baliye* expressed confusion about the programme, 'Where is the classical dance? I wanted the children to do some classical dancing' (male foreign funder). Local elites including businesses called *Azeem* to complain, most expressing disbelief over the performance, 'this was not the type of cultural show we wanted to fund' (local businessman). These reactions highlight debates over participation and ownership of Indian culture – debates which often take place at cultural centres of power, but also at the local level. Orientalist views of Indian culture that speak to Edward Said's ideas of the Western view of India as 'exotic' and 'timeless', were expressed by the foreign ambassador. The preference of local powerful businesses for a 'decent' and 'cultured' show also reiterate a classist view of decency and respectability. These are fused to create an understanding of 'authentic Indian dance' which is not Bollywood, and not from the slums. Debates around authenticity did not take young people's opinions into account:

> Sometimes I do wonder how Bollywood is so accepted as a film or *time-pass*, but the real life in Kolkata has not caught up to it. Doing (the show) is a way for us to live out this dream in real life, and in time we can show people that we can do more than *Rabindra Sangeet*.
>
> (Asif, male 19)

Asif articulates his frustration with understandings of 'traditional' Indian dance. Although he felt that Bollywood was a legitimate form of modern dance, and participating in this dance strengthened his membership in Indian youth culture, his skills and membership were not recognised by those in positions of power. Asif felt that over time his identity as a cool youth (or *hero*) would be recognised, while time was also needed for traditional dance culture to make room for Bollywood. The Organiser (21) echoed young people's frustrations, 'no one (youth) does *Rabindra Sangeet* anymore, not even Bengalis. Bollywood is what young people want, it's what is cool'. He argued that artistic expression was not static, but flexible, and thus wanted to support young people's desire to learn and participate in a 'cool' culture of their choice.

Asking some of the young women why there is so much resistance from non-family, Heera (20) volunteered, 'some people in the *bustees* don't want to see us all grow up, they want to keep us as babies ... some people also think that as Muslims we should behave in a Muslim way, not in a modern way.' Here Heera articulates that some aspects of modernity are tied to the adult world that, as unmarried youth, the *Nach Baliye* participants should not have access to. She also argues that many in the slums tie perceived 'traditional' behaviours to an authentic Muslim identity. As a minority group in India, the pressure to sustain a particular understanding of Muslim identity is felt by young women who are seen to be challenging cultural norms by participating in 'modern' Bollywood dance.

Not all members of the slums discouraged Bollywood dance. The CEO of *Azeem* vigorously and publicly defended *Nach Baliye*:

> When I heard what everyone was saying about the performance, I was just sickened. I had tears in my eyes. This child (his son, the Organiser) worked so hard for so many months to put this program together. He didn't sleep for one week before the event, running around here and there to get things done. This young boy did what the people wanted him to do, this is a great thing.
>
> (*Azeem* CEO)

I believe that the CEO did not actually overtly support young people's sexually provocative dance; rather he supported his son's claims that young people desire to dance in a Bollywood style. The CEO's support for *Nach Baliye* was strongly underpinned by a desire to protect his son from potential backlash, while maintaining a firm generational hold on the NGO. His public support was strategic as it enforced his son's identity as a community worker 'for the people', and this supported the Organiser's dreams of a future career in politics. A few days after the event a group of very angry fathers also came to the NGO which is best expressed by a local youth worker, 'Oh God I remember they all came wearing *lungis* (sarong) tied to the side like a bunch of *goondas* (hooligans) from a village (ghram), like in a movie. Everyone was full of tension' (NGO worker, female). This group of fathers spent a good part of the morning shouting at various members of the NGO, their main area of concern was 'the corruption of our girls'. The Organiser (21) received most of the blame, which he gladly accepted, 'That second year what had happened when the parents came ... they were angry that their girls had danced and that we forced them to dance ... they couldn't accept their free will to dance, their rights'. Although he faced criticism, the Organiser knew that it was due to kinship ties and *Azeem's* strong reputation that he was not terribly hurt, 'it is because I am (my father's) son I got the protection and they couldn't do anything to me'.

Not all *Azeem* employees supported the programme and the week following the show a majority of those employees who were not members of the organising committee started a petition to not have their names associated with *Nach Baliye*. The *Nach Baliye* Organising Committee members later revealed that they were expecting some backlash from the community, but not from their co-workers:

> I think for us that [fellow employees' reaction] was the biggest shock. Why are we working for an NGO then? It is to give the girls a place for them to make choices and decisions and live out the dreams in their lives!
>
> (*Nach Baliye* Organising Committee member, male)

For most of the opposing NGO employees, *Nach Baliye* was a dangerous activity and they signed the petition to protect their employment, as they were fearful of the community reaction to the performance. Staff, critical of the programme, were all older and not youth members of the *Nach Baliye* organising committee. Their disapproval of the programme highlights generational conflicts in the NGO. As adult members of *Azeem* tried to hold onto their status they were challenged by newer younger powers who are supported by contemporary infrastructures including popular media, new technologies, a changing economy and changing social structures. The Organising Committee members were hurt by the reactions of their co-workers, but were adamant about the importance of the participants' freedom of choice, and they underpinned this through a contemporary discourse of rights. One could argue, thus, that this belief in and awareness of children's rights is important in contemporary youth social justice movements and contemporary global youth culture, particularly in the Minority world.

After the show the majority of young women who participated in *Nach Baliye* were verbally and physically reprimanded by their family members. The most substantial abuse, however, occurred after parents received criticism by community members:

> Of course I did get into trouble, but more so after some *changra* (losers) started calling me a *nach* girl ... some of those *changra* were invited (but) they were not meant to be invited, that is what caused all the problems.
>
> (Shirzad, 16)

Shirzad recounts that some of her family members were proud of her participation, with her parents and dad in particular commenting that she 'looked
like a foreigner' on the stage, tying perceptions of a modern India with a
colonial past and a racially aware present. Community members also clapped
and whistled with glee watching the show. But at home she was physically
slapped and verbally abused by her father, which is something she felt 'he had
to do' because 'he still' needed to show discipline. She was not, however,
removed from school and Shirzad felt her punishment was appropriate. A few
days later the same boys who cheered her on at the show began calling her a
'dancing girl' which further upset her parents and she received more abuse
from her mother and father. Until her character was insulted publicly, her
family's response was tame by *bustee* standards.

Female peers also played their part in defaming the dance performers as
well. After the public *Nach Baliye* performance, some young women who
were not able to perform in the show were eager to gossip about the raunchy
behaviour of the female and male dancers. Young women's jealousy and petti-
ness is best described by Heera (20), who understands 'in the slums girls think
"if I can't have it, she can't have it either" and then she will go out of her way
to *badnam* [defame the reputation] of another (girl)'. As I will detail in the
next chapter, young women compete against each other and defame their
peers' public reputation in order to gain status as a good girl, gain protection
in a patriarchal society and release internal jealousy.

These incidents of gossip and *badnam* exponentially increased risks; Shirzad's father, for example, explained to me that it was only after his daughter's
izzat was threatened that he became really angry about her dance performance. Catcalls made by young men and *badnam* by young women publicly
affected the honour of Shirzad and her family. Her father explained that
his anxiety over his daughter's marriage potential and public reputation
caused him to punish her more severely after the dance. But Shirzad's
father also commented that he was sympathetic to her desires, and
expressed time-bound tolerance for transgression, 'she can make this mistake, we of course have to forgive her, she is a child'. He felt that his daughter
was entitled to make mistakes during her youth, and he as a parent must tolerate
such transgressions.

By publicly positioning his daughter as a still learning child, Shirzad's
father was able to temporarily support her dance performance. Of course he
did not really believe his daughter was a child in all aspects of life. Unlike real
children, who could make multiple mistakes in various avenues of life, Shirzad
would never be allowed to publicly experience mixed-sex dancing again. This
discourse of 'mistake making' allowed the community to temporarily support
young women's dance, without approving the social changes that allow for a
culture of individualisation to occur. Publicly defending 'childhood' mistakes
gave young post-pubescent women one chance, and often only one chance, to
undertake serious transgressions. Mistake making was a strategy to support
certain transgressive aspects of youth culture, with the knowledge that they

should not permanently challenge social and cultural norms that are maintained by, and through, adulthood.

Most of the rage over *Nach Baliye* was, predictably, in reaction to young people's overt transgression of traditional gender norms, and many community elders reprimanded *Azeem* and their children. Understanding that schooling was used to participate in *Nach Baliye*, many parents asked, 'Is this what I send her to school for?' The action that caused the most controversy, however, was not *Nach Baliye* – it was the sudden elopement of a 14-year-old girl, Sheena, soon after the *Nach Baliye* performance. Members of the community were upset that:

> The *Azeem* show made [the girl] run away with her boyfriend and elope on Saturday. The show gave her the strength to do it and now all the other girls will get this type of idea.
>
> (Male member of the community)

The entire community feared that *Nach Baliye* gave Sheena the 'strength' to pursue an individualised and selfish love course. This strength was understood to be derived from mixed-sex interactions including friendship, as well as mixed-sex dance. Socialising with boys made Sheena 'bold', which contributed to her gaining the courage to run away and marry. Here participation in *Nach Baliye* is not seen as a child-like mistake, but rather as an act that 'planted a seed in the girls' minds' (Community Member) and allowed young women to act selfishly. Within the community eloping and marriage are not seen as silly childhood mistakes but a long-term public defiance of social norms. Interestingly Sheena was a member of the girls-only dance group and had very little contact with other young men on the roof. My discussions with Sheena after her elopement revealed that she was aware her parents did not approve of her partner, whom she had been dating secretly for over a year. She knew that it was a matter of time before they were forced to separate. They planned to run away, but ironically it was Sheena's commitment to rehearsals that delayed the process.

Upon discovering that Sheena had eloped, executive members of the NGO explicitly informed community elders and her parents that they would not tolerate such 'selfish' behaviour associated with individualised love and marriage. Though the NGO was happy to be seen as an advocate of young women's temporary dance desires, the official line was that they were not in the business of supporting individually directed life courses which seeped into adulthood and that created long-term challenges in the community. Context is important here: neither the community nor the NGO would probably have reacted this way if Sheena had eloped with a middle-class and successful boy. Rather her partner was a local boy who did not have steady work (although he was from a more economically secure family than Sheena).

Sheena's peers had mixed reactions to her elopement; a number of young women felt what she did was the right thing, as the young man was more economically secure than Sheena. Many felt this marriage would be a benefit to her long-term future, 'because he has a flat and can give her a better life' (Tania, 16). In contrast some young women felt Sheena's actions were under-pinned by Sheena's 'traditional' outlook and low-class status, 'sometimes girls just *phataphat* (rapidly, without thinking) marry, like that is the only thing in her life' (Mumtaz, 15). In spite of her dance knowledge Mumtaz felt that by eloping Sheena positioned herself as a 'low class' girl. For an 'uneducated girls like Sheena' a boyfriend was the only thing to look forward to. Moreover Mumtaz alludes to the fact that Sheena could only secure sex through marriage, and thus married to experience a physical relationship. Mumtaz understands that Sheena reinforces her own poor economic class and low social status through an early marriage. By reacting this way Mumtaz and many of her peers are able to write identities of higher status relative to Sheena. For Mumtaz and her friends, many of them *Nach Baliye* performers, rushing into marriage and not 'losing your mind' when in a relationship with a boy are some of the hallmarks of a higher status. By critiquing Sheena in this way, Mumtaz aligns herself with a 'modern' Indian youth culture, where youth are able to work, socialise and dance without limiting themselves to a poor life in the *bustees* and marriage and the commencement of adulthood by the age of fourteen.

Conclusion

The opportunity to perform mixed-sex Bollywood dance in the *bustees* was made possible by individual and group negotiations of risk and with the support of family members and the NGO. Through performance of the 'good Muslim girl', young women used time-honoured strategies to transgress gender and social norms. *Nach Baliye* opened up new chances for young women, but just as significantly it brought new conflicts and pressures. These conflicts are most visible in Mumtaz's experience of physical violence and in community reactions after the final performance, where indignation was expressed at an eloping participant. Given the post-show fallout, I doubted that another show would ever take place in the *bustees*. To my surprise in 2007 a third show made its debut on a similar stage, and again in 2012. The 2012 show saw the use of props, including umbrellas and balls, while in the 2007 show mixed-sex couples exuberantly danced festive *Bhangra* routines. In both of these shows dance did *not* involve sexually suggestive contact. On the surface it looks as if based on the 2005–2006 fallout post-*Nach Baliye* none of the local shows wanted to continue sexy dancing styles. However Nabila, a member of the girls-only group in the 2005 show, expresses this shift as a cultural change,

> When we did *Nach Baliye*, that was 2005–2006? That was the style, like Kareena-Kapoor-sexy. But now 2013 people like (television show *Dance India Dance) Li'l Masters*. They want to see Prabhu Deva (popular choreographer) style.
>
> (Nabila, 23)

While it seems all subsequent shows were less sexy because of fallout from *Nach Baliye*, Nabila is quick to point out that the shows are still being staged, and that the dance styles being performed are following dance trends which are learnt from television, films and from popular dance choreographers (like Prabhu Deva). Young people in the community, then, are engaging with dance culture that is current in Bollywood, and not learning dance that is just transgressive (like *Nach Baliye*) for the sake of being transgressive.

After the 2005–2006 *Nach Baliye* fallout it was hard to imagine how *Azeem* would secure funding for another show, but both subsequent shows were funded, and attracted throngs of young women who wanted to participate. Directly after *Nach Baliye* every participant from the previous year expressed interest in joining the *Bhangra* performance, and many approached the NGO to sign up. However on the *Bhangra* stage in 2007 only Aysha and Raya made a repeat performance. The Choreographer made the executive decision not to include all young women from the previous year, 'we need to be fair and give all the girls a chance'. She also admitted that Aysha and Raya were invited back because their families would support their return. In the case of Raya, her family support was well known in the community, while Aysha received limited support to join a second time from all members of her family, with the exception of her father. The young men, in contrast, were mostly the same dancers from the previous year. Unlike *Nach Baliye*, the Choreographer sought verbal permission from one guardian before she accepted young women in the new *Bhangra* show. The need for permission resulted in the Choreographer choosing *Bhangra*, and not sexy 'Western dance', as the theme for the new show, but that too was following the trend at the time, 'this is what is cool now, actually' (the Choreographer, 23).

Although some of the female *Nach Baliye* dancers from the previous year were eager to be involved in the new show, many were aware that dancing and getting caught again would no longer be viewed as a mistake: 'We had our chance I guess ...we used our chance' (Mumtaz, 15). For Mumtaz dance did not represent a new modern youth culture in the slums. Rather it was a calculated transgression which young people discovered, or were already aware of, that they only had one chance to pursue. Many young women compromised with their families and accepted that mixed-sex dance was a one-time opportunity to be read as a 'big childhood mistake' which moved them from immature kids to a path closer to an adult waiting for marriage. Other young women were angry for not being chosen again, including Reena (15) who grumbled to me, 'it is so unfair that we can't enjoy ourselves again, but they can'. Reena was not willing to compromise and participate in mixed-sex dance only once, but she quickly found out that entry into the world of *Nach Baliye* was controlled, apparently for her own benefit. She was disappointed and made strong accusations of favouritism.

When asking Raya about this accusation, she reveals that she sees herself as different to her *Nach Baliye* peers, 'I guess I am different, but I have the family support' (Raya, 16). Aysha was bolder in her explanation, 'well I guess [the Choreographer] recognised a little bit of her in me, she was confident in my abilities ... I know these steps and these lifestyles'. Unlike a onetime chance or mistake, Bollywood dance became a public part of both Raya and Aysha's identities and contributed to their building a reputation – like that of the Choreographer – of 'modern' young women. The other female *Nach Baliye* performers also held this 'modern' reputation, but unlike Raya and Aysha, they did not have sustained support for their Bollywood-inspired identities. Raya and Aysha's examples showcase how both kinship support and private and public supporters were required to publicly live challenging aspects of their lives, and how this support can mitigate violence and slander.

Nach Baliye gave its participants valuable cultural capital, particularly amongst their younger peers. Importantly this capital showcases rifts between youth who thought of themselves as 'modern' and those who were not. Many non-dancing peers saw their dancing friends gaining experience akin to modern youth culture. Indeed, youth view dance as a little step (like education and work) to gain status in the slums. Reflecting on the growth of the women's movement in the West, Beck-Gernsheim and Beck (2002) asserts:

> It is not the major systematic changes, power struggles and revolutions on which history and sociology have long concentrated, but rather the many little steps in education, work and the family, which have given the women's movement in the last two decades its momentum and brought about palpable changes in society. For these little steps have been creating an awareness of traditional inequalities.

In addition to dance, other little steps which young women saw as helping them become more 'modern' and improving their cultural capital and status over their peers include choosing one's own partner for marriage. Unlike dancing, however, the pursuit of love and romance can lead to long-term lifestyle changes that are not contained by the period of youth; they are not 'silly mistakes'. The fact that elopement and marriage effectively ends childhood means transgressions of love and marriage cannot be forgotten or forgiven easily. As the next chapter shows, love and its associated marriage propel young women into adulthood and there is permanence in transgressions, and permanence in developing a particular reputation or status that cannot be easily undone.

Notes

1 Drawn from my fieldwork notes 2005–2006.
2 See for example Morcom 2013; Ram 2000; David 2007a, 2007b, 2010; Dudrah 2008; Gopal and Moorti 2008; Shresthova 2004, 2010.
3 "Star One terms *Nach Baliye* a universal success" accessed 2007 at: www.indian television.com/headlines/y2k5/dec/dec271.htm.
4 Roy was fairly unique in the slums. He was a Muslim orphan and came to the slums as a young boy to live with extended family. His family was very poor and

had to send Roy to a care centre a few years earlier as they could no longer support him. He obtained a place in a Christian orphanage near the *bustees*. He recently converted to Christianity but was quick to share with the community that this was done to gain financial and social support from the orphanage, in addition to mini-mising the everyday pressures he felt to convert. He tried to keep practising *namaz* in private and observed some fasting during *Ramzan*.

5 During rehearsals most of the community and even members of *Azeem* were not aware of the details of the programme. After the public performance debuted and the mixed-sex dancing was revealed *Azeem* vocally defended the actions of all involved.

6 The Muslim call to prayer.

7 Muslim prayer to be performed five times a day.

4 Love, desire and disappointment

Introduction

The pursuit of premarital relationships, underpinned by discourses of hetero-sexual romance and love, is another transgressive aspect of Bollywood-inspired youth culture that young Muslim women in the *bustees* pursue. Risk taking is essential in young women's pursuit of love biographies. Like Bolly-wood dance desires and identities, young women depend on public and private supporters, group risk taking and a shared literacy of love in their premarital pursuit of love, sex and romance. Like dancing, young women develop premarital relationships in third spaces, including on the *Nach Baliye* rehearsal roof, in shopping plazas, at parks and within the *bustees* themselves.

Bollywood plays an important role in setting up the ideals of romantic love and providing instructions on how to move these relationships forward. In the slums Bollywood is used as an educational tool to help understand the rules of love, dating, courtship and sex, and for many young people the desire for premarital romance has altered marriage expectations. While using this role model helps to build confidence, Bollywood can also perpetuate misinforma-tion, gender stereotypes and unequal power relationships. Sodhi and Verma (2003: 93) argue that Bollywood encourages 'girls to idealise the notion of "true love" and encourage[s] boys to seek sexual gratification'. Rather than viewing Bollywood-style love as inappropriate in real life, as in the case of other communities in India (Derne 2005; Rao 2007), young women in the *bustees* mould these popular cultural guidelines within third spaces to suit their own social environments, limited mobility and economic circumstances, to pursue premarital relationships particularly during leisure time.

In India individually directed premarital romances are not the norm for many young people (Jeffery and Jeffery 2012). Derne (2005, 2008) describes how Bollywood romance is viewed as a fantasy by young men in North India. For these men the culture of arranged marriages is strong and can be useful for various levels of support. In the slums of Delhi, Grover (2009, 2010) describes how arranged marriages are also conducive to maintaining kinship ties which women often rely on later as mothers and wives, and this is similar to work in South India (Osella 2012; Osella and Osella 2000, 2006). Indeed arranged marriages, joint family systems and the dominance of hetero-normative social systems throughout India are some of the key ways young people gain status and power within their communities.

In many communities across India having a premarital relationship and a 'love marriage' can impact upon one's public reputation. A young woman entering into a love marriage, particularly with the wrong sort of boy, can be seen as being 'too modern' and her family unable to control her, something Donner (2002, 2008, 2011) discusses in middle-class Kolkata. Sara Ahmed (2004) explores how the bodies of two lovers can be imbued, through a discourse of emotion and affect, with contemporary ideologies, and we see this in the slums. A 'too modern' or 'selfish' girl is one who rejects 'traditional arranged marriages' in favour of self-directed and individually positioned love marriages. This discourse is particularly used when a young woman makes a poor marriage choice, which sees her in a difficult social or economic situation (marrying an unemployed drug user for example), rather than having a boyfriend who is of upper class/status.

In the *bustees* entering an arranged marriage allows both young men and women to maintain *izzat*, and arranged marriage actors are discussed as 'good' boys and girls who maintain religious and collective ideological practices. This way of linking families can also help to reinforce an Indian patriarchy that continues to favour working men (even in places where employment opportunities are poor, as Grover's 2010 book in the slums of Delhi details) and their families. In discussing premarital relationships, romance and love marriages, it is important to recognise the complexities of relationships. As Osella argues 'many commonly drawn oppositions: "love" versus "arranged"; "companionate" versus "economic-pragmatic"; "till death do us part" versus "easy divorce", are representational fictions requiring sharp critique' (Osella 2012: 241). In the *bustees* young Muslim women significantly idealised the pattern of premarital relationship resulting in a community-approved marriage and joint family living, but this ideal is not always achievable, nor does it net the results they desire.

The context of studying young people's premarital relationships in a community where public display of a premarital relationship is frowned upon, and where love marriages are a growing trend, but only if one marries the 'right' kind of person, is complicated. *Azeem* reports that almost 80 per cent of current marriages amongst youth in the slums are love marriages. Other non-governmental organisations (NGOs) in the area report more conservative estimates between 40 and 60 per cent. The shift within one generation has been noteworthy as most community elders and parents have had predominantly arranged marriages. However like Grover (2010) I show that a shift towards love marriage does not equate a movement towards a more individualised equal and life course, and that the equivalence between modernity and self-directed love (Giddens 1992; Beck-Gernsheim and Beck 1995) is highly problematic.

A suitable match: arranged marriages in the *bustees*

In India, traditional arranged marriage culture aims to achieve a suitable match between a young man and woman, while keeping the values, personalities and goals of both families in mind.

> The collectivist culture of India manifests itself in the beliefs and practices that reflect the individual's embeddedness in his or her family and the influence of the family and extended family on the individual in all important aspects of life, including mate selection and marriage.
>
> (Medora 2003: 211)

In theory, compatibility with and adjustability to the entire family is gauged and there is no need to fall in love with one's partner before marriage. Pursuing one's own marriage, in particular one where there is love and romance before marriage can be seen as breaking the rules (see Mody 2008; Jeffery and Jeffery 2012). For some in the *bustees* falling in love and marrying a person of one's choice can tarnish the *izzat* of a young woman and her family because young people often make poor choices. Many families explain their preference for arranged marriages through the discourses of 'best interests'. Community elders in *bustees* articulate that they often do not trust the abilities of children and cite inexperience and immaturity in young people's partner selection. Moreover, many young people in the *bustees* contend that 'my parents know me better than I know myself, so they can choose better than I ever can' (local NGO worker, female, 22). When a young woman's family negotiates an arranged marriage, there are standard criteria to identify a potential son-in-law or 'suitable match'. Consideration is given to the young man's potential or present income, and the overall social status and reputation of his family. Class and social status are of particular concern and ideally most families desire to marry their daughters into families of equal, if not higher class. If the young man is not of a higher class, families aim to arrange a match with a young man with higher social status, which can include boys with greater education and religious knowledge, families with more visible consumer goods and families with relatives abroad. Arranging a match with a lower-class boy of a lower social status is seen as both a parental failure and a young woman's bad luck.

Religious identity and dowry expectations

In the *bustees* an ideal son-in-law should have a good family history and reputation, employment and minimum dowry demands. In this community, education, although rated highly as an individual characteristic, only holds weight if the young man is employed as a result of his studies. Physical attributes such as height, weight, skin tone, teeth condition, disabilities and general attractiveness are also taken into consideration. These criteria are weighed on a scale – parents expect a handsome son-in-law for their beautiful daughter – and a less attractive mate for their less attractive daughter.

Local Islamic culture also plays an important role in marriage. Religious identity and affiliations have always been important guides during marriage negotiations in the slums, and they continue to be of importance. In thinking of an appropriate groom for her 18-year-old daughter, Noor's mother expressed to me during 2006 *Ramzan* (the month of fasting) her desire for a practising young man for her daughter, one who was 'well learned' and aligned with a particular Salafi *masjid* near to their home.[1] One year later, and with no suitable prospects in sight, Noor's mother said that her family 'was really looking for a prospective groom who observed (just) the basics of Islam with a good personality'.[2] When I recalled our previous conversation she confessed that her daughter did not 'have the right brains' to be married into a middle-class and higher status family. Moreover she explained that such a groom was not ideal for her family, as her family observes a variety of faith-based practices including participating in particular festivals during *Muharram* (including flagellation on the day of *Ashura*, a Shia practice) and worshipping at the local *mazar* (symbolic tomb for a Sufi saint). Noor's mother was particularly articulate about her family's recent positive experience with a *pir* (Sufi mystical man).

Almost all of the people I worked with had a very similar relationship with *masjid* and ritual as Noor's family had. They mixed different schools and traditions in their faith. Some young people choose not to classify themselves as wedded to one school. Rather they see their religious identity as fluid across schools. This fluidity did not exist for everyone (see also Osella and Osella 2008 in Kerala). Whether from lower or upper class families, Sufi practicing or Sunni practicing, I know young people who are very committed to their religious school and carefully observe the rituals of that school. People like the Coordinator (male, 21) whose family were trying very hard to follow Salafi traditions were adamant that these examples of observations and rituals kept poor *bustee* dwellers in their low-class positions. The discourse of purity and proper Muslim practice inflect many middle-class descriptions about their alignment to one school (usually Salafi or Deobandi) and for the growing Muslim bourgeoisie in the *bustees*, mixing Shia and Sufi practice 'is the indication of someone backwards from the slums' (local Muslim elite, female).

This fluidity, in combination with poor wage income, is at the root of middle-class (especially Salafi community) perceptions of a 'low status/low class' slum dweller. Over the course of one year I believe that Noor's mother's change from wanting an upper-class Salafi groom to a 'practising Muslim' was due to her inability to secure such a groom. While initially excited to find a higher status/middle-class man, it is not easy for many families to secure grooms outside their community because of poverty and because of their fluid religious practice. A year later she resigned herself to finding a groom within the same class and social status as her family. In the *bustees* relationships with, and acceptance of, certain schools of thought and certain practices (whether conservative, mystical or of foreign lineage) shift according to context (see Soares 2005; Simpson 2008). Even during crucial marriage negotiations one's religious demands fluctuate and for many families their ideals could be bent to accommodate a suitable boy. Of course not all families are flexible. Pinky's family certainly was not. Their family lived in a flat in the *bustees*, and they were very invested in maintaining a middle-class reputation. For their 19-year-old daughter a suitable boy could be no less than an educated and steadily employed conservative practising Deobandi Muslim, who prayed at the same mosque as the family.

> We accepted this family because they are well learned, well educated. Both brothers passed through (the local) *madrasa* and go to our *masjid* to listen to the discussions ... they both participate in the debates as well.
>
> (Pinky's mother)

Religious positionality is very important in marriage negotiations, and in my experience in the slums religious considerations can be as important as dowry considerations. *Azeem* is a strong supporter of the abolishment of dowry, as well as vocational training, greater education and public employment opportunities for women. While the NGO itself is secular it does not shy away from its goal of uplifting the Muslim masses in the slums. *Azeem* provides opportunities at their centres to hear and discuss lectures by popular Muslim reformers on the importance of education and abolishment of backward practices, including the dowry.

Dowry in this community (and many others in India) is the practice of the girl's family providing money and gifts to the boy's family. The general consensus in the *bustees* is that a 'good boy' has high dowry demands because he has more to offer. Conversely, higher dowries are expected from a family whose daughter is not a good catch. Dowry is a burden to poor families. Thus it is not surprising that parents of young women who felt they had a good marriage 'offer' (i.e., little dowry) often did not delay in approving these matches.

In the *bustees* the pressure on many poor families to offer a good-sized dowry to secure their daughter's marriage very clearly contributes to early marriage. For example, the father of *Nach Baliye* winner Tazeema explains: 'I know [my daughter] is 15 years old, but we found a good boy who didn't demand anything, so we accepted ... What if another offer as good as this does not come in the future? What if we can't afford it later on? I cannot take that risk.'

Dowry demands are understood to increase as one's age increases, as the value of the young women wanes with age. Parents explained to me that marrying their daughter at 21 meant doubling the gifts, cash and gold that a young woman at 16 is expected to bring to a partnership. Given the pressures of dowry, elopement, although publicly chastised, is often initially seen as a welcome relief to many poor families who cannot afford large dowries. This respite is often only temporary. A few months after 17-year-old Romi eloped with her boyfriend her father commented:

> When they first came to me and said they had married ... I will tell you the truth, I was worried about how I could afford to marry her ... but now her mother-in-law is making her life a hell, angry at her because she could not collect a big dowry through her son's marriage.
>
> (Romi's father)

Romi's father explains that his daughter was being 'punished' for eloping, 'his mother is angry because of all the items she missed out on, and is taking it out on Romi'.

Interestingly while dowry is a symbol of backwardness that reformers in the *bustees* rally against, many reformers do not shy away from marriage dowry. Indeed I am aware of many middle-class families committed to the Salafi school that engage in the practice. Saba (20), for example, describes how her sister married into such a family in 2013: 'She was married into a good family ... initially [the family] doesn't come out and make demands, they say "If you want to give gifts it's your choice", but what they mean is give (us) everything!' Saba described how her sister currently faces 'problems in the home' due to her mother-in-law. She experienced contempt and it was obvious that the other daughter-in-law in the home who arrived with a size-able dowry was favoured in the house – all this in a progressive, and publicly outspoken 'middle-class' Salafi family.

Education and marriage

Education is also an important consideration in young women's marriage biographies. In the *bustees* it is understood that the peak of a young woman's 'worth' is when she is literate, but not highly educated, and domestically trained, but not homebound for a long time. A young woman at home is a liability for most families as it is perceived her maturing body and mind puts her at risk of sexual connections outside of the home. Consensus in the slums is that younger women adjust to marriage and a new husband with greater ease because they are not set in their ways. Girls of younger age also have less education than their male peers, and thus are appealing as brides. Highly educated young women are seen to be difficult, with stronger opinions, as Farah (21), the sister of a young man of marriageable age describes:

> My family was thinking of one girl near our home, she was good, she passed 12th standard and was of good reputation, but after much con-sideration we decided against this ... if he told her to do something and she spoke back, how would he feel? He would be insulted.
>
> (Farah, 21)

Since many young men in the slums do not complete their secondary schooling (and hardly enrol in graduate studies) due to the pressure to obtain paid employment, parents of young women try to give their daughters the correct amount of education to be marriageable, but not so much as to be placed out of the marriage market.

Not all community members view higher studies for young women in this way, 'I think that when a girl is more educated than her husband, he gives her full respect' (Layla, 20). Layla's comments are shared by many of her peers and currently there is an education revolution taking place in the *bustees* and young women are at the centre of this revolution. For example *Azeem* sponsored nine female college-goers in 2007. In 2014 that number jumped to 29 and this represents an important change. Secondary school completion rates for young women over this time have almost doubled as well. Unlike a decade before *Azeem*'s sponsorship scheme, which financially supports high performing students, has become a very competitive programme with long waiting lists. Interest and support for young women's education, particularly the completion of secondary schooling, has been growing rapidly. The NGO's support for young women's education is similar to other NGO and central and state government schemes which have prioritised educational opportunities for young women, particularly in marginalised areas. However this 'success' needs to be unpacked: families struggle with the hidden costs of schooling including books, transportation, escorts and *tiffin*, a light lunch. These are exacerbated by the accessibility of 'good' schools in the *bustees* where this research has been conducted. As Medena's mother argued, 'We have no objections to sending her to the best seats, but where are they? Over 20 minutes away! Whoever will take her there will then have to wait to take her back, and we can't afford two people out like that.' Medena's mother's comments remind us that while many young women are gaining access to higher levels of learning, access is still very much tied to young women's limited independent mobility. Medena's family was much more established than most of the families of young women in this research. Their requirement of a full-time escort to bring their daughter to school was a privilege and concern only for those more economically stable.

While increased school attendance by young women is impressive, the reality is that most secondary school completion in the *bustees* is done at private institutions. Good schools in Kolkata are those which are recognised by the State government and often have State affiliation of some kind. In the slums most private schools that operate at primary and secondary level have limited recognition.[3] Roohi (2007) contends that the lack of recognised and affordable schooling continues to marginalise the educational achievements of young Muslim women in Kolkata. Access is not the only issue; when *Azeem* has been able to secure access and a small stipend for girls to attend reputable public schools close to the community, most families do not send their daughters to 'good' schools. Juni's mother, whose daughter acquired a place at a Central Board of Secondary Education (CBSE) school through *Azeem*'s support confessed, 'we were afraid she would become too big … after that who will marry her?' After a few weeks at her new 'good' school her parents pulled her out. Anxieties around marriage often override both the will and desire of many families to support higher education of young women.

Many young women who obtained a space at good schools found travelling and funding to be an obstacle. 'Everyone there had extra money for auto (rickshaw) and they would do things after class like go for *phuckha*, I just couldn't participate because of my budget' (Layla, 20). Layla here describes the isolation she felt as a poor student, and while she did eventually complete her studies at this school, she made no real friends and felt the entire school experience very lonely. These experiences are highly personalised and intersect strongly with religious identity politics, which Layla also found. 'I was the only Muslim in my small group, and while many girls did help with my budget on outings, I always felt so insecure because I was poor ... they didn't talk bad about me, but I felt like others might have.' Intersecting factors of mobility, family responsibilities, loneliness and exclusion saw many young women choose not to pursue recognised education or vocational training when the opportunity presented itself.

In communities where schooling role models are limited and higher level schooling can be a lonely experience, many young women used schooling time to develop relationships and pursue other desires and identities which they saw as important. Sheena, who eloped after the *Nach Baliye* performance, felt 'I didn't have the brain for school, I was always a homebody' (Sheena, 14). Her choice to marry young was underpinned by her difficulties at keeping up with school. Inconsistent school attendance results in a wide range of ages in one class, accommodating young people who are attending for the first time, those who have failed several times, and those who have dropped out and re-entered school on numerous occasions. The bulk of young women in the slums – *Azeem* estimates well over 60 per cent – are unable to pass through their schooling years with regularity.

Young women who attend school on a regular basis, such as Layla, Heera and Aysha, describe this majority as 'simple', 'uneducated' and 'low class'. Layla and her friends understand that to gain higher social status and class mobility in the poor slums, a variety of perceived 'modern' practices should be undertaken, including marrying later, having consumer knowledge and participating in good schooling. A global discourse of rights like UNICEF's International Day of the Girl (Svanemyr *et al.* 2012) supports Layla's viewpoint as a 'progressive' one. But as Saba's experience of dowry discrimination in her home shows, the contradictory behaviours of so-called modern families complicate the ingredients and practices of modernity, which seem to shift between persons and communities in the slums.

The good girl and love/romance

While traditional social and religious attitudes in the slums do favour arranged marriage and female premarital chastity, premarital relationships, underpinned by love and romance, do develop between youth in the slums.

There is evidence that young people throughout India are creating love-cum-arranged marriages in complex ways (see Netting 2010; Donner 2008; Mody 2008; Kapur 2010; Patel 2010; Grover 2010; Trivedi 2014). The results of such marriages, as Grover (2010) has shown in the slums of Delhi, are not always the ideal of blending two distinct systems.

Desiring the love of a romantic partner is not new in India. Indian culture is rich with tales of religious, family and romantic love (Dwyer 2000; Orsini 2006). What has changed after liberalisation is the expanding opportunities to engage in premarital romance for youth in particular. With greater work, schooling and social opportunities, the opportunities for finding premarital partners have increased for young people. For young women in the *bustees*, school is the main avenue to develop relationships, and families were exceptionally concerned that their daughters not use this freedom to meet boys. Though parents struggle with their decision to allow their daughters to pursue further study, they are aware that in a globalising India, educational capital is a necessity for all youth, and they often relented by sending them to school: 'We have to let her go, or she will be left behind' (Shirzad's father). Parents often cautiously sent their girls to school, but as one parent warns, 'she should not think that just because we let her go to school the door will open to other things [boyfriends]'. To prevent misuse of this freedom many young women are escorted to and from school and wear the *burqa* to embody *purdah* in public spaces. However, young women find ways around these protective measures, such as not paying the tuition master and organising to skip school together with friends. These group strategies open avenues for premarital love, romance and sex.

In the *bustees* young women's desire for premarital relationships are not separate from cultural constructions of a dominant girlhood, traditional gender roles and kinship structures. The pursuit of love, romance and sex exists in a society that places high value on the importance of marriage, childbearing and hetero-normative ways of being. Thus, it is not surprising that for most young women in the *bustees*, falling in love is achieved by obtaining a boyfriend, and marriage is their stated goal of dating, and these had to take place within heterosexual unions. Pursuing premarital romance with these articulated goals reduced the risks of dating.

Another way for managing the risks associated with premarital relationships is having a relationship with a *suitable* boy, as Shirzad (16) explains: 'If you bring home a boy who is the President of India's son, no parent will disapprove.' Shirzad felt that having a boyfriend *per se* was not the problem; rather it is the partner in question that caused conflict in families. She contends that if parents discovered a young woman is in a relationship with a suitable boy the consequences would not be great. While it would not be acceptable to prolong the dating process, Shirzad felt her family would allow them to 'quickly marry each other', to decrease the shame of the clandestine relationship. Though her assertion is highly exaggerated, and given the reality that the parents of a suitable boy have their own criteria of a suitable girl,

Shirzad was earnest in her belief that if a young woman is caught pursuing a relationship with a decent young man, they could just marry, and many of her peers felt the same way. Many young women gave examples of girls who have been caught in a relationship with a 'good boy' and were allowed to marry. For young women in the *bustees* dating an appropriate young man who meets the criteria of 'suitable boy' could prove to be the least risky way to pursue premarital relationships.

Playing games

Finding the right kind of partner in the slums is difficult. In a community where the employment and educational achievements of young men are low, and drug use is problematic, suitable boys are few and far between. Moreover, the social rules around mixed-sex socialising in public mean that meeting non-local boys is difficult. Visibly engaging in romance goes against the normative cultural constructions of female sexuality and the good Muslim girl. Young women understand these rules: 'dating is just not acceptable in our culture because people think the girl will be spoiled before marriage' (Layla, 20). A 'spoiled' young woman is understood to have had relationships with young men (sexual or otherwise). She is thought of as 'used property' and assumptions are made about her physical and emotional experiences.

Not everyone views mixed-sex interactions this way. The middle-class Choreographer, for example, understood that it is 'the lack of social education in these slums that makes boy-girl interaction bad'. Equating all mixed-sex interaction with the potential for romance, sex and attraction is, according to the Choreographer, a consequence of poor education. She argued that greater education would eradicate such negative connotations. 'The boys here, they are not good, they don't go to school, they work in the garage, they have two wives and one girlfriend ... social and religious education both are needed, not just one or the other.' The Choreographer suggests that non-formal education and vocational training in combination with religious education could improve the slums. Such education would address poor employment prospects and multiple marriages by young men.

Given the implications of obtaining a 'spoiled' moniker before marriage, pursuit of premarital relationships has to be discreet. In her research with young Indonesian Muslim women Bennett (2005a, 2005b) describes how young women's success in negotiating their romantic desires is dependent upon their ability to maintain a faultless public reputation. In her work many single women found ways to pursue multiple romantic relationships by performing the 'good girl' in public. This performance also had the support of many family and community members. For Muslim young women to have premarital relationships Bennett conceptualises a negotiation between a public performance of purity and private desires as a 'game' that young women have to play within their traditional society:

It is useful to apply the analogy of a courtship as a social sport. In doing so we must imagine that: the sport has explicit rules – the hegemonic sexual ideology; an umpire – the community in which women live; mechanisms for disciplining recalcitrant players – the social regulation of courtship through gossip, stigma and exclusion; and finally expulsion from the game for reckless disregard for the rules – that is, for visible sexual transgression ... when women play the game in the public area and bend the rules without visibly breaking them, they exercise resistance. Women who bend the rules with discretion, do so because they do not wish to be thrown out of the game, they remain fixed on the ultimate trophy of marriage, yet wish to enjoy the game while it lasts.

(Bennett 2005b: 103)

In the *bustees*, premarital romance is also achieved by playing by the rules. For young Muslim women to win freedom and time outside of the home, they behave publicly pure, thus maintaining a respectable reputation in the neighbourhood and within the home, but the 'good girl' is not entirely an act, as Aysha explains she also envisions courtship as a game:

I play the good girl for everyone, for my parents, for my teachers, my neighbours, for myself. There are things about [the performance] that are true to me, but there are things that are not. I play the game so that I can build trust and buy time. This way I can pursue my other desires. Without the trust, my parents won't let me leave the house for schooling or tuition ... I take these opportunities to live my desires that I know they will not approve ... I am willing to play the game.

(Aysha, 15)

Aysha's performance of the good girl reflects her understanding of both the necessity, and personal desire, to play by the rules of a dominant femininity. She admits there are aspects of the good girl that are true to her personality, but there are other aspects that are only presented to build trust. The complexities of her hybrid identity shift depending on the context. She explained to me that she felt particularly 'good' during holy times of the year (which Schielke (2009) also reports in Egypt). Aysha also deliberately maintains a naiveté within the home by showing her parents that she enjoyed playing children's games, playing with toys, and watching children's programmes. For example, she employed a strategy of watching safe television programmes when her father was home: 'There is a button on the controller, it lets you go to the last station you were viewing. So I put some programme on one and the music video channel on the other and jump between when he is not looking.'

Of course her parents did not view her as a small child and she often complained to me about the cooking, cleaning and child-minding responsibilities that she was required to undertake at home. Aysha believed that by drawing attention and manipulating her childlike qualities at times, she was able to reduce her adult responsibilities. This manipulation often worked, 'sometimes my father says to my mother, just let her rest'. By toeing the line of childhood games and adult responsibilities, Aysha positions herself 'between the freedom and autonomy of adulthood and the constraints and dependence of infancy, neither child nor adult' (Matthews, Limb and Taylor 1998). It is this liminal space that young women in the *bustees* occupied as they cautiously used schooling time to develop romantic relationships.

Although young people are well versed in manipulating the good girl to win freedom, the performances themselves are not risk free, especially when the acts of public purity do not match the expected outputs of such a performance. For example, most young women play up their interest in school, talking publicly about homework, lessons and school activities within the home and with neighbours. Scholars have shown that young people's school identity is very important in the Indian context (Still 2011). Indeed during our early meetings I believed that I was working with a group of keen students, as every conversation we had was about school. Only after rapport was built did I discover that some young women did not even go to school, and one participant had been enrolled in the same grade for three years.

Parents generally gave young women a two-strike policy, giving them two years to pass their grade. If they did not succeed by the second round most families removed their daughters from school. While they might be able to enrol again later, permanently removing young women from school sent distinct messages to the community: this daughter does not have the skills for further schooling; we require help in the house and cannot afford and/or are unwilling to continue the education of this girl; this daughter will be ready for marriage soon. Removing a young woman from school for several weeks or months is also used as a punishment, as seen post-*Nach Baliye*. For young women who want to use school time to ensure public mobility, they must find ways to obtain decent school marks and pass at least some of their courses. To facilitate school attendance, young women regularly copied texts and notebooks from each other. Some young women also purchased the services of a tutor to complete their homework, but this service was only utilised by those who could afford to do so. Other young women brought their homework to the NGO, where sympathetic staff assisted them with completing their assignments. On several occasions I witnessed senior employees of the NGOs dictating essays to groups of young women.

Some young women whom I worked with felt there was a difference between young women who were genuinely interested in schooling and those who were not. While a young woman might rely on peer networks to scope out homework assistance, and skip classes to pursue relationships, she might also try her best to complete her schoolwork and not let her grades suffer. Other young women had little interest in schooling, but used school attendance to pursue alternative identities and desires, letting their grades slip. Thus merely attending school did not automatically make someone a 'good girl'.

The *Nach Baliye* rehearsal roof further problematised what it meant to be a good girl. In this space, as described in the dance chapter, fluency in dance and Bollywood literacy was required and rewarded. Initially, however, young women expressed apprehension concerning the physicality of Bollywood-style dance. They explained that their reactions were a result of their modest upbringing, but an analysis of their anxieties reveals multifaceted negotiations of risk, personal goals and discourses of desirability. Most young women were careful not to rush into mixed-sex dance because they did not want to acquire the distinction of being promiscuous. Young women understood that both their male and female peers played a role in classifying a young woman. Young men concur:

> (Boys) decide early on to which category this girl belongs, whether she was in the marriage category or if she was not. If she was 'good' for marriage the boy would be very serious about protecting her, keeping her good and making ways to have her accepted in his family. If she was not, then he would flirt with her and would take almost every chance for getting with her physically.
>
> (Parvez, male, 20)

By performing the selfless server of food and observer of prayer on the *Nach Baliye* roof young women hoped to not act as, and be labelled as, a bad girl. This meant that even if a young woman does develop feelings with someone on the roof, she does not express her feelings, as Shirzad explains:

> In our mind we know that we might like him, but we don't express our feelings. Even when the feelings develop we won't say anything and keep it inside ... Girls don't express their feelings; we wait for the boy to do it so as to keep our character.
>
> (Shirzad, 16)

By not overtly expressing preliminary interest in a potential suitor, even in the mixed-sex and transgressive geography of the *Nach Baliye* roof, Shirzad supports practices that constrain expressions of female sexuality before marriage. By maintaining these norms on the roof young women try to secure a reputation of a 'good girl'. This distinction allowed her to play the game of dance and courtship without a *timepass* label and an unmarriageable reputation. A *timepass* relationship is a casual relationship that is not rooted in the discourses of love and long-term commitment (see Abraham 2002), and while love may not have been the goal of all relationships, to admit such a thing would certainly be outside the rules of the game.

Changing expectations?

The experience of love and intimacy before marriage, the development of premarital romance and marrying one's chosen partner, are growing trends within the *bustees*. There are many reasons for young people to long for, and enact, romantic unions leading to marriage. Obviously we cannot under-estimate the power of romance and the feelings of love that develop within a romantic relationship. The euphoria, the tenderness and the trust that devel-ops in a romantic union are some of the feelings human beings of all back-grounds can experience when in love. Bollywood culture plays a significant role in inspiring young people to seek out true love. In fact the English terms 'true love' and 'life partner' have found their way into normative discussions around love and romance in the *bustees*. Premarital romance is standard fare in popular culture and Bollywood often positively depicts individually direc-ted romantic love as a life goal. Although romance usually exists within the communal structures of the joint family in films and television, a growing number of films and television shows depict a nuclear family way of life and young women in the *bustees* enjoyed these programmes. Fernandes (2006: 86) contends that the dominant public narratives of middle-class identity – including those within modern Bollywood films – emphasise shifting patterns of consumption and the emergence of new lifestyles that value freedom, individualisation and nuclear family systems. In the *bustees* many young women fantasise about living alone with their partners after marriage. Fur-ther discussions with young women reveal that what most are looking for is the ability to blend premarital romantic love with joint family living. 'Very few girls live in that (nuclear) way. They prefer the joint way, and only separate if there are problems' (Layla, 20). In fact all the young women I knew felt that the 'best' kind of man is one who took active steps towards protecting his wife 'during family conflict', as Layla explains:

A really good boy is the one who tries to work hard and find a separate place (*ghar*) for his wife so that she does not have to put up with abuse of his family. He should start to save for this when they are dating so that he will be prepared for married life after.

(Layla, 20)

Family conflict is seen by all participants to be inevitable in joint families, and young women understood that they had to *adjust* to the reality of conflict. But many young women felt that romantic love might be a protective factor later in life. Layla understands, for example, that the nuclear family systems protect young women from difficulties associated with the 'burden' of the daughter-in-law, including dowry violence and domestic violence. Popular Bollywood culture supports the fantasy of problem-free nuclear family arrangements, as Layla comments: '(in films) when the couple finds love and lives on their own do you ever see a wife being set on fire?' Speaking to young people the desire for nuclear living is felt in peaks and waves. I felt young women's desire to run away with their partner and fantasise about nuclear living after I returned to the community in 2013, where several months earlier 19-year-old Miriam was burnt to death by her brother-in-law over dowry demands. Dowry violence is certainly a reality in this community. In the face of horrific examples of gender-based violence, including Miriam's murder by members of her joint-family, we see many young women creating nuclear family fantasies and (at times) striving for nuclear family formation.

For young women premarital romantic love helps the creation of a nuclear family, because it is the 'power' of love that drives a young man to protect his partner in joint family conflict. Netting's (2010: 720) observations in Gujarat show that young women 'felt that a self-chosen marriage would alleviate the danger, as a loving, egalitarian husband would help preserve a woman's rights within the man's family'. However, the reality of nuclear living is far from Bollywood depictions. Nargis's experience supports this view. Eighteen-year-old Nargis had been together with her partner for over two years. Both from very poor households (Nargis's mom was a widow), she and her partner had a love marriage shortly after *Nach Baliye*. They immediately moved into her husband's home afterwards. At her in-laws' home Nargis experienced both verbal and physical abuse. Like Saba's sister, Nargis was punished by her in-laws for not providing a dowry. She was physically beaten on many occasions during arguments over money and household duties. According to Nargis she used 'love' (in English) to persuade her partner to find a *ghar* (home) on their own after experiencing sustained conflict. By crafting a home for just the two of them her husband proved to her, and to other young women in the slums, that 'obviously he is her soulmate because he put her happiness first' (Layla, 20). Although I am only aware of a handful of people who live in nuclear family systems like this, Nargis's life course was held up as ideal by many of her peers. Some young women looked to Nargis as an example of how they too should hold out or look for a young man who was willing to 'find a separate *ghar*' and put his wife first in the face of in-law conflict. For some young women the fantasy of living alone with their partners did not challenge their ideas of being a good girl, particularly if the need to live away from one's in-laws is the result of violence or employment opportunities. Although the Bollywood fantasy of a problem-free nuclear life is widespread in the slums, I understand that young women are idealistic about nuclear family living, and in particular Nargis's situation, because they have limited real-life role models.

The reality is that nuclear family living is very risky in the slums. While never admitting it to Nargis herself, many of her friends saw Nargis's nuclear life as scary and lonely. This is a community where co-sleeping and shared private space is the norm, and where it is not uncommon to ask relatives to stay with married family members if they are left alone in the home for any reason. Within this context Nargis in 2011 commented with great sadness that her home felt 'vacant'. She also had other concerns, 'sometimes I think that when it is just us, is he bored? And I don't want him to leave this house looking for something to do, I am scared of that.' Nargis was fearful that their quiet and independent life could prompt her husband to find another partner, and that he was secretly searching for a more lively life with more people and more companions, in other words, a joint family.

Unlike many of her peers who viewed her life course positively, Nargis had many regrets about not being able to *adjust* to her in-laws. In spite of facing abuse, her feelings fluctuated between giving joint family living another try, and loving the independence and freedom she enjoyed with her husband. In India the joint family system provides high levels of kinship support, which Grover (2010) describes in detail in the slums of Delhi. In a nation where there are limited resources for the urban poor, low levels of literacy, high levels of bureaucracy and where corruption is a normative transaction, kinship support is often necessary just to get by. As an NGO colleague explains, 'you need someone, somewhere, to do anything in this country'. Renting an available *ghar* in the *bustees*, for example, was an extraordinary task for Nargis and her partner. Indeed her partner was only able to secure their home through the aid of a workmate's father.

Community elders also had mixed feelings about Nargis and her partner living alone in the slums. For most women Nargis's lifestyle was not ideal, 'I have heard what happened at her in-laws so I can understand why she is here, but this is why I tell my daughter "look carefully at her"' (Mirza's mother). Although she expressed sympathy for Nargis, whose in-laws were abusive, Mirza's mother cautions against poor marriage decisions. She reminds her daughter to marry wisely according to the family's choice so that she does not end up in a similar situation. For elders in the community arranged marriages are safer for women. 'No one here is against love, we are against poor futures … this is not a good *bustee*, so the boys here are also not good. If you marry a local loafer what does that make your future? If it is not poor then what is it?' (Mirza's mother). Community elders argue that arranged marriages secure the safety of young women because a family will try and choose the best possible mate (who is often local), rather than a young man who may be a deadbeat, but charming. Community concerns are that young women develop relationships with the wrong kind of local boys because of inexperience, while elders have experience and access to more preferable local boys. When nuclear life exists in the *bustees* it is an anomaly and not necessarily permanent; in 2013 after years of difficulty conceiving, Nargis and her husband were expecting a baby, and this prompted a reconciliation with her husband's family, and they were again living in a joint family system.

A seemingly happy compromise is the arranged love marriage, or 'love-cum-arranged' marriage model (Mody 2006, 2008). Mody describes in detail this system where a couple have a facilitated meeting (through friends or relatives), some level of romance is pursued (dating, courtship) before a family-supported marriage and joint family living is enacted. She shows how these unions develop a bridge between individually designed love and arranged unions. Some of the most appealing films and television serials that young women in the *bustees* viewed with interest were ones that 'combine love with the family' (Medena, 14). Many young women felt films like *Dilwale Dulhania Le Jayenge* (DDLJ 1995) and *2 States* (2014) were good films to be inspired by, since they reinforce a reality for many in India that 'you are nothing without your family' (Medena) and that family support is crucial for marriage success and overall happiness.

However, love-cum-marriage are not always ideal. Young women were sceptical of their partners' ability to protect them over the long term. In addition, many girls questioned their reputation within their new home, as Fiza (19) explains, love-cum-marriage systems 'only works if the family accepted the girl wholly, only then do these arrangements suit love'. She felt that a family must accept this new person as a 'daughter-in-law, and not as just their son's girlfriend'. The distinction between the two, according to Fiza, was 'the daughter-in-law is a part of the family, while the girlfriend always remains the outsider (even after marriage)'.

Young women gave many local examples of how even the strongest romantic relationships were strained because of an uncooperative family-in-law after marriage. Similarly Grover (2010) states that when a couple marries for romantic love in the slums of Delhi they can face uncertain and uneven kinship support throughout their married lives. Her findings show that for some couples 'declarations of romantic love that characterised the courtship period have been replaced by discourses of male dominance and female deference in the post-marriage phase' (Grover 2009: 26). Related to these discourses of male dominance is the culture of triple *talaq* in the *bustees*. In this male-initiated practice a man utters *talaq* three times to divorce his partner, which is in accordance with *Shar'ia*. Religious leaders in the slums describe the correct way to use *talaq*: each *talaq* is read as a warning of bad behaviour. Warnings are not consecutive but involve a waiting period between each warning. In the *bustees* many men had multiple wives and abused triple *talaq* – often by not allowing the waiting period between declarations – as a way to pursue multiple relationships.[4] In fact the CEO of *Azeem* felt that outside of the growing use of heroin, the abandonment of families by men in search of new girlfriends and wives was 'the biggest epidemic in these slums'. The NGO spoke against these practices:

> We need to show the boys that what they are doing is wrong, they are making their family suffer, their children suffer ... it is ignorance that is causing this of course, if people actually read the *Qu'ran* and analysed what it means then they know that (using) triple *talaq* is very very serious. Not because you are angry you say it ... it is over many problems, many years, many problems ... listen to Dr. Naik, read the *Qu'ran*, go to *masjid*, talk to *imam*, then rid yourself of this ignorance.
>
> (The Organiser, 21)

Here the Organiser explains that improper understanding of *talaq* has contributed to a culture in the slums where young men marry and start a family, only to abandon their wives for a new partner. The Organiser points to the poor understanding of the *Qu'ran* that has caused this epidemic. 'People here walk around and say "yes I have read the Qu'ran" but do they even understand what it is saying ... because Arabic is not something people can fully understand without some help.' He advises that because Arabic is poorly understood young people should educate themselves about *talaq* through consultation with religious leaders and community leaders (including himself and particularly televangelist Dr Zakir Naik). The Organiser's asser- tion of 'good' avenues for learning, however, reinforces his class status; asking Sheena (14) about learning from Dr Naik, she responds, 'who's that?'

The reality in the slums is that love marriages, arranged marriages, joint families and nuclear families all exist within a patriarchal society. This is a community where marriages (especially arranged) bring a substantial dowry and where men have control over (and improper use of) *talaq*, and where newly married young women are often placed at the bottom of a family hierarchy. With this reality in mind, many young women in the slums *choose* independently to pursue premarital romantic relationships with the *hope* that this partnership may lead to marriage and that her new family would accept her as a daughter. Many young women believe that falling in love gave them some measure of control to shape their married lives and the 'power of love' would keep young women safe from various abuses in relationships, regardless of the family system they lived in.

While there is a strong desire amongst young women to pursue individually directed premarital relationships, these romantic directions do not always lead to marriage. Nor do the marriage unions that result from premarital court- ship last long-term, nor do couples in these relationships move towards a more egalitarian partnership between husband and wife (as proposed by European scholars such as Giddens 1992). However, premarital relationships are actively pursued by *almost every* unmarried young person I know. Pre- marital relationships are becoming an important path towards marriage, and are changing young women's expectations of premarital relationships in the slums.

Although there is a strong undercurrent of individually styled love and romance amongst most young women in the slums, not all of them wanted to participate in premarital romance. Tales of heartbreak as a result of love were abundant throughout the *bustees*. Young people told me stories of peers who had fallen in love, but were not able to continue their relationship with 'their one true love'. Young people also reported many instances where peers secretly eloped, upsetting and hurting their family in the process. Thus there were a handful of young women who did not want to ever experience premarital love.

Role models

For those who wanted to have a premarital relationship, complete with love and romance, stories of neighbours and families whose love grew from within an arranged marriage did not prepare them for their romantic escapades. 'You hear older people saying (love) grows within the marriage, but they've won, they've already got the marriage, we want to know how to move there (towards love marriages)' (Heera, 20). Heera suggests that a love marriage is the goal of dating, and arranged marriage couples did not provide them with the advice they needed because they have already achieved marriage. Young women turned to new role models to inspire their love lives, and here Bollywood tales of romance are held as inspiring. When asked to list some of their romantic ideals and role models, Bollywood film and television couples dominated their preferences.

Gone were Laila and Majnun, an Arabic tale of star-crossed lovers, like Romeo and Juliet. It was Shah Rukh Khan (SRK) and Kajol in *Dilwale Dulhania Le Jayenge* (DDLJ – 1995) and Alia Bhatt and Arjun Kapoor in *2 States* (2014) that young people hold up as ideal. It is the *jodi* (pairing) of SRK and Kajol whom many describe as the 'ideal loving couple'. DDLJ as a great mix of romantic love, understanding, patience and eventually family approval (see Uberoi 1998 for further detail) was the *ultimate* Bollywood romance. While the movie is considerably old, made while most young people were not born, the popularity of the tale, the wide availability of DVDs, posters, soundtrack and in particular the constant television viewing opportunities, have made this film probably the most popular film in the slums.

In the film the two non-resident Indian (NRI) characters meet while pursuing independent travel with friends. The travel was given to Kajol's character as a one-chance reward for being a good girl, specifically by doing

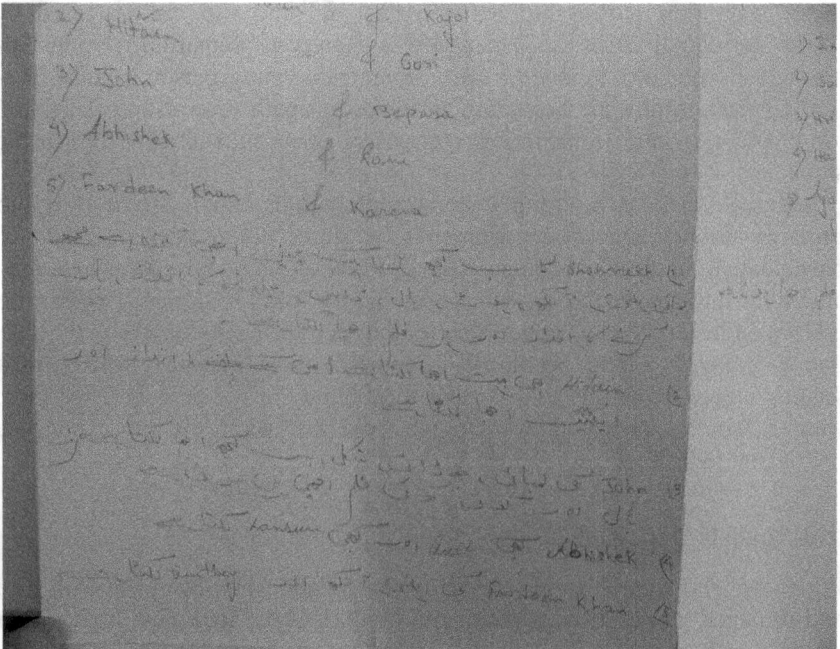

Figure 4.1 'My best couples list' (Aysha, female 15)

well in school and agreeing to an arranged marriage. On her trip she meets SRK's character, whom she initially dislikes; however, he was able to prove his decent moral fabric by keeping her safe and chaste, leading both characters to fall in love. After the trip, however, Kajol is swiftly taken back to India for her arranged nuptials. SRK's character follows Kajol's family to India and assures Kajol that he will find a way to convince her family to let them marry, and that he would only marry her once he obtained her parents' approval. The film ends with Kajol's father agreeing the two should marry, after being convinced that no other man could love his daughter as much as SRK's character.

Young women spoke of this love story as a good example of a successful romance, and desired such a love story, as Aysha (15) explains, 'I hope I can achieve such a love match in my life'. Importantly for Aysha it is not just that their love was romantic, but at the end of the film that their love was approved by all. Young women acknowledge that for romantic love to be truly successful within the context of the *bustee*, it has to play by communal rules, and thus must be approved by both families. What made SRK's character an ideal partner for the young women in this community was his ability to love within a communal system. As Raya (16) describes, 'his deep love and his patience' gave him the strength to wait for parental approval. SRK's character was valued for his positive interactions with Kajol and her family.

Bollywood film heroes also proved to be good aesthetic role models as well – Raya describes her ideal man:

> Salman Khan's body is very fine. I like John's height, but not his hair. I love everything about Shah Rukh, his lips, eyes, clothes, dance and acting, and his deep love. I also like Hiten's face.
>
> (Raya, 16)

Raya's ideal man is a mix of different Bollywood stars and popular television characters.

'Raj' is SRK's character in DDLJ (1995), and Hiten is a television actor. Interestingly, Raya's description of ideal men lacked popular music singers, sports personalities or models. Being asked about this, she felt she could only tell a good man by his interactions with females, and this can only be viewed in popular culture. Young women viewing and idolising movie stars and characters as romantic partners is not a novel phenomenon, but in a changing India where individually styled romance is growing, idolising a celebrity plays an important role in a young woman's newly developing romantic identity. Engle and Kasser's (2005) critical analysis of why young women idolise celebrities makes the important link between a young woman's developing romantic identity, and male stars. Their findings show:

> For many adolescents, identity is partially constructed by interacting with popular media, which of course includes many celebrities ... idolisation is

an avenue through which girls explore romantic views and attitudes toward interpersonal relationships ... thus, celebrity idolisation may relate to the types of relationships girls form.

(Engle and Kasser 2005: 264–265)

In the *bustees*, for example, young women idolise particular stars with good screen characters, and not actors with bad relationships with women on screen. As Mumtaz (15) explained, 'Emaraan Hashmi is just a disgusting man, he is the worst character, his character takes advantage of and behaves badly with women'. Actor Emaraan Hashmi is popularly known as the 'kiss-king'. He plays a playboy-type character in most films, having intimate relationships with many female actors on screen. In the slums he is disliked by young women for his womanising ways, even though they all agreed he is a committed husband in real life. In contrast male actors who were typecast to play charming men on screen – like the community favourite Salman Khan – was held up to be an ideal boyfriend, in spite of his womanising and violent behaviour off-screen, 'oh that's the kind of boy I want ... so cheeky, so strong and handsome' (Reena, 15). As depictions of intimacy increase rapidly in contemporary Bollywood it will be interesting to see how idolisation changes in the slums.

Geographies of relationships

Applying knowledge gained from Bollywood, peers and siblings, young women in the *bustee* learn the rules of courtship, how to perform on a date and how to move relationships forward. For most young women finding a partner and developing a relationship generally occur on the way to school and in the local neighbourhood. Young women can also develop relationships in spaces like shopping centres and parks. These non-local spaces require more mobility negotiations, thus more risk taking. Most young women in the *bustees* usually fall in love with their neighbours, family friends and cousins, and these are often reported as first romances. Once in a relationship with a young man, as Abraham (2001) has discussed, they can participate in many types of relationships: *Bhai-behen*, *timepass* and 'true love' relationships. *Bhai-behen* literally translates to brother and sister, and these relationships are understood to be platonic and non-sexual. *Timepass* relationships are relationships that are understood by one or both parties to be impermanent in nature, while true love relationships are romantic in nature, and underpinned by goals of marriage. The boundaries of these categories, however, are fuzzy and young women can participate in all three of these relationships with the same person.

Most premarital romantic relationships develop within third spaces like the *Nach Baliye* roof and laneways. In spaces like the *Nach Baliye* roof and shopping centres outside of the slums, relationships can develop with more ease as they are outside of the prying eyes of community members. Local laneways are also spaces where love can develop, but courtship here is more problematic. Girls caught overtly challenging *purdah* and appropriate gendered interactions in public laneways put themselves at risk. While their movements are monitored, young women do find local and public places to participate in romance.

One of the places romance usually does not develop is within the home itself. In the *bustees* young women are seldom alone at home, as the home is a place where small babies and elderly grandparents, and home-based mothers spend most of their time. The rules of *purdah* also position the home, especially during the day, as a female space. There are, however, times when young men come to the house as acquaintances of family members, or to service things within the home. If a young woman is interested in a guest, she discreetly makes eye contact with him, and he discreetly makes eye contact with her. To begin a relationship requires skills that favour subtlety. For the most part, direct eye contact and a discreet smile between two people is often all that is needed to signify interest. Not surprisingly, mistaken interest as a result of eye contact is also the cause of episodes of stalking and one-sided love in the *bustees*. In fact in the slums, incidents of eve-teasing accelerate when young men misunderstand looks received from young women. If a young woman clarifies her disinterest, the ego crush might prompt men to harass and tease the young woman on the streets for a length of time. Eve-teasing is often translated as the public sexual harassment of women, however this is not a very good definition. Eve-teasing can be complicated by women's feelings of both fear and annoyance, coupled by feelings of romantic/sexual interest. Teasing can be verbal (such as singing a song to a passer-by), sonic (like whistling) and/or gesticulatory (such as thrusting one's pelvis) (see also Sodhi and Verma 2003). Eve-teasing can play an important role in the development of romance in a community where *purdah* is observed.

Unlike young women whose heterosexual desire needs to be monitored and contained through marriage, strong heterosexual desire is an important indicator of a 'normal boy'. The *bustees*, not unlike other public places in India, have spaces where overt exhibition of heterosexual desire is prominent, such as at tea stalls and rickshaw stands. Dominant public discourse in India suggests that teasing is related to young men's poor education outcomes, low socio-economic status and marginalisation (Jeffrey 2010). For such young men teasing can be a *timepass*, something to do to kill their time. However these dominant discourses have been challenged by the 2012 gang rape and murder of a college student in Delhi (see Schinder and Titzmann 2015) which saw unprecedented public debates about eve-teasing as a national problem. In the *bustees* eve-teasing is viewed in different ways by different people. Some young men understand eve-teasing to be a duty they perform in order to 'test' the character of young women. If the women they tease remain silent and submissive in public, they prove their 'good' character. Most elder women view eve-teasing as a disrespectful act, but that this act is a normal part of the growing up process. Young women view eve-teasing as shameful and scary; the act draws attention to young women's bodies and their general presence in public, which is embarrassing. However, teasing can also be read as flirting and inviting, in particular if a young woman feels safe and is attracted to her teaser. Given the gendered geographies of public and private spaces, eve-teasing is a tool young men use to mark their dominance in and of public male space. While eve-teasing can make public space difficult to negotiate, it is also a socially acceptable means of expressing interest. Sodhi and Verma (2003) show that eve-teasing allows a young woman to know if a young man is interested in her. In this way teasing can also be understood as 'a contextually appropriate way to approach girls' (Sodhi and Verma 2003: 120). This view that eve-teasing is an act of flirting is not shared by all, 'only low class *changra* (losers) think flirting and teasing are the same' (Aysha, 15). Aysha suggests that higher-class boys and even poor boys with greater status (obtained through education for example) would not mix flirting with harassment. She felt that good boys express interest using respectable means, such as writing a love letter, a *filmi* inspired gesture very popular in the slums.

Within the *bustees* if a young woman accepts a young man's initial interest (whether through a letter or teasing) she responds to his gestures, questions or comments. After some communication and eye contact, a young man will go out of his way to find out more about the young woman, such as where she lives and where she goes to school, and then frequent these areas. If a young man is able to do so, he delivers a love letter (by hand or through an acquaintance) to the young woman. Since the popularity of mobile phones in the slums, the seeking of mobile numbers is also another strategy of young men. However, phone number sharing is not always possible and young people often share their mobile with other family members, thus privacy is not always guaranteed on the mobile. Younger siblings can also play a role in delivering messages between young women and men, as they do not have *purdah* restrictions. Young women rely on their suitors to frequent areas where they will have a chance to meet and exchange information, telephone numbers and letters. The most popular local meeting times are during walks to and from school and tuition. These laneways become places where interest is gauged and contacts are forged and it is here that the first steps towards neighbourhood romance develop.

Schools and tuition centres have limited romance opportunities because most young men enter the work force at an early age. Thus even when tuition centres are mixed-sex, they are often made up of younger boys, not potential suitors. Young women's experiences of schooling differ from the idealised co-ed college environment depicted in Bollywood. Bollywood idealises 'the college years' as the most important time to explore love and live self-directed lives before marriage. These depictions of college life, however, also contribute to a poor public perception of the few young women who attend college in the *bustees*: 'They think we are bad girls, we go to college and meet with boys all the time like in the movies' (Layla, 20).

Most young people in the slums lack the 'college experience'; they do not have extended periods of mixed-sex interaction at school and this may be one reason for the quick pace of romance in the community. From the time of meeting, to declaring one's love, to eloping can be very brief and may take only a few months. Layla, for example, describes a young man who once gave her a love letter on the way to school. In the letter he wrote, 'I've fallen in love with you after watching you walk to school over the last one month'. Asking her about this suitor she laughs, 'He was young, you are a romantic at that age, you watch films and that's what you want: love, romance, a girl-friend ... yes to him it was real love, that is what he knows it as (real love).' The rushed entry into love is received in different ways. For Layla a rushed declaration of love without knowing each other is unacceptable and silly.

For others like Abia (16) true love can take a short time to develop. Abia met her partner, a flower seller, while being escorted to school (in a *niquab*) by her younger brother:

> I was in class nine and my brother walked me to school. He noticed me when I was walking, he knew my brother as well. So he would *salam* (greet) us together ... I did not feel anything at first. He became more friendly with my brother and I suspected that then he must have feelings for me, then he proposed to me. He began to meet me during school time, asking how I was, if I ate, how I was feeling, brought me presents as well. We talked nicely ... I believe it was *kismet* (fate) ... we did *nikah* (wedding) with his aunty and my sister's friend (as witnesses) in one month (outside of the slum).
>
> (Abia, 16)

Abia's husband pursued her through decent behaviour (greeting both her and her brother, asking about her feelings), buying her gifts and meeting her at her school. She accepted his request to be his steady girlfriend (an action called 'proposing') and she enjoyed his decent behaviour towards her. Abia felt fate (*kismet*) brought them together. They eloped in a community outside of their own, where she was supported by her sister's friend (who had also eloped), and her partner's aunt as witnesses. For Abia, the feeling of love that developed in one month was real and directed by a higher power. In this way love is almost like a religion:

> Such attitudes, wishing and hoping for the ultimate in love, constitute a belief; a religious state of mind ... the essence of our faith in love can best be shown by comparing it with religion. Both hold out the promise of perfect happiness, to be achieved along similar lines. Each offers itself as a way of escaping from the daily grind, giving normality a new aura; stale

old attitudes are tossed aside and the world seems suffused with new significance.

(Beck-Gernsheim and Beck 1995: 175)

Abia's experience also speaks to Sara Ahmed's (2004) understanding of love as two actors moving towards an ideological, in this case metaphysical and spiritual, goal. Pinning their hopes and dreams onto one another, Abia and her partner eloped with the support of believers in the metaphysical power of love. Abia was aware, however, that many of her peers ridiculed her, and that the community response to this act was that she was a selfish little girl who made a very bad life decision. Abia's analysis that a higher power brought her and her partner together, directly responds to criticism that she married too young. To subscribe to a faith-based approach to negate her 'selfish' actions is a calculated response to critique that she is not only selfish, but 'backwards', which again speaks to Ahmed's (2004) analysis of physical bodies imbuing ideologies in relation to discourses of love.

In the *bustees* it is not unusual for 'dating' to begin as early as nine years of age, and elopements to occur after a few months of knowing each other. These stories of love are increasingly discussed by many members of the community and the NGO as 'low class'. Many young women who aspire to higher status or class mobility, like Layla and Heera, do not view elopements like Abia's favourably: 'Those girls don't do dating for long, as soon as there is interest there, they are married with a baby in the stomach in one month' (Zafreen, 17). Here Zafreen believes peers like Abia are not well versed in the vocabulary of 'modern' courtship. Moreover since marriage is the proper way Muslims can have sex, Zafreen felt that ill-versed young women elope in order to experience intimacy as quickly as possible. By putting down peers who marry quickly Zafreen depicts her identity as a more upwardly mobile young woman, one who wishes to acquire higher status.

To young women like Zafreen it is Abia's poor choices that keep her in a low-class and low-status position, while Zafreen uses tools like learning dance, education and long-term dating with a suitable match, to gain higher status and upward mobility in a poor community.

Abia resists this low-class labelling by introducing *kismet* into the discourse of self-chosen love; she also uses moral superiority to address her peers' comments towards her. 'By participating in *badnam* (Zafreen) thinks she is so *hi-fi*, everyone knows that she goes with so many boys'. While Abia might agree that her love course was short, and has kept her in poverty, she believes her love affair is morally superior to other young women who in her mind 'are using boys' to gain social mobility. Discussions around appropriate times and ways to marry, and discourses of modernity and moral superiority – imbued in these discussions – are very complicated. What is not complicated is that early marriage has been identified by *Azeem* as one of the causes of poverty in the slums. According to the NGO young women get trapped into poverty when they are young wives. Education opportunities cease for them, home-based work increases for them, and duties of being a wife and mother start at a young age.

The dating process

Once a couple have made clear their interest in each other they embark on a dating process that goes through a number of phases. Since spending time with same-sex friends continues to be the most acceptable avenue for sociali-sation amongst Indian youth, a relationship can develop when same-sex friendship groups meet. For most, if not all of the young women in the *bus-tees*, skipping school or after-school excursions are a common way to meet with their same-sex friends outside of the home. The main way a romantic relationship can form with a boy during these outings is if someone within the same-sex group has a boyfriend and brings his friends, or if the group meets young men during their excursion. Of course, many young women develop relationships within the *bustees* on their own and manage to meet up with their partners unbeknownst to anyone else. However, even then, peer support is also needed as Aysha explains: 'there are some girls here who can keep their relationship a secret. They meet their boyfriends and do dating all in secret, but they still use our names to meet him.' Aysha (15) explains that even if young women are secretive about meeting boyfriends, they tell their parents that they are with their girlfriends and that this secret peer support contributes to the success of premarital relationships.

Peer support is more than just a strategy to meet prospective suitors; young women meet up with young men while in their same-sex groups because it is fun. Like dancing, they do not want to experience the fun and frolic of dating on their own. Thus not surprisingly group dating, where several couples meet to hang out, flirt and spend time together, is a popular way to begin the courtship process. Group dating also has strong support in popular culture, with television shows and films depicting group dating and even a group honeymoon (*Hum Saath Saath Hain* 1999).

Planning for group dates begins at school or in the neighbourhood, where friends discuss best times, locations and activities for their excursions. Young people may decide to skip school and meet up with friends, including young men, at a specified location. The frequency of these meetings depends on the ability of young women to negotiate good school marks and organise funds, and on the availability of their peers. On average young people tried to go on a group excursion once in a few months. Some members of the NGO *Azeem* also organised events in an effort to support mixed-sex interaction several times a year. The excursions involved visiting a space outside of the slums, eating food, spending time teasing each other, telling jokes and having fun. Single young women may mingle with many young men during this stage, and may be pursued by several suitors.

To reduce sexual jealousy and competition amongst candidates, a young woman may quickly make brothers (*bhais*) out of young men she does not have an interest in. She does this by addressing him as *bhai*, perhaps even tying a *rakhi* on him to symbolise their relationship. Taking on a *bhai* signals a platonic brother/sister friendship and these interactions can be, but are not always, a socially permissible way for young men and women to engage in public. *Bhais* by definition are 'decent' young men (see Abraham 2002) who are assigned a non-sexual protective brother role. Their duty as *bhais* mean that they can spend time with their *bahens* (sisters) in public as an escort, provide social support when called upon and counsel young women in relationship matters. Publicly these relationships are viewed as protective relationships, and while not all families approve of or condone them, in some families *bhais* are given brother-like responsibilities, such as monitoring a young woman's public behaviour, and can be in charge of escorting. In the slums it is not uncommon for couples to manipulate the *bhai–bahen* relationship by using it as a cover for a romance. In other cases a young woman may find herself falling in love with her *bhai* (and vice versa). This latter scenario is particularly problematic if the feelings are not mutual.

According to young women initial group dating is some of the most enjoyable in the relationship process. It provides the opportunity to meet up with friends and potential partners without the pressures of one-to-one conversation and fear of possible intimacy. During this phase young women look to find a young man who is her 'best friend'. Parveena (18) explains, 'I am looking for a good friend, a best friend, in my boyfriend. Someone I can tell everything to, someone who I can share things with.' On the *Nach Baliye* roof, however, the first phase of the dating process was problematised by dancing. Rather than slowly growing a physical relationship with their 'best friends', young people were immediately forced into intimate dance situations. This close physical contact confused many young women on the roof, and the performers divulged their feelings to the Choreographer, who gave several talks to the entire dance group regarding intimacy and dance:

> I told them that the nature of dance is to express oneself creatively. Just because you are dancing and touching each other does not mean you are in love, or are boyfriends and girlfriends to each other. That is another matter for the heart … this is only dance.
>
> (The Choreographer, 23)

The Choreographer was able to reaffirm her socially progressive middle-class status through her expertise in dance, friendships and romance. Her clarification of the difference between dance and intimacy helped some young women process the confusion they felt when being touched by unknown young men; however, all of the romantic relationships that did develop on the roof were between dance couples. While the close relationships dancers shared with each other can turn into rich and meaningful relationships, it is also important to recognise that by dating the young men they were in a close physical dance relationship with, young women can negate the *haram* nature of premarital intimate contact.

Proposing

When a young man 'proposes' to his partner, he expresses his desire to be her boyfriend. He then waits for her response to officially become a couple. Although young women can propose to young men, by appearing too dominant and sexually charged, young women who propose may find themselves labelled as *timepass* partners, which greatly compromises their ability to enjoy serious relationships that end in marriage. Upon receiving a proposal a young woman weighs the risk of bending the rules:

> You also need to know with 100 per cent surety he is a good boy, that would make (the decision) easier for you ... obviously you think of the future and what your parents will say. But by this time, if you acted right, you would say yes.
>
> (Shirzad, 16)

Shirzad describes her concerns about engaging in a relationship with a good boy. She argues that if she 'acted right', or obtained all the relevant information about the young man and developed a good friendship with him, then she would accept his proposal because she would have picked him out as a good character and grown to like him as well. Dating and romance, however, are never linear processes and some young people move between caring about someone as a friend, lover and brother over time.

The expert

When young women find themselves unsure about proceeding with the dating process, or find themselves experiencing problems in the relationship, it is not uncommon for someone to step in and offer advice. This 'expert' talks to the couple about the situation. These can be cousins or friends, or mutual friends. The significance of the expert's role in the relationship process was revealed during the *Nach Baliye* rehearsals when Aysha initially rejected a proposal from Javed. Parvez (20), a mutual friend and respected peer, stepped in to offer advice and 'sell' the idea of the relationship to her:

> When Parvez approached me I knew it had to do with the proposal. The reason I said no was because I was unsure about going into a relationship. I have seen so many girls in my neighbourhood get hurt, or their parents got hurt because of love. I was not interested in love. But (Parvez) said to give it a chance, and I did ... I suppose I always wanted to give it a chance, but needed some reassurance.
>
> (Aysha, 15)

One dominant discourse in the slums is that young women are vulnerable targets for romance or are coerced by unsavoury young men. Aysha addresses this by explaining that she had control over the process and was able to make calculated decisions. In negotiating whether to start a relationship with Javed, one risk she contends with is the possibility of the relationship being made public. Another consideration, Layla (20) explains, is '(some) girls end up marrying the boyfriend when their relationship is exposed, only to find out he is not good. Or their parents force them to marry someone of their choice.' The potential permanence of marriage also contributes to risk taking, 'because *izzat* is for boys to take and girls to lose, it is silly to just accept a boy's proposal after a few days' (Heera, 20). Thus when accepting a proposal, young women judge whether their suitor is worth the risks of getting caught, hurting one's family, and damaging one's *izzat*. But this is not always the case. Many young women I spoke with were adamant that boys 'put on an act' for most of the courtship period, and accepting proposals is dangerous. Their evidence lies in the many unhappy love marriages in the community, where post-marriage love-stricken boyfriends turn out to be deadbeat husbands (see also Grover 2010; Osella 2012).

The pressures of accepting the right kind of boyfriend are compounded by the expectations of limited dating experience amongst young women. In the *bustees* commitment is commendable. Fiza (19) explains, 'we don't just choose boyfriends to throw away like those (bad) kind of girls'. The reality is that in the *bustees* many young women go through more than one premarital relationship during their youth. For a young woman to participate in the game of courtship, however, she must master the persona of the good girlfriend, who is chaste, has limited relationship experience, and is focused on one man alone. Her public behaviour must conform to this, and her private behaviour (like shirking away from a dance partner) must conform to this. Through these actions she prevents a *timepass* label, protects her *izzat* and is able to continue to enter relationships with the possibilities of marriage. A 'good' girlfriend, then, is written with the same rules of sacrifice, adjustment and fidelity as young women entering arranged marriages.

Developing a relationship

After accepting a proposal the young woman and young man officially become a couple, and the dating processes they undertake emphasise their 'couple' status. On a group date couples break away from the group to spend more quality time with each other. Some couples also leave the community to spend time alone. On dates the young man may surprise the young woman with a gift of chocolates, which shows that he has been thinking of her. A working boy may find most of his expenses (outside of money which he should give his family) going towards a rendezvous with his girlfriend(s).

A lot of cultural capital is attached to gifts during the dating process, with young women who receive more expensive presents like clothing and jewellery becoming the envy of their peers. Expensive presents signify that a boyfriend is employed, earns decent wages and cares enough to think of his girlfriend.

Gifts that can be viewed in public, like clothing or trinkets, are often displayed prominently in third spaces like parks and the *Nach Baliye* roof, but also amongst close peers in schoolyards. Gifts prove the existence of romance, and are an important way to demonstrate one's global romance literacy, particularly during global and commercialised holidays including the plethora of commercialised themed days in India like Friendship Day and Rose Day. Heera (20) signalled the importance of these days: 'Obviously for Valentine's Day he will get me a rose, maybe a showpiece? I am not too sure of his plans.'

On these celebratory 'Days' shopping malls are filled with youth from all class backgrounds parading their gifts and their relationships throughout the day. In Kolkata these performances are viewed by higher-class women in a particular way. I had many friends from elite backgrounds who were sure that 'such obvious displays means they are low class' – which is actually not at all true if 'obvious displays' of class are gauged in a nightclub during Valentine's Day – but these statements remind us that youth police youth spaces where romance develops. *Bustee* youth who engage in a public romance have a heightened awareness of their class status and make a significant effort in public displaying their knowledge of global romance culture. By learning and undertaking the rituals of dating young people understood that they too are participating in a global youth culture:

> Obviously we would love to do the type of dating found in the films; that would be the ideal. But we don't have that much freedom to take vacations or go to expensive parks with our boyfriends. So we adjust (laughs). We go to (a large park) and the mall to spend time (together). (On the date) most important is food (laughs) and spending time somewhere with your boyfriend. But yes, it is from these films we learn what is a date and what to do on them. Before, how would you know, it is not like they teach you these things in school (laughs).
>
> (Heera, 20)

Heera explains that although the types of dating presented in films were beyond the socio-economic capabilities of *bustee* youth, they were not excluded from dating culture. In popular films a couple may meet and date while on a European holiday and go on dates in scenic locations like ornamental gardens, nightclubs and high-end restaurants. Young women in the *bustees* modify Bollywood dating to fit their lives, and use the general theme of visiting a space and having some food, as found in all Hindi films. By going to the local mall, eating at a food court and strolling through an ordinary park, romance is 'individually styled, invented and adorned' (Beck-Gernsheim and Beck 1995: 181).

Love, sex and intimacy

One of the more risky stages of relationship building is when intimacy develops, when couples proclaim their love for each other, or as Zeena (female, 15) explains, 'when we become serious in the relationship'. Asking her to photo-graph some of the important people in her life, Zeena offered an image of a young man and woman (Figure 4.2). She explained to me that her one true love was her boyfriend and she loved him more than anything.

The image, however, was of her boyfriend and her sister, but she described this photo to me as 'a photo of my boyfriend Rashad'. When I asked her why she did not have a photo with her partner, she explains, 'I wanted to, but in case this photo gets leaked I can't take the chance'. It was permissible to have a photo of her sister with Rashad because Rashad had publicly taken on the role of *bhai* to Zeena's sister. No photo of the romantic couple existed because Zeena did not want to leave any visible public 'proof' of their relation-ship, even after their declaration of love. Unlike idealistic Bollywood depic-tions of love conquering all, many young women in the *bustees* were not under the impression that declaring one's love would magically decrease the risk or legitimise a relationship. In fact, declaring one's love amplified the risks involved in a relationship, especially if the couple decided to share sexual intimacy.

My first contact with public displays of affection came on a day excursion organised by some young *Azeem* employees. I was asked to meet everyone at a bakery near the slums and to my surprise a minivan pulled up with four couples and a youth worker. All of the young people had pooled their money together, with *Azeem* contributing the most, to rent the vehicle and driver. They planned to travel to a resort town outside of the city. Within the van each couple was positioned to maximise privacy; I sat with the *Azeem* employee up in front with the driver. Individual shawls (*dupatta*) were used to cover each of the four couples in the van. One of the young women removed her *burqa* (she was wearing a *salwar kameez* underneath) to provide extra cover under which she and her partner could hide. Couples created privacy under the veils and used this space to kiss and be affectionate and talk to each other. When the shawls were lowered the group came together to chat and joke around. Subsequent group dates saw the same kind of group intimacy sessions, but adjusted to the physical context. In a park large trees provided privacy and couples scattered around the park to secure their own private spaces. In another memorable instance at a private home outside of the slums I witnessed two couples engaged in a kissing competition, with one couple kissing and challenging the other couple to match their accomplishment.

I must admit here that this type of group intimacy shocked me, and it also made me uncomfortable. My shock was initially because I was just not pre-pared for a group make-out session, and the context of a group make-out was very far removed from my own realities of intimacy. Here it is important to heed Mahmood (2005) who reminds us to look carefully at our own under-standing and biases around sexuality/performance and liberal ideologies. My discomfort came from my own understanding of physical intimacy as private, and not requiring peer assistance. My discomfort also came from a feeling that some aspects of group intimacy were competitive. Heera (20) explained

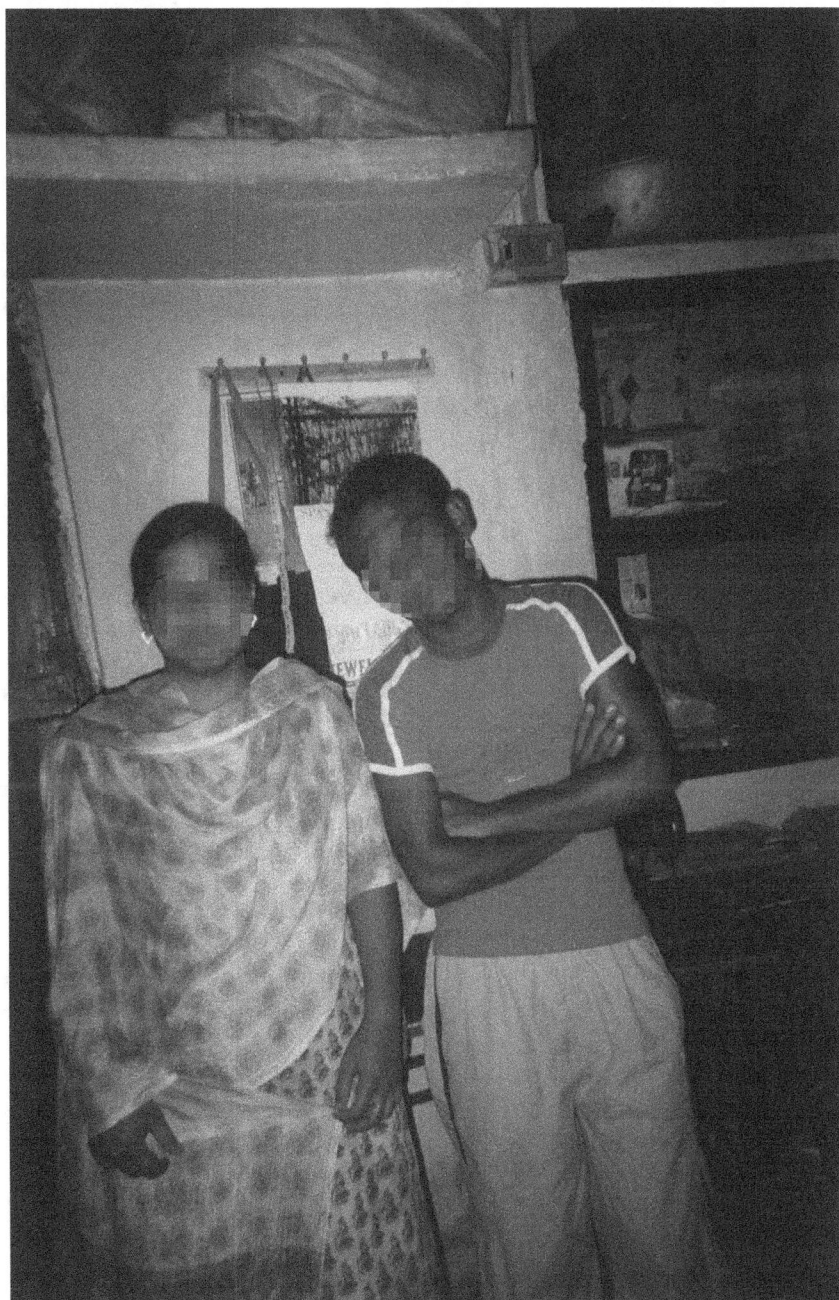

Figure 4.2 'A photo of my boyfriend Rashad'

that, as a participant in the kissing competition, she was performing in a particular way. However, she later regretted the decision, 'I made a mistake taking part in that ... had I been thinking that Rahul was recording on his mobile I wouldn't have done it, this is how girls get blackmailed ... but (another girl) said "oh you can't do it" and I knew I could...'. Here Heera identifies some important aspects of premarital relationships in the slums. When youth do have time to leave the community, intimacy becomes an important performance amongst peers, just as displaying one's gifts at the shopping mall during Valentine's Day. Even when they are not completely comfortable, many girls wish to show that they too can participate in a youth culture which values having a boyfriend and intimacy. Heera did not want to face accusations of not playing along because by not taking the same risks as her peer, Heera was herself at risk of losing peer solidarity. Heera's comments also reveal that young women's sexual and romantic transgressions can be used against them, something I discuss later in this chapter.

For young women group intimacy can be a support system that helps them to feel more at ease with displays of affection, especially during the initial stages of dating. 'When we first started going together I was shy, but my friend is doing it, I feel I too can hold his hand' (Layla, 20). Public displays of affection allowed young women to behave affectionately in ways they viewed on screen, and which could not be found in the *bustees*. Those who participated in premarital romance knew that their ability to be affectionate did not negate social, economic and cultural obstacles. 'Our time with our boyfriends is so precious ... such limited time we have to squeeze in our relations' (Layla, 20). Layla complains that quality time with her boyfriend is often limited to dates outside of the slum. She felt that, unlike upper-class youth, she 'can only be myself' with her boyfriend a few times a month.

Heera (20) felt her ability to have an affectionate relationship with her partner without marrying was not common amongst her other peers. For most girls, 'holding hands is like a big deal, a boy holds her hand, and she immediately falls in love.' Heera suggests that young women like Abia (14), who are not fluent in a global romance culture, read every sign of affection as 'a big deal'. Taking cues from Bollywood, holding hands and kissing are normal parts of the courtship process, so by holding their boyfriend's hand on their dates, Heera and her friends like Aysha and Layla are able to write their higher status. Of course these comments are unfair because none of these girls were privy to Abia's premarital romance, but their articulation of a difference between those who practise affection and wait to marry, and those who marry early after experiencing affection, intersect strongly with understandings of class and status.

Bollywood and informal sex education

A couple's decision to have premarital sex (*zina*), including both oral and penetrative acts, amplifies the risks within a relationship. Premarital sex for women carries great social stigma and if the community discovers that a young woman has had *zina* she is at risk of violence and hasty marriage. To be clear, this stigmatisation of young women resulting from their premarital sexual behaviour is a 'double standard of sexual morality' (Sleightholme and Sinha 1996: 5). As Sleightholme and Sinha (1996: 4–5) have noted in their work in the slums of Kolkata 'a man can "get away" with sex before marriage, while a woman's virginity is seen as an absolute necessity'. In the slums family reputation is maintained through the regulation of female sexuality and a high premium is placed on female virginity. It is this double standard that accounts for the stigmatisation of young women who socialise with young men in public or have sexual relationships before marriage.

Although *zina* is *haram* for *both* men and women in Islam, in the *bustees*, conservative interpretations of Islamic texts and misunderstanding of religious teachings result in what Bennett (2007: 375) describes in Indonesia as a 'tolerance of male promiscuity and the hyper-regulation of female sexuality'. Premarital sexual revelation thus is more risky for young women, but this did not dissuade *Azeem* from teaching young women about their sexual and reproductive health. *Azeem* was able to organise a 'girl's class' which I helped to run (in an action-research project, see Chakraborty 2010a, 2010b). Importantly this class was supported only by *Azeem*; the community was unaware of the nature of the class and only 'mature' students were invited by *Azeem* to attend. In the class health lessons were planned, and there was time allotted for young women to talk about issues they faced in their lives, including sex. These times were met with stony silence. In order to discuss sexual and reproductive health, and to draw out questions and concerns, I used clips and examples from Bollywood film.[5] In this way young women began to talk about sex and romance through characters in films and television, which did not directly imply personal experiences.

In the *bustees* popular Hindi cinema helps to locate sexual learning within a culturally specific context, as sexual knowledge and discourse are normalised within the context of Bollywood. Bollywood culture also provides insight into young women's romantic fantasies and expectations of relationships and marriage. Thus for many young women it is 'safe' to discuss sex through Bollywood. Bollywood, however, is a poor sex educator. As Heera confesses, films have not provided her with a clear picture of sexual activity:

> When I first watched *Raja Hindustani* it was the first time I saw an open smooch. Even then I didn't know I also had to move my lips; I thought that was only the boy's part. But for sex, I didn't really know the details ... rolling in the bed and bath I thought that was the extent ... that the boy's [penis] is put inside [the vagina] was not clear. The first time my friend told me these details and explained it I wanted to vomit. I thought I'd vomit if it ever happened to me; it was some kind of sick thing.
>
> (Heera, 20)

Although young people turn to Bollywood to educate themselves, many express confusion over sexual relationships and a couple's rights and roles in a relationship, an area where Bollywood provides little advice. While *Raja Hindustani* (1996) represents some of the first popular groups of films to show kissing in the 1990s, there have been many films since about 2010 which are more detailed in depictions of love and romance. In my most recent fieldwork, it was *2 States* (2014) which shows two upper-class college students creating a quasi-live-in romantic relationship while studying away from their home towns. Throughout the film both protagonists find ways to convince one another's family to accept their relationship and allow them to marry, or as Saba (20) explained to me, 'it's like a modern DDLJ!' Young people really enjoyed this movie, and felt that it was a positive example of blending premarital intimacy with the obligation to marry afterwards. The topic of depictions of intimacy in Bollywood created two very different camps amongst girls in the *bustees*. Some felt the depiction of intimacy to be 'more helpful to understand what it is that is going on' (Saba). While Saba felt the kissing and romantic scenes in films really helped her understand the mechanics of intimacy, Sakina did not appreciate detailed depictions:

> Our family went to see *Yeh Jawaani Hai Deewani* (2013) together. We were seven of us, myself, my cousins, elder brother, aunty and uncle. This was during when it was opening, but there were lots of families like us … every time Deepika and Ranbir kissed I thought, 'I'm going to die'. I was so embarrassed. If it was just me and my cousins, okay, but with my brother and uncle, and that too a *housefull* show, every guy up there was shouting and passing comments.
>
> (Sakina, 16)

While public displays of affection are not normally socially acceptable in Kolkata, reading Sakina's experience we see that she would have been fine with viewing kissing and intimate scenes with similarly aged cousins. However, she was mortified watching such scenes in front of her elders, whom she also knew were embarrassed. This embarrassment was intensified by the (sold out, *housefull*) audience's reaction, and in particular young rowdy men who drew attention to the provocativeness of the entertainment. Further discussion reveals that this embarrassment stems from ideas of respect (that kissing in front of elders is disrespectful) and shame (or *sharam*, that public kissing and viewing such, is shameful because it is a private matter). Sakina believes, 'I don't think we (society or *samaaj*) are ready for lip-to-lip kissing in every film, at least not in the *bustees*'.

Though most young women view popular culture as an important educational tool, many admit that they turn to Bollywood culture and popular television serials in private to see how characters resolved issues as Shirzad explains:

You don't want anyone to think you are so uneducated that you don't know about these matters [of love] and that you need some television serial to help you with problems with your boyfriend … it's fake, just *timepass*. Even though we all know that Tulsi gives good advice, you won't tell anyone you take it seriously or they might think you don't have your own personality.

(Shirzad, 16)

While Shirzad thought the protagonist Tulsi from the popular television drama *Kyunki Saas Bhi Kabhi Bahu Thi* had excellent advice, she also knew the limits of this advice in her real life.[6] Shirzad's comments are supported by Banaji's (2006a, 2006b) findings amongst middle-class young people in India who often publicly reject advice from Bollywood. Banaji shows how, amongst South Asian youth in Bombay and London, there is a sense of shame amongst young people in admitting that they have been influenced by the media.

Western films and pornography, public health campaigns and peers, all help youth across India to learn about sex (Abraham 2003; Alexander *et al.* 2006). In the *bustees* young men, more than young women, turn to internet pornography to educate themselves on the logistics of sex. Most young women have limited access to internet cafés because of mobility and financial restrictions. While there is a small but growing trend of young women trying to cultivate virtual friendships and romance (Chakraborty 2012b), internet cafés in the slums are male-dominated spaces. Like Bollywood films, pornography is also a poor sex educator and young men were critical of its performative nature (Chakraborty 2010b). Outside of the internet, other sources of pornography in the slums include cheap DVDs with detailed sex scenes from Hollywood films like *Basic Instinct* (1992), Western pornographic films, as well as Indian b-movies. These are passed around in mostly male friendship groups and viewed in private homes. Young men and women also view Western film sex scenes on cable television/DVDs at home or in the cinema.

Even after drawing on these different sex educators, many young women report that they were initially unsure of how to have sex and young women relied on further discussions with their partners. Peers, older siblings and family members were also sources of informal sexual knowledge. *Bustee* youth received certain information about sex from older family members. The experiences of youth in the *bustees* are similar to observations in Pakistan where frustrated youth receive information about sex at certain times, such as before one's wedding (Hennink, Imran and Iqbal 2005).

Zina *and gender roles*

Unlike their male peers, who may brag about their sexual conquests in same-sex groups, young women tried not to confide in female friends about their sexual relations. Here we see a divergence away from group risk taking, which is underpinned by the very *haram* nature of *zina*. To be clear, dating is acceptable, and even kissing and flirting in public can be acceptable in third spaces; however, sexual relations before marriage is absolutely unacceptable. Young women who do experience premarital sex must keep this information very secret. They could not risk the stigma which revelation of *zina* would bestow upon them. In fact it was other young women who could really harm them – we will see later that Raya loses all her friends after it is suspected she engaged in a sexual relationship before marriage. Sodhi and Verma's research in the *bustees* of Delhi also reveals that when *zina* is exposed, young women put themselves at risk of sexual blackmail and harassment by men in the community. Unfortunately once a young woman develops this reputation it is very hard to undo. For young women eager to write their 'good girl' identities, reprimanding the 'bad' behaviour of peers in front of family and community members is one way to perform the 'good girl' in public. This makes group solidarity and risk taking unstable, and Shazana (15) acknowledges that as a result of this instability 'girls are girls' worst enemies here'.

Discussions about *zina* really brought out the essence of gendered double standards in the community. For example, in one of our focus group discussions we talked about 'good' and 'bad' films which lead to many young women describing *Neal and Nikki* (2005) as a bad film. In particular young women felt that the main female character was 'bad' because she was too promiscuous, and that the male character was equally 'bad' for being a promiscuous flirt. But further discussions of the film reveal that not all promiscuous behaviour is considered equal:

> That film was nonsense, about these two immoral characters who were just flirting with too many people ... but still the woman should have at least tried to keep her character, even though the boy didn't. We know boys are like that, but she should have been strong in her convictions.
>
> (Shazana, 15)

Shazana publicly supports a normative performance of female sexuality where young women remain chaste, while men can obtain sexual experience before marriage. She implies that if young women desire sex and intimacy before marriage, they should remain strong and fight these sexual urges. Young men, in contrast, could not control their urges, and thus it was up to women to practise self-control. Fast forward almost a decade after that film was released, where in *2 States* (2014) the male and female leads have a pre-marital relationship while away from home, youth I spoke with who unequivocally loved the film felt the female protagonist should have more control and not have had sex. 'Maybe it would be better if she just didn't have sex so that her heart wouldn't have been so broken when they had to separate' (Sakina, 16). Sakina suggests that risk of hurt in sexual relationships is greater for girls. Mumtaz agrees; she explains that while young men could get away with sex before marriage, young women could not even publicly attend sex and reproductive health class in the slums. 'If people come to know that you know something about sex, then the boys will be on your back and then you'll have trouble' (Mumtaz, 15).

In discussing *zina* both young men and women agree that a young woman's decision to have sex amplifies her risks of abandonment by her partner, and violence by the community:

> According to the Society the girl is like a soap which is Used whereas the Boy is the user of this soap and is never used.... so, most of the time the boys say that they have used the girls and thrown them in a garbage [dustbin]. These remarks can never be said by a girl atleast (*sic*) a good respected girl would rather die than say anything like this. Nobody wants to loose (*sic*) their respect and dignity. 99% in the neighbourhood lies that they didn't have sex even if they had it once or twice or more. While some [boyfriends] come to know from their girlfriend's ex-boyfriend they have had sex, I have seen the boy who was mad for the girl; after hearing this [she had sex] left her at once and never turned back.... Nobody wants a use (*sic*) product. So in Indian society a girl has to be really very conservative if she wants her image and character good. Then she would be respected in the society.
>
> (Parvez, 20, email correspondence)

Parvez understands that in the slums honour and discourses of shame really impact young women. Parvez, however, articulates that young women resist the burdens of *izzat* by lying and keeping a conservative image. Thus, for a young woman to be viewed as 'respectable' she must always lie about sexual experience and knowledge, and must always perform the good Muslim girl, especially in public. Both men and women, then, work to reinforce sexual double standards that tie a family's pride to a 'good virgin' bride and reinforce a femininity that prizes virginity. The desire for a virgin bride negatively impacts upon the life courses of sexually active young men and women in the *bustees*. Young men in particular admit that due to a young woman's performance of the good girl, they could inadvertently marry a 'used' product. Many view this type of marriage as the ultimate risk.

I have had countless conversations with young men (some who I knew were sexually active) who were adamant they would use triple *talaq* if they found out after marriage that their wives were not virgin brides. Thus in the slums marriage may not protect young women from a negative reputation or abandonment. In this way young women must also deny sexual experience and sexual knowledge even after marriage, which accentuates the sexual health risks of both young men and women. This virgin/whore dichotomy – that the female virgin is to be protected and the whore to be used – has been and remains of central relevance to patriarchal power in India, and indeed around the world (McRobbie 2000). Far from a sexual revolution that brings young people towards more egalitarian relationships, having sex in a relationship places young women in an incredibly difficult position, as it operates within a patriarchy that both young men and women play their part in supporting and reinforcing.

The importance of virginity also sheds some light on why sexual violence against women is such a powerful tool in this community and why eve-teasing is so successful in supporting male dominance of public space. Nobody wants to be 'that girl' who is deemed overtly sexual. Implications of such branding could seriously affect mobility, marriage and family honour.

Geographies of sexual encounters

Despite the risks, in the slums there are some young people who have pre-marital sex with their partners. While on the surface of the community it does not look like this can even occur, especially given mobility restrictions and dangerous repercussions particularly against young women, transgressions exist in various spaces. Over the time I have been in this community I am aware of a handful of young women who engaged in premarital sex. In line with the taboo nature of *zina*, many did not admit their sexual encounters directly to me, and used obscure 'I'm asking for a friend' language. However throughout the last 11 years I have been approached for reproductive health support by some young women (and some young men). These incidents are surrounded by fear of being caught, and shame regarding their actions. I feel I was approached because I was a familiar *didi* (older sister) but I was also an NRI and Hindu, and I was leading a 'girl's class' – making me a total outsider by community standards. By teaching the class I did develop a reputation as an 'expert' in these matters, and many young people called me Buladi, a female puppet who was the star of a very successful HIV/AIDS campaign. While young people did share with me some information about their sexual lives, because of stigma it is clear that vital context was missing in their discussions (I have discussed this elsewhere, Chakraborty 2010a). Thus I do not claim to fully understand the intricacies and logistics of premarital sexual relationships, and I probably never will.

Based on the information I have been able to gather, it is clear that the time period from when a couple meets to when they have sex varies considerably, from a few weeks to few months or years. In the *bustees* some young women felt that social status underpinned discourses of sexual debut: 'We think that if a girl has done sex say in a few weeks after she met her boyfriend, she is not very educated' (Heera, 20). Comments with this judgemental undertone are common in both boy and girl groups. For most young people premarital sex in the *bustees* is opportunistic. Previous studies on sexual coercion and the consensuality of sexual experiences in the *bustees* reveal young women's experiences of forced sex in their relationships (Sodhi and Verma 2003). Likewise young women who approached me often expressed how their first sexual experience was a surprise. Although none disclosed any incidents of sexual abuse in their partnership, some discussed how they were persuaded or tricked into sexual intimacy. In their study of young people's sexual behaviour in Pune, Alexander *et al.* (2006: 152) report that 30 per cent of young women were 'persuaded' to have sex for the first time; that is, they 'refused at first to have sex, but then agreed to have sex the first time with at least one partner'.

It is possible to read discourses about persuasion differently than Sodhi and Verma (2003) who understand that non-consensual sex is as serious a problem in the slums of India. Although I do not in any way deny the unequal power relations within relationships in the *bustee,* and there is a problem of forced sexual contact throughout India (the rape and murder of Nirbhaya in 2012 reminds us of that), discourses about persuasion can also be read as an extension of the good girl performance. Branding oneself as an 'innocent girl' who was duped into a sexual relationship can protect a young woman if her sexual activities are ever revealed in the *bustees.* Within a relationship, to be naïve suggests sexual unawareness, limited social experiences and self-control, characteristics of a good girl. Indeed research on sexual communication in India reveals that in many relationships it is not always clear if saying 'no' to sex really means that, or simply a required performance of virtue (McDougall, Edmeades and Krishnan 2011; Pande *et al.* 2011; Chakraborty 2012a).

In the slums the opportunistic nature of sexual activity has strong social status links. If a young man is exceptionally poor the couple may meet in the back alleys of undesirable locations in the slums, such as close to a garbage dump or a factory that is closed for the day. Here sex often occurs fully clothed and can be standing up. I know of couples who used work places and a schoolhouse after hours. Most poor youth are unable to secure stable locations for a consistent sexual routine. Bushes in dark parks near the *bustees* were not desirable locations as sex workers frequently use these spaces. Many young men and women scorned having sex in parks, viewing it as 'low class'.

Some couples in the slums, especially upwardly mobile youth, try hard to plan their affairs. Planning a sexual encounter in the conservative *bustees* requires careful preparation; young men are responsible for planning sexual encounters while young women provide limited input on location. Young men in long-term relationships have discussed with me how their girlfriends are 'surprised' to engage in sex, even after jointly planning a date in a secluded area. These acts, as with discourses of sexual trickery, maintain a girls's modest identity and exhibit the qualities of a controlled girlfriend, and possibly a 'good' future wife.

For sexually active couples who can afford to do so, intimacy takes place on dates away from the *bustees*, at tourist spots and secluded areas away from prying eyes. The middle-class experience of having sex on a bed in private, or in a rented space so that they could lie down, was ideal for all. This is unlike sex in the *bustee*, where married couples often have sex in one-room homes with other people in the room. In one-room *bustee* homes there is generally only one bed and it is customary to give the newly-wed couple, a couple without children, or elders and the sick the bed to sleep on. There is an unspoken rule in *bustee* homes that you 'don't look up' at the bed when the rest of the family sleeps on the floor at night. This gives couples a chance to have sex within their own home, fully or semi-clothed, in the darkness of night. The small quarters and poor privacy of slum homes can make sex a public act – and discourses outside of the *bustees*, including in major newspapers suggest that children's access to sexual observation makes poor slum dwellers sexually knowledgeable from a young age and more prone to sexual experience. While all young women embarrassedly did tell me about witnessing particular acts when they were younger, there certainly was no correlation between witnessing acts and sexual knowledge or experience.

Public discourses which suggest sex in the *bustees* is low class because of lack of privacy supported young people's idealising the private and very middle-class sexual encounters that they view in popular culture. Some young men went out of their way to achieve this fantasy. If a young man can afford to, the couple leave their *bustee* for another community a distance away. Here he rents a room that has basic furnishings and perhaps a television for an hour or so. The television might have DVD options and they may come prepared with blue films. When I started fieldwork in 2005 a room could be booked for 100 rupees; in 2014 it was difficult to find a room for anything less than 300 rupees, and some young men had to secure up to 800 rupees, depending on the size and facilities in the room. This is a middle-class outing, but like young women who depend on peer-support to date, 'all boys get help from their friends to go on these (sex) dates … they borrow money, they use their motorbikes' (Talah, male, 22). Their use of these rooms points to new geographies for sex for the urban poor who are concerned about status, and the growing middle-class consciousness around intimacy and sexual privacy certainly plays a part in its rise.

On the outing a young woman may wear a *burqa* so as not to be identified. This also assists with her public performance of purity. Although landlords understand that the couple has come to have sex, they may assume that they are married and getting away from their crowded homes in order to be intimate. Performing intercourse away from their own *bustee* reduces the risk of a couple being caught by family or community members. Perceptions of respectability also influence the couple's behaviour during the sex act itself. Young men and women try hard not to make a lot of noise during sex for fear of being heard. Young women in particular suppressed vocalisation during sexual intercourse because according to young people only sexually experienced or promiscuous girls make audible noise during sex. The soundless act of sexual intercourse allows a young woman to perform an identity of respectability, conveying that she is a decent girl who is not wild about sex – a good girlfriend, and a good future wife.

Sexual negotiations

Like dance, premarital sexual activity has both private and public supporters in the slums. As discussed, some members of *Azeem* are very supportive of mixed-sex interaction, but never *zina*. They organised the *Nach Baliye* shows, picnics and activities throughout the year and encouraged young men and women to attend. The availability of government-sponsored abortion services, as well as local and illegal abortion services are other examples of infra-structural support of premarital sexual activity. These services, however, are not overt and public denial about premarital sex is the norm in this commu-nity. Most families organise the swift marriage of a couple or arrange for a quick abortion or removal of pregnant young women to distant communities in order to maintain that 'premarital sex does not occur here' (community elder, female).

Sex education is an important social reform that the youth workers at *Azeem* support. The younger employees of the NGO have been steadily moving forward plans for premarital sex education for *bustee* youth since 2006. Few Islamic leaders in Kolkata support such programmes, but I spoke to many religious and community leaders who were more than happy to back programmes addressing maternal health issues. Layla (20) explains that, 'here it is easier to talk about sex education like you are going to help young women get pregnant after marriage'. Religious support is not available for young women who participate in *zina*. Breaking the social and religious rules of premarital sex is thus a stressful decision. Those who did engage in *zina* struggled with how to reconcile their Muslim identity with the realities of their sexual lives. Like young people's negotiated use of Islamic discourse in relation to mixed-sex dance, young women moved between upholding the *haram* nature of *zina* and operating a self-directed biography, guided by their own life choices.

Many young women pick and choose aspects of Islamic discourse to suit their sexual lives. Most justified this action by claiming individualised choice, *meri marzi*. During a discussion about *haram* acts and Islam, Mumtaz (15) contemplates: 'Yes, *zina* is a sin also, but sin is a choice as well. One can argue that *meri marzi*, it's my choice if I want to sin.' Mumtaz uses the con-cept of individual choice to philosophise about premarital sex. But this use of Islam and individual desire does not favour young women, as Talah (male, 22) explains, 'no girls would say *meri marzi*, I choose to have sex … any girl who has sex even with her boyfriend of seven years, whom she is certain to marry, will be considered a *randi* if this is exposed … and he maybe won't marry her after this'.

Talah believes that if a dating couple was truly in love, and the couple's sexual experience was revealed in the community, even a young man who professed his utmost love for his girlfriend would face pressure to leave the relationship. Layla (20) also felt that boys lost respect for girls whom they have sex with, 'it's like in *Band Baaja Baaraat* even when Shruti loves the guy he totally loses respect for her – even as a friend – that is reality. Guys will lose respect for the girl (after she sleeps with him) even if she would die for him.' Here Layla gives an example of a popular film *Band Baaja Baaraat* (2010) which depicts best friends starting a sexual relationship, only to have the guy not able to commit afterwards and abandon her. Layla felt that in the slums the reality is that young men lose interest and respect for young women after sex, in spite of strong friendship.

A young woman's ability to make sexual choices depends on her ability to keep the matter private. One female participant Zuri (female, 15) who was engaged in a sexual relationship with her partner, had mixed feelings about her experience. She approached me for pressing reproductive health support, and was one of very few young women who approached me directly (rather than through a partner) about issues in her own sexual life. This was a very stressful and shameful time for Zuri. Between the awkward silences and questions about specific treatments, she explained that she made a mistake but also admitted she was deeply in love with her boyfriend. She was sure he was going to marry her, but on the other hand she wished she was a 'better Muslim' who could 'stay strong' and wait for marriage. Being asked why she just did not elope with her partner, she reveals her class and status aspirations and the changing position of marriage in a globalising slum:

> During my mother's time you could just marry at 15 and that was your life. But now, how? You have to go to school, you have to make some-thing of yourself. Marrying now … I'd be like those uneducated girls who just think the purpose of their whole life is just to come together with their boyfriend.
>
> (Zuri, 15)

Zuri explains that in a globalising India a young woman should complete some secondary school, develop her own identity and meet the right kind of boy for marriage. In doing so Zuri saw a future better than what her parents were able to achieve. Zuri wanted to have a chance to take on some of the new possibilities available for her – specifically further education and paid employment. By abruptly marrying her boyfriend those opportunities would slip away, because the community still wholeheartedly believes that married women should not attend schooling, regardless of their age.

While Zuri was not in the minority for accessing emergency reproductive health services – as mentioned earlier there were countless public and private clinics which had these facilities – she was certainly in the minority in viewing the prospect of early marriage as unsatisfying. *Azeem* reports that over 80 per cent of all young women under the age of 19 were married in the *bustees*, and of these many had eloped. The issue of elopements prompted the NGO to offer special girls-only classes addressing the importance of marrying later. 'We don't say "love is bad", we say "wait to marry". But many of these girls, they want to experience sex and love, and they are insecure, so they rush' (female NGO employee). This NGO employee explains that some young women in the slums rush into marriage to experience intimacy and to secure their relationship through sex. She also suggests that young women are very anxious about securing a good boyfriend, and are afraid he will leave if they do not comply with requests for sex.

Sheena and Abia, who participated in quick romances and marriages, were stigmatised by this discourse, and they were very insecure about the stigma that they were 'simple' girls. To Sheena (14) 'modern' young women like Heera and Aysha came from 'good families' with different opportunities: 'Layla is with (her upper-class boyfriend), so she can work in an office'. Sheena felt that since Layla had 'secured' a higher-class boyfriend, she gained social status that allowed her to pursue activities like public paid employment without fear. Sheena did not have a similar opportunity, and was happy to have met her partner and marry him quickly. These examples remind us that individual young women interpret religious texts and discourses differently, and that negotiations of faith and piety in the world of romance are both subjective *and* contextual.

Disenchantment and disappointment

While young women in this research were of relatively similar social and economic status, participation in dating and romance culture created a division between young women. The most successful way to gain upward mobility in the *bustees* is through marriage. Conversely young women with the potential for higher status and upward mobility can undo their trajectory with a bad marriage. If one's poor marriage partner was arranged, families often feel obligation to retain various levels of kinship support after their daughter's marriage. But if a young woman undertakes a self-directed romance and love marriage, and that marriage is poor, she often cannot draw on similar support networks post-marriage. Grover (2010) reports similar findings in the slums of Delhi. To illustrate just how powerful a poor love marriage is, and how self-directed love can shape one's life course post-marriage, I draw on Raya's story.

Raya (16) was the female dance captain of the 2005 and 2007 *Nach Baliye*. She was, according to the community and to Raya herself, on the right path towards a 'better life' after these shows. Unlike many families in the *bustees* her mother and father encouraged Raya to pursue her dreams of dance, and encouraged her further education and paid employment. 'My parents said to me if you want to study, then study, if you want to work, then work.' With so much support and such a promising future I was sure Raya would be able to 'make something of herself'. After a few years of being unable to connect with her, I finally met up with Raya in 2011 when she was 22 years old, and was shocked to see her selling toys on the pavement in the slum. This once fit girl was now quite thin with sunken eyes. Since our reunion I regularly meet up with Raya to discuss her life and about her *Nach Baliye* memories. Unlike most of the young women I work with who Facebook me and who I chat and text on the phone with, Raya was unable to continue any form of telecommunications with me, and this speaks to her socio-economic situation. Raya recounted that about a year after the 2007, show she began an affair with a married man who had a child. They fell in love in spite of peer discouragement. Eventually he left his family for Raya and they secretly eloped. Years later she was struggling with the realities of life including the difficulty of maintaining a steady income because she did not finish secondary schooling. She also was having problems at home because of her husband's philandering tendencies; she lamented to me 'I have seen him hanging around the schools, talking to different girls'. We met many times and these meetings were underscored by deep regret, 'I am married now *didi* ... those days of the shows are my past ... If you told me five years ago this would be my life, I would have laughed. I thought I was going to be on television' (Raya, 16).

All of the young women that I knew, and Raya herself, viewed her life course as littered with mistakes. Poor decisions anchored Raya to a life that was similar to her own mother's. Rather than moving forward socially and gaining status through educational, economic and cultural participation, Raya was 'stuck with (her) own poor decisions' as her peer Parveena (18) explained to me. For young women participating in the game of courtship, seeking social change and holding out for a different life course should be as important as falling in love and experiencing romance. By seeking a suitable partner one's romance goals could eventually obtain parental approval. Raya did not have a chance at this; her parents felt betrayed by her poor decision, and to her peers her life was a tragedy of her own making. Speaking of Raya, Layla (20) comments, 'it is absolutely her fault she is in this situation, she misused the freedoms she was given, and actually she was given too much freedom it seems'.

Layla explains that when the community found out that Raya had eloped it caused stress for her peers as her public transgression put the spotlight on premarital romance practice in the slums. Moreover, falling in love with a married man gives self-directed romance a bad name, something many girls were trying to mend. After Raya eloped her close *Nach Baliye* peers were forced to take extra precautions to cover their own transgressions, which left little time to support Raya who had poorly played her hand. Raya expressed hurt that her friends from *Nach Baliye* no longer wished to hang out with her: 'they didn't want to continue the friendship after my marriage'. To her peers Raya was a selfish girl, whose actions could possibly jeopardise and expose their own relationships. She was a risky friend, and was cut loose from many social circles.

Breaking up, stalking and violence

While many young women in the *bustees* desire premarital romance, not all romantic relationships last happily ever after. In the slums there are many ways to end a relationship. A break-up may be mutual, with the couple parting ways with little drama. Young women felt that although this was the best way to break up, it did not always happen this way: 'Yes sometimes you just easily break up with the guy, other times he gives you problems' (Fiza,

19). Other break-ups are more complicated. Some young women who are unhappy in their relationships discuss their problems with *bhais* or friends. Romantic relationships that grow out of *bhai* relationships problematise the brother–sister union. Young women who bend this fictive kin relationship often do so knowing that they are jeopardising the way this union is viewed in the community, 'that's why many families don't like you taking a *bhai*' (Fiza).

Stalking and harassment after a break-up is also frequent; young women in particular describe how ex-boyfriends engage in harassment. Heera explains how after a recent split from her ex-partner:

> He made trouble for me. He used to come to *Azeem* and just wait out-side. He said he would reveal everything we did to my mother and to my new boyfriend also. He is unable to see me happy, he thinks he owns me.
>
> (Heera, 20)

More than an innocent heartbreak, harassment post-break-up reveals a patriarchal culture that condones male dominance and violence against women. Harassment and violence find strong support amongst young men in the community. Like eve-teasing, many young men describe their 'duty' to blame and shame women who have engaged in romantic relationships, 'we show everyone "hey, here is a bad girl"' (Asif, 19). The idea that an ex-girlfriend can be owned sits comfortably within a patriarchy where young men gain status through their control of young women's movement and behaviours. Even if he may no longer be interested in his ex-girlfriend, many young men feel the need to shame her and own her.

Young men use strategies of stalking, gossiping and slander against ex-partners to shame them, and to prevent other young men from engaging in a romantic relationship with them.

> For many boys they feel victory if they can shame their ex so much so that she cannot have any romance. They harass out of habit, and then over time get bored with this game and move on, and if her name is not that muddied, the girls try again.
>
> (Heera, 20)

Heera explains how young men harass and shame young women out of sport; she later uses the example of cat and mouse, where the cat feels he owns the mouse and toys with the mouse out of amusement, even if it hurts the mouse. While many young men are intent on shaming their partners out of revenge and to exhibit ownership, Heera does not believe they really wish for girls to kill themselves, or never marry. While initially they may be emotional about the breakup and wish for harm, Heera understands male harassment as a game young men play to exhibit power over women, and over time young men lose interest in the game. However some young men are intent on ruining their ex-partners lives because they can; I know of an engagement which was broken off after an ex-partner many years previous, came back to tattletale on his ex-girlfriend's past romance.

This view of girls and young women as an ex/boyfriend's property is very dominant, and has seen little shift, even in the wake of unprecedented advocacy around gendered violence and the treatment of young women in Indian society. It was the 2012 rape and murder of a college student in Delhi which saw unprecedented national action to challenge the normative experiences of sexual discrimination, violence and harassment against women in the country. In this incident a group of boys and young men lured a college student into a bus where she and her friend were brutally assaulted. As a result of the sexual assault 23-year-old Nirhbaya died of her injuries, and her death sparked both national and international outrage (see for example Schinder and Titzmann 2015; Sharma, Unnikrishnan and Sharma 2014; Kabeer 2013). Protests across the country urging for safer spaces for girls and women, and changes to Indian laws on gendered violence, ignited the country. Most of these protests were led by young women and men, college and university students in particular. The guttural reaction of youth across the country saw public space being occupied by *lacs* (hundreds of thousands) of young people in large city centres. One of the state's immediate responses was to organise a committee led by late chief justice J.S. Verma to review and recommend amendments to criminal laws, and this saw for the first time stalking and voyeurism as crimes against women.

In the slums Nirbhaya's death saw both NGOs and CBOs organise petitions and statements against violence towards women. I am aware of a handful of NGOs/CBOs that organised the community and marched in rallies which took place in Kolkata after Nirhbaya's death. But back in the field in 2013 and 2014 relationship patterns which see violence and stalking increase during the break-up period remain stubbornly the same. To understand this I draw on Shabnam's (female, 18) explanation:

> Some people at that time (of Nirhbaya's death and the subsequent rallies) thought that things would change, but not one person in this entire *bustee* believed that, not for one minute. Even if she (Nirhbaya) was his own sister, when it came time for his own girlfriend moving on, he himself would send her 100 SMS (text messages) to say 'if you accept his proposal I'll kill myself' for no good reason but to torture (her). None of this is going to change because boys are not going to change, and the *samaaj* won't change.
>
> (Shabnam, 18)

Shabnam believes that men control women out of pleasure to see them suffer ('to torture her'). Her pessimism is rooted in a deep-set patriarchy where violence is commonly used to control women and girls, and where ideas of male ownership are embedded in the culture (an example is being asked for the father/husband's name on official documents). Even as the community sees shifts in young women's educational output, Shabnam is careful to pinpoint that it is young men who are reluctant to change because their status and privilege in the home remains supported by society (*samaaj*).

While many young women fear stalking and harassment, some read ownership in a more positive light, 'when you see those guys who keep trying to win her back (through stalking behaviour) you feel pity, you understand how deep his love was' (Heera, 20). Thus for some young women, harassment and violence can be a normative part of the relationship process, one which they try to mitigate by staying silent and not responding to accusations during the break-up period. If a young woman can successfully weather this period of harassment, she is able to pursue romantic relationships at a later time. A young man's ability to shift from a loving partner to a violent ex-boyfriend is another risk young women negotiate when they enter into sexual relations. Young men who seem possessive quickly develop reputations as 'emotional' '*senti*' (sentimental) and 'crazy' and young women try to avoid relationships with these men.

Young women also have their own strategies of negotiating conflict and break-ups. As Bhatia, Verma and Murty (2006) show, young women in India often turn to suicide and self-injury when faced with problems in their love lives. Their study of suicide in Delhi reveals that a disturbed love affair is the most common reason young women under the age of 30 kill themselves, usually by hanging themselves in the home. Bollywood supports the use of self-harm during conflicts in love. Many films depict self-harm as a way to 'prove' to their partner how much they love them (for example *Raanjhanaa* 2013) while some films mock the use of self-injury or attempted suicide within a failed love affair (*Lage Raho Munna Bhai* 2006).

Self-harm differs from attempted suicide because there is no intention by the actor to take his/her life. Discourses around self-harm in the slums reveal how harm is used to send a message to a partner or family, and it is a common strategy for both young men and women in relationships. Language such as hurting oneself to 'win back' a partner, to 'punish' a partner, as well as to 'prove' their love is normative. Importantly self-harm in the *bustees* is an important way to gain the attention or sympathy of a lover.

> U (sic) know yesterday (girlfriend) and I had some serious problems in our relationship, and you know what she did. She took tablets and Vitamin Capsules. I made her drink a lot of water on the spot. Atleast (sic) 4 lts of water. This is not at all good. That should not be a wise way to punish or teach me something ... I don't want anything to happen to her because of the Big love that I have for her.
>
> (Parvez, 20, email correspondence)

Lovers on the receiving end of these messages can analyse self-harm in many ways. For Parvez self-harm by his girlfriend was viewed as a punishment, a tactic he felt would cause maximum hurt for him because of his love for her. In some relationships self-inflicted injury allows actors to 'prove the sincerity of love' (Layla, 20), while at the same time promoting sympathy.

Self-harm can backfire as a tactic to punish a partner. The relationship between *Nach Baliye* winners Tazeema (15) and her dance partner Waqar (17) highlights the complexities of using self-harm as a strategy. The couple met in 2005 on the *Nach Baliye* rehearsal roof and subsequently dated for a couple of months, sharing the euphoria of winning the *Nach Baliye* competition. Tazeema's peers were convinced Waqar was going to marry Tazeema. In 2006 Tazeema discovered that he was planning to break up with her. According to Waqar '(Tazeema) has a different personality from the beginning of the relationship ... she is too controlling'. Tazeema confronted him about his intentions, 'I felt betrayed by him ... we should have lasted forever'. One day, after arguing with Waqar, Tazeema went home and took about twenty of her mother's heart medication tablets. By her own admission she consumed too many pills, fell ill, fainted and had to be admitted to hospital by her family. She subsequently had to spend over a week in the hospital after suffering an adverse reaction to the medicine and the ordeal, having her stomach pumped several times. When Waqar became aware that she had self-injured, he sent a message to the hospital saying that he was walking away from the relationship. At the hospital Tazeema's parents were very concerned about how this situation would affect their daughter's marriage-ability. Fearful of his daughter obtaining an 'emotionally unstable' reputation, Tazeema's father quickly arranged her marriage, and she left the hospital as a married woman. Rather than exact sympathy from her peers, Tazeema's friends were critical of how she dealt with her romantic troubles 'When (Tazeema's) father came to our house to tell us what happened; I knew right away he was also coming to tell me that he found a boy that did not hear of this attempt and was going to marry her off when she was in the hospital Tazeema should have know better' (Parvez, 20).

Self-poisoning is a culturally acceptable method of self-harm in India (Eddleston and Phillips 2004). Parvez's assertion that Tazeema should know better, reflects a knowledge of self-injury/poisoning, amongst young people in the slums. Young people have learnt from television reports and peer networks about the impacts of certain medicines and pills, and many are careful not to 'go too far' in their attempts. This awareness has resulted in most young people taking 'soft' pills like vitamin capsules in small quantities. This literacy has also led to a marked decline in using fertiliser and other chemicals in self-harm attempts. Conversations with community educators reveal that throughout the 1980s and 1990s these chemicals were preferred in the slums. Greater awareness about the consumption of fertilisers and insect sprays by poor farmers – and the consequences of this consumption – has been shared through media stories for several years now. This knowledge alerted most young people in the *bustees* to the fact that consuming fertiliser or Baygon (a powerful insect spray) will unquestionably kill them, as Aysha (15) attests, 'Baygon will surely do the job'.

As with Raya who poorly played her hand by entering an unsuitable partnership, Tazeema also found herself with little peer support after her marriage. For her friends, banishment from the game of courtship and dating was of her own doing: 'She was a stupid girl to know 20 (tablets) would be too much' (Layla, 20). With the support of popular culture and a knowledge of injury amongst peer groups, self-harm is an important and dangerous strategy young women use to cope with love's woes, particularly in the premarital phase where poor decisions can impact one's entire life course. While Tazeema's actions caused her to be labelled as emotionally unstable, on the flip side is male self-injury which promotes responses such as '*bachara* (poor darling) his only reason for living was that girl, see how much he loves her', as Mumtaz once discussed of a local boy who harmed himself over a break-up. Thus it is important when reading self-harm as a strategy in relationships to remember that this act, like almost all acts associated with intimacy in the *bustees*, is deeply gendered.

Conclusion

Young Muslim women in the *bustees* of Kolkata navigate very risky social and cultural terrain when they search for premarital love, romance and sexual relations. Youth in the slums turn to popular culture, peer networks and partner support to write their own love lives. Like dance, third spaces such as the *Nach Baliye* rehearsal space, laneways, parks and shopping plazas are important geographies of romance. Young women mediate their desire for love, romance and sex by drawing on religious discourses and gender norms in an effort to write an identity of a good girlfriend. Once married, however, their opportunities to play the games of courtship are halted. They are propelled into adulthood and the permanency of their life choices is set in place. While the youth period allows them to make mistakes and enjoy different kinds of transgressions, marriage cements their roles and responsibilities as adults, and their 'proper' participation in an adult-dominated world.

Although love and romance are goals for many young women, dating life and married life are two very different realities. As young single women, optimism about what love and romance can mean for their relationships makes way for the realities of a bad marriage, where few women find their desire for social mobility fulfilled. In 2011, 22-year-old Raya offers:

> If I advise someone younger than me I would say that single life and marriage are very different. When dating they say they love you, but after marriage they are looking around for another wife.
>
> (Raya)

Marrying the 'right kind of boy' who loved them and protected them was the ideal. But the power young men yield with triple *talaq*, as well as their social and economic status, does not shift in love relationships. Love relationships, when operating in a patriarchal slum, do little to change male privilege and female insecurity (see also Grover 2010).

Premarital romantic desire has greatly influenced paths to marriage in the slums, with many young women searching, and marrying, for love. For better, or for worse, these love marriages take place amongst a majority of youth in the *bustees*. It is not an exaggeration, then, that premarital love culture is impacting upon marriage culture in the slums. Drawing on Giddens's (1991: 51) insight in relation to a globalising world, of the changes going on in the *bustees*, 'none are more important than those happening (in) personal lives – in sexuality, emotional life, marriage and the family'. *Bustee* youth are a part of a global youth movement that is questioning 'how we think of ourselves and how we form ties and connections with others'. As in other parts of the world we see that in the *bustees* this revolution is 'advancing unevenly ... with many resistances' (Giddens 1991: 51). This is also the case with their consumption of material culture and their identities as middle-class consumers. Like dance and the 'right' romance, however, the practice of consumption does little to change the status of young women in the *bustees* as 'poor slum girls'.

Notes

1 A conservative school originating in the Middle East. The school moves away from so-called *haram* practices like *mazar* worship, associated with Deobandi and Braveli schools in the slums.
2 A man who practises some major pillars in Islam: reads the Quran and believes in the teachings faithfully, does *namaz* (prayer) five times a day, practises *sawm* (fasting) during *Ramzan*, gives *zakat* (donations to the needy), does not eat pork and does not drink alcohol.
3 Examples of 'good' schools are Central Board of Secondary Education (CBSE) schools or schools that administer Indian Certificate of Secondary Education (ICSE) exams, see Akhtar and Narula (2010) for more discussion on schooling options for Muslims in India.
4 Most of the girls I spoke with felt triple *talaq* was a form of violence and intimidation that men used against women (in Indonesia, see Bennett, Andajani-Sutjahjo and Idrus 2011).
5 Madan-Bahel's (2007) research within the South Asian diaspora looks at how Bollywood can be a culturally sensitive tool to talk about sex with young women.
6 Tulsi is the main female protagonist from *Kyunki Saas Bhi Kabhi Bahu Thi* (2000–2008) which is considered to be India's most popular and longest running television drama serial.

5 Changing youth culture, changing consumption culture

Introduction

Another way in which young Muslim women in the *bustees* are living more Bollywood-inspired lives in a globalising India is through participation in middle-class consumption practices. Through their participation in self-perceived modern clothing and food consumption, *bustee* youth try to resist dominant societal discourses of being 'poor Muslims' and try to experience a lifestyle that aligns itself with a contemporary youth culture which they view through Bollywood. The chapter shows how young women manage their money and how they use consumption to gain status and cultural capital amongst their peers. While shifting their class position is an aim for many young women, it is shifts in status – through the acquisition of cultural capital like dance knowledge and higher education and particular to this chapter, participation in a variety of perceived middle-class consumption arenas – that is more realistic for young women in the *bustees*.

Like young women's participation in dance and romance culture, consumption can be a risky endeavour and these risks are directly related to the expectations of normative femininities, accepted gender roles and one's relationship with Islam. Youth's consumption desires, practices and identity politics highlight the importance of Bollywood as an expert in their lives. As in the previous chapters, young people's relationship with this new expertise creates tensions with normative and patriarchal knowledge keepers, while expanding discussion of what it means to be a contemporary young person in the *bustees*.

Young women in the slums have many role models to help them navigate through the new shopping complexes, fast food shops and other outlets that are providing them with fresh consumption opportunities. Bollywood popular culture is the most glamorous of role models, and young people in the slums enjoy watching characters partake in a myriad of shopping, travel and lifestyle possibilities. Peers and boyfriends also help them make the transition from viewers to physical consumers. Cultural Studies scholars have had a long and rich history of documenting how consumption and consumer practices are critical to identity formation and re-formation – that is, what we own, eat, drink and wear signify who we are and who we wish to be. Rather than being a straightforward act of acquisition, consumption 'is a social process whereby people relate to goods and artefacts in complex ways, transforming their meanings as they incorporate them into their lives' (Jackson and Holbrook 1995: 1914). Consumption in this chapter is both practice and work, accomplished by young women who are skilled social actors with finite resources (see Jackson 2004).

Within Asian Cultural Studies one of the most exciting areas of scholarship is the rise of the middle class and the cultures of middle classness in India. These discussions are far from uniform, with some touting the power of this growing class, and others reporting on their inability to change systems of oppression in the country (Fernandes 2000a, 2000b; Srivastava 2007, 2009; Ganguly-Scrase and Scrase 2009; Lukose 2009). Discussions about India's growing middle class can be heard on every corner in the *bustees*. In my conversations with young people in the slums, non-governmental organisation (NGO) workers, and even strangers reveal that there is a sense of pride around Kolkata's perceived growing economic power and global connections. For example Aysha (15) once boasted, 'the fashions you find in Paris can be now found in the shops of Kolkata'. Part-and-parcel of growing opportunities to buy and spend are the changing employment opportunities for many middle-class youth, who may desire to join, in various capacities, expanding private and multinational employers including banks and the IT industry. Indeed many young women hoped to use their education to 'work in an office and learn the computer' (Aliah, 16).

Greater opportunities to participate in consumption culture have raised questions about the impacts of materialism on the country's social fabric, particularly around links between family connection and materialism (Fuller and Narasimhan 2007). In the *bustees*, for example, many parents reflect on how changing socialising opportunities impact upon family home culture, as Aysha's mother expressed to me with sadness: 'we all used to play Ludo (a board game) at night but now everyone is on the phone or we watch television'. It is within this changing socio-cultural sphere that young women use limited consumption opportunities to fulfil particular desires and identities in the slums.

Money, work and *purdah*

Within the *bustees* the opportunities to write one's identity through middle-class consumption are gendered as a result of access to money, mobility and social circumstances. Like street and slum boys the world over, most young men in the *bustees* worked and earned their own money with employment being temporal and inconsistent. Pressures to work from an early age saw most young men leave school in their teen years to bring home a paycheque. In contrast young women were not obliged to find paid employment from a young age, but were expected to contribute significantly towards unpaid domestic duties. While young men perform the 'good boy' and leave home to work, the 'good girl' cares for her siblings, washes clothes, prepares meals, collects water and attends school. This does not mean young women do not face *pressures* to earn money. However, for most unmarried young women, segregated work responsibilities in combination with growing domestic and international support for young women's education (see for example Balago-palan 2014 in India; Asadullah and Chaudhury 2009 in Bangladesh) have resulted in the beginnings of a skewed male–female education ratio in the slums. This is a trend that is also emerging in other parts of India and Bangladesh, where 'educate the girl child' campaigns have had steady funding from various sources.

Azeem estimates that for every 10 young women who complete class 10, only 2–3 boys are able to achieve the same. Moreover, of the young people I know to have completed their Bachelor degrees in the slums, all are young women. In a community where traditionally men have had greater educational skills, the *bustees* are now confronted with a very new problem – over-educated women and undereducated men. This unique dilemma is particular to young people of this generation. Some NGO and community members are starting to articulate that as long as young men are pressured to enter the work force early, their overall educational achievements, and the overall achievements of the community will remain low. This is a marked difference from discourses only a decade ago where moderate education for boys and minimal education for girls was the norm.[1] The differential in education levels is a problem for young women's marriage potential, as Aliah's mother explained to me when describing her college-educated niece, 'will she marry a cook with her Bachelors? He needs to be educated too … if not, then she'll marry a cook and is the same, right?' (Aliah's mother). Aliah's mother understands that a young woman's educational achievements can be used to obtain higher status and upward mobility – in this example by marrying upwards in class – only if young men have similar, and in particular higher, educational achievements. Her reasoning is strongly linked to the preference for young men to marry brides with less education. Current education strategies that focus on women have, according to Aliah's mother, left men behind and this is problematic for highly educated young women because they have no one (local) to marry.

Although there is growing acceptance that young women in the *bustees* seem to be more educated than young men, young men continue to wield economic power because they earn money from a young age and continue to work after marriage. Young women's limited mobility and a culture of *purdah* see few young women enter lucrative public workplaces, especially after marriage. For the majority the very narrow window of public work occurs when young single women have completed their education, but have not married. However, the majority of young single women who have minimal education and have completed their schooling typically join their married peers in home-based work. This last point is important to note, as it reminds us that not all young women are taking up opportunities to go to school, nor is home-based work diminishing in the *bustees*. Young women who are school-going may also help their home-based family members, but pressures to work impact those who have completed schooling much more strongly. The dominant conversation about home-based work suggests that working from home allows Muslim young women to keep *purdah*, while attending to the needs of the family.

The realities of being employed from home, however, often do not live up to expectations. In the *bustees* the most common home-based work for minimally educated girls is leather piecework including the cutting of insoles, the gluing of shoe parts, and the application of decors and embroidery onto material. Young women engaged in this work report that it is monotonous, boring and not without its impact on one's mental and physical health, and self-esteem: 'I would love to do beauty salon training instead of this work, it is so boring and I have to do so much gluing, it makes me dizzy ... I feel like I am capable of so much more' (Fiza, 19). For higher educated girls employment is private tuitions. As described by Roohi (2007), home-based work by Muslim women in Kolkata is both exploitative and limiting. The flip side is that home-based work allows young women to multi-task in the home, set their own work schedules and spend time with family members. While being at home does have some advantages, the private nature of this work means that workers' rights – including adequate pay, training, hours of work and workload – are not transparent or easily monitored. In contrast, girls' paycheques are closely monitored and their spending is fodder for family and community tension.

Young men's paycheques are also scrutinised and as with young women, what young men do with their money is the source of a good deal of discussion and debate both within the family and within the community. According to community leaders – including religious leaders, NGO workers and even the local MLA – the *bustees* are currently facing a crisis around young men's failure of responsibility. 'The young men in our community have been taken by drugs and crime and their own individual satisfaction. They are no longer looking after their family' (local *Mullah*). The perception of community elders is that many young men fail to be responsible. They use their paycheques to support personal desires, including addictions, their relationships with girlfriends, and their desire for *ishstyle* – Bollywood style (*filmi*-inspired clothing and accessories, for example. See Nakassis 2013). For those unemployed young men the situation is worse:

> If he can't find jobs, if he went to school and can't find jobs, then how do you think that makes him feel? What does that do to his motivation? What does that do to his view of himself as a man?
>
> (Local NGO employee, male)

Young women are aware of men's pressure to work, and they participate in the talk of irresponsibility; however, their position within this debate depends on their relationship with the man in question. If a boyfriend is providing a young woman with things she needs and wants, she is usually supportive of his ability to spend money on her. That her boyfriend may be taking away income from his own family, and other young women in his family who cannot/do not work, is rarely acknowledged. In fact a boyfriend who spends a significant amount of time and money on his girlfriend is considered to be a 'good boyfriend' and a desired husband. Limited access to money means that young women's consumption practices differ from, and can be dependent on, young men.

Many single young women in this research pursued home-based work: Abia (14), Reena (15) and Fiza (19) all engaged in home-based piecework, mostly embroidery. Due to mobility restrictions, family perceptions of work and issues related to *purdah*, only a handful of young women within the research engaged in public paid employment. Layla (20), Heera (20) and Sakina (16) all worked for *Azeem*; Layla as a full-time programme coordinator for the young women's education programme, and Heera and Sakina as part-time assistants at the library and computer centre. Raya (16) sells toys on the pavement, and was one of a few young women I knew who worked in public, but not for an NGO. The formidable presence of NGOs in *bustees* has opened up new employment opportunities for many young women, and NGO work is becoming a very real career path for hundreds of youth.

Young women's venture into public work was met with ambivalence by the community. For example in 2010 twenty-year-old Aysha started a part-time position at *Azeem*, but was forced to leave her job a year later. 'My father didn't like me working, he said it looks bad. He said that people will say "you are making your daughter work and living off her back". But then he also took all of my paycheque as well, so ... I don't know.' Aysha describes her father's uneasy relationship with young women's work outside of the home. Female paid work, especially paid public work by married women, is a direct threat to the dominant constructions of both a femininity which supports the public identity of women as mothers and wives, and a dominant masculinity which supports the public identity of men as breadwinners and heads of the household. At the same time adding to a family's income and contributing to household expenses is a welcome relief for all, and public work in the slums often brings in more income than private home-based work.

Kibria (1995: 306) notes that in Bangladesh 'working-class men associated women's wage-work with their own economic impotence; seizing control of women's income was a gesture that affirmed their economic headship'. Aysha's experience highlights how the money earned by young unmarried women is more closely scrutinised than the income of young unmarried men. Like Kibria, women's income can also be a source of conflict as Sakina (16) shared, 'for example Putul works at one of our NGO centres and she tried to keep some of her paycheque for herself by putting it in her underwear, but (one day) her husband put his hand down there right in front of everyone in the office and took it out'. Violence as described by Sakina is closely associated with young women's earnings and is commonplace in the slums. For many young women, however, such violence is viewed through a particular lens. Speaking of her own husband in 2011, 22-year-old Raya explained to me, 'he is not very educated, so he thinks "I don't want to lose my face because she is working, what will people say"… so he compensates by hitting me'. Lower status boys in the slums, ones with little education and poor cultural literacy, are understood to be more likely to participate in violence, but this is not accurate as violence against women was widespread throughout the slums in all communities and men from every class background participate in violence.

With the exception of Layla and Sakina, young working women explained that they gave a large portion of their income to their families, particularly if they were married. As described in the previous chapter, both Raya and Abia had early marriages. They saw all their income being spent on their own family needs. They had little avenue to use their income to buy expensive mobile phones and cosmetics, for example. Even though they were younger in age than Layla, early marriage pushed them into the role of responsible adults who sacrifice for their family. Their personal spending is seen as selfish in the slums, however working women are more sympathetic. Speaking about Abia, Sakina (16) sympathises, '*Bachacri* (poor darling). This is why you don't marry early, not even a proper brassiere she can buy for herself.' Young women in the *bustees* share experiences with women the world over who are encouraged to spend money in ways which strengthen their roles as mother, daughter and wife, and praised if they do so.

While married young women supported their families, the same cannot be said for young married men. Raya's husband did not satisfactorily contribute to the family, and a lot of the income he was earning did not make its way into his new family, rather Raya (16) complains, 'he doesn't support us, but has money for his *ishstyle* and girlfriends'. Raya explains that long gone are the days when her partner was courting her and buying her gifts. Rather as a married woman, 'no man will try and please you with gifts and an outing to see a film once married'. In Raya's experience during courtship her boyfriend spent time and money on her, trying to woo her. She recalled being attracted to her boyfriend because of all of the attention and gifts he showered over her. It was only after marriage that she discovered that such romantic behaviour (in her case) was temporary. I read this as young people's limited experience with love marriages (given the community has had a tradition of arranged marriage), but also Bollywood presentation of romantic *dating* but not romantic *marriage*. She explains that once married her husband 'won' by getting the girl. When she does try to get him to take her out for a film 'he says "I don't have to treat my wife like a girlfriend"… that hard work is done for them'. Asking girls how it is possible that young men 'get away' with using their money for *ishstyle*, but married young women could not, Raya responds 'they get away because they are boys, and what can I do about it now? I am stuck in this marriage, he can always pick up another wife, but me, I'm stuck. So I know my limits when complaining about money.' Post-courtship saw many young women reflexively understanding that a boyfriend who takes income away from his family to pursue a girlfriend may become a husband who does not always think of his family's needs. Moreover we see that many young women fear the power of (the incorrect use of) triple *talaq* and this made daily fighting over finances risky.

Public face and *izzat*

In the *bustees* the complicated relationship between breaking *purdah* and work seemed to have little relationship to poverty and status. Families who live in grinding poverty in some of the most deprived squatter settlements are as likely as families with several earning members in established slums to not have women work in public. Both economically deprived and economically secure families are also likely to have women work in well-paying areas of public employment including the very lucrative area of rag picking. Moreover small families are as likely as families with large support and kinship networks to be ambivalent to the idea of public work. So when it comes to young women working in public, in these *bustees* there is no clear trend other than young women tending not to work in public especially the newly married. There are shifts to women's public work only later in life; if a married woman is widowed or has to provide for pressing needs at home including supporting medical expenses we see a break of *purdah* for public work.

When speaking to married adults about public employment, the obligations of *purdah* and the pressures to maintain *purdah* for the sake of *izzat* were often used to explain why it is acceptable for young women to work 10 hours a day in the home rather than work five hours a day in public for equal, if not more, pay. 'At home we can maintain our families' reputation (*izzat*), we look after the home and our husbands can work' (Farah's mother). Farah's mother argues that a lack of child-care and homemaking responsibilities make home-based work ideal for women. She also alludes to how public presence is tied to dominant constructions of femininity and masculinity. Young women who work in public challenge the norms of a successful father/brother as an adequate provider. Home-based employment allows a family to maintain a public face of young women being committed homemakers and men being dominant earners.

It is also important to recognise that home-based work is an example of mobility control and restrictions placed on young women by both men and other women. In the slums rules over young women's behaviours and move-ments, and men's perceived ability to control these behaviours and move-ments, are rewarded with the honourable reputation of a man and his family. Control over young women is more than just a patriarchal tool to create an honourable public face or justify their dominance. Control over young women can also be seen as an extension of a man's own self-control, as one Muslim informant in Nilan, Howson and Donaldson's (2007: 9) study explained, 'not only (do) we have to control ourself, but we have to control our wife'.

Men controlling their own behaviours, and controlling women's behaviours, however, should not be viewed with the same lens. In his research with Hindu men Derne (1994: 204) argues that men in India understand clearly the advantages and rewards of controlling women and thus 'they consciously act and talk to maintain those advantages'. As a result, 'women's strategies of pursuing power and security in their husbands' families ... often lead women into "bargains with patriarchy" that also contribute to the reconstitution of gender inequality in India' (Derne 1994: 203). Annie George (2006) argues that in a globalising India masculinities are changing and being re-written to include non-traditional behaviours, including acceptance of women's public work. In some families in the *bustees* this is the case – Layla's father was supportive and encouraging of his daughter's career life. His support should be placed in context, and is underpinned by his own inability to obtain secure employment. Over the last decade many tanneries, once the major source of employment in the *bustees*, have shifted out of the slums. This has left entire (male) generations without a clear source of employment. Layla's father chose to encourage all of his daughters to gain further education and work outside of the home, and he sees their success as a result of their own initiatives, 'I am nothing in this house, my daughters are everything because of their own hard work'. While he places all the onus of success on his daughters, to be fair to Layla's father this could not have been a straightforward decision, and he certainly would have to hear about his own failure as a man, and his inability to keep his daughters inside the home. Layla's father was rare in the *bustees.*

For Layla, ambivalence to young women's public work occurs only in certain groups. 'In uneducated families ... if a woman works, she loses, and if she doesn't work, she loses.' Layla understands that in many homes a young woman who works outside of the home is seen as a shameful thing, regardless of whether they have a 'good position'. Men in the family may feel emasculated and resort to violence because of this inadequacy; families may think a working woman shames the men in their family, or that her actions are boastful. While for some families it is the work in question, honourable work (teaching for example) as more tolerable than dishonourable work (rag picking for example), Layla is critical of these created boundaries. In 2012, right before her marriage, Layla was able to secure a more senior position at the NGO. This was a great source of pride, but she was careful in her celebrations, 'in this *bustee* there are people who think that this (promotion) is something not to boast about'. Positioning herself as an advocate for young women's public employment (and social mobility) helps Layla to validate her identity as a contemporary, educated and upper status young woman in contrast to others. Like dance and extended courtship, working in public was another way some young women in the *bustees* tried to differentiate themselves from their lower status peers.

Public employment – fantasies and realities

Regardless of a family's attitude towards paid employment, especially that of public employment, all young women I spoke with dreamt of careers outside of the home. One way I was able to get young women to conceptualise their futures was by using yoga as a method, and I usually did this at the local *Azeem* community centre where we have privacy. To use yoga as a method I first darken the space and get young people to be comfortable. We do different stretching and breathing exercises, with a focus on clearing young people's minds. As I did not want young people to think of this as yoga for spiritual purposes I do not use Sanskrit names for poses, rather just describe the movements and get young people to follow the poses. Sometimes I play relaxing music, while other times there is no music, and after different stretching postures we sit on the floor with our eyes closed, focusing on our breathing. I ask young people to clear their minds and focus on themselves. In this example of understanding young people's future desires I go through a series of visualisation exercises (for example, 'you are 25 years old and have just gotten out of bed. Where are you?'; 'You are now at your *nikah* and an aunty is doing your *mendhi*, you look down at your hands and smell the paste ... where is your groom? Who is he? What is he wearing?'). In the meantime I have placed blank paper and pencils in front of them. After a visualisation exercise, I slowly get young people to focus and turn on the lights. When they open their eyes I ask them to draw the scenario which they had visualised in the yoga activity. Yoga as a method takes well over an hour; getting young people to relax may itself take an hour and the visualisation requires some silence in between each statement. The drawing is the object of our discussions (either as a group or individually). While interviews about the future are rich, combining them with drawing has been more successful with this particular community. In Shirzad's drawing of her future in five years she prominently depicts her desire for paid employment outside of the home and financial independence (see Figure 5.1).

Speaking with Shirzad (16) about her drawing, she confessed that she 'could not choose' between several career paths, that of a 'Tacher' (teacher) an 'offsheal Job' (official job) or as an NGO worker. The latter job was a good fit because according to Shirzad, 'I like sosalesarvis' (I like social service). Her drawing transgresses normative femininity in many ways: she clearly articulates her own desires for monetary independence, placing her wish in the centre of the page and stating 'I Like hit Indpinden' (I like independence). With her financial freedom Shirzad wished to participate in consumer culture 'Give the fist seelari; I going to market. I making a Dresh. She is my Drime' (With my first paycheque I am going to the market to buy a dress, this is my dream). Important also in Shirzad's drawing is her use of English, which she felt was a ticket to future success.

Shirzad's desire to buy a dress moves away from the normative expectations that female income should primarily aid in supporting the family. Shirzad's drawing did not include her as a wife and/or mother, which by the age of 21, would be the norm for this community. Her career desires were greatly inspired by both her lived experiences in the slums, and Bollywood popular culture. According to Shirzad an 'offsheal job' (official job) is a career path where computers are used 'to type and make notes for the office'. Though she

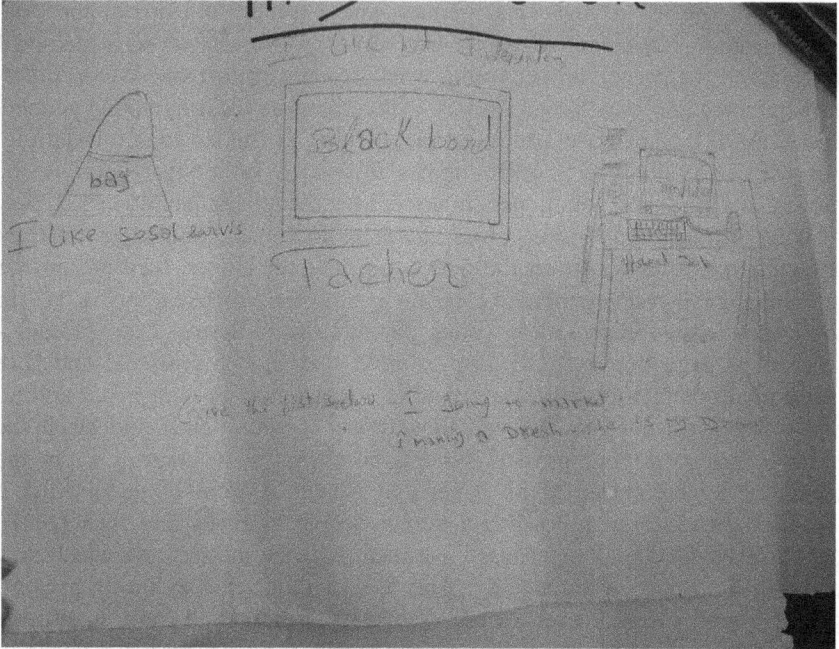

Figure 5.1 'Me in five years' (Shirzad, female 16)

admitted to me that she had limited computer training, she was familiar with their operations. She also saw computers being used by both female and male staff at the *Azeem* and library centre, thus NGOs are providing young *bustee* women with new kinds of working role models.

Azeem employed over 20 community outreach workers, some of them young women from the local community with whom Shirzad had sustained interactions. The visibility of young female NGO workers, and non-formal education (NFE) teachers certainly influenced many young women to aspire to become teachers, NGO workers and join other social service careers in the future. Her interaction with Layla, for example, sustained her desire for paid work in the future, 'I would like to become exactly like Layla *didi*, she works outside, she makes money for herself and she is independent and no one can keep her down ... I'd like to be like that' (Shirzad, 16).

To Shirzad, Layla personified a confident, independent working young woman. Shirzad believed that Layla kept her paycheque and was independent because she could spend her money any way she wanted. Indeed Layla is one of the few working women that I knew who self-managed almost all of her earnings. The flipside was that Layla managed her entire household, including groceries and her sisters' schooling costs. With power over one's finances, Shirzad felt that young women like Layla cannot be dominated by different members of the community ('keep her down'). For Shirzad, unless women have complete control over their finances, they are not independent. Asking

Shirzad what steps she was taking to be like Layla she explained that Layla was able to become an NGO worker because 'she is from a good family, her family is supportive'. Shirzad understood that status and class ('good family') play an important role in Layla's ability to transgress the rules of *purdah* and work in public. Desire and ambition alone did not propel Layla from an ordinary *bustee* girl to a visible worker. When I asked her if her family would support her in the pursuit of a career, Shirzad felt that 'they would, but if we lived in a good neighbourhood'. Shirzad felt that it is not her family that would keep her from working outside of the home, rather the community would make it difficult for her to obtain a career. She understood the barriers the community would place on her family to include gossip about Shirzad's whereabouts, her *izzat* and the kind of work she was doing, 'they would say I was too forward, or that my parents don't have control, or ask, "what is she doing outside at work". They are not educated people, they won't understand.'

These public discourses about paid employment are inflected with accusations of impurity, loose character and modern values, which seriously impact the *izzat* of young women and their families (see Maslak and Singhal 2008). Shirzad argued that it is the low-class *bustee* community that pressures her parents to prevent her from becoming a teacher, office worker or a social worker – not her family itself. Her understanding that career subordination is community driven, not a family problem, has also been discussed in other South Asian Muslim communities (see for example Amin 1997; Rosario 1992; Kabeer 1994). Examples from these studies show that some families give their daughters and wives the freedom to work and live multiple identities outside of their own communities.

In a later conversation, however, Shirzad confessed that her family probably never conceived of her as a pubic worker, '(my) schooling is (for me) to be educated, to read and write, to teach my kids. I don't think my parents think I will be a lawyer.' For Shirzad female education in the *bustees* was not linked to potential participation in the workforce. The recent acceptance of further education for young women is thus publicly supported within the norms of a local Muslim culture – with the assumption that education will make them better wives and mothers, and to be used to find a suitable marriage partner.

This makes young women who do work in public the subject of gossip and jealousy. 'I see (Layla) in the (*Azeem*) office, I just get my stamps and go … she thinks just because she went to college and works behind a computer she is better than us' (Abia, 14). Abia explains that when it comes to getting assistance from *Azeem*, she just does what needs to be done and leaves '*kaam se kaam rakhne, aur kuchne*' (I just mind my own business, that's it). She tries to keep her interaction with Layla – at one time her tutor – to a minimum. Many young women who did not work in public feel that with education and public employment Layla became a snob, who 'thinks she is better than us'. Many young women actively engaged in *badnam* (defaming) against Layla. For example, during one of our talks Abia told me that she suspected Layla had more than one boyfriend because of her extended time away from the slums. 'She does all these fieldtrips for the office away from (boyfriend). Who knows whom she mixes with? I once heard that at the fieldtrips (male and female workers) share a hotel together.'

Layla felt that young women in the community practised *badnam* against her to compensate for their poor status. Layla (20) was conscious of her public reputation amongst other young women, 'I am working and so most women talk bad about me, that I am bad, I went to college, I mix with boys … but when they need to open an account at the bank, who do they come to?' While she is critical of the *badnam* the community engages in, she also recognises that her skills are in demand and are the source of jealousy amongst her peers. She understands that many, if not most, young women in the *bustees* want to work but 'their parents don't want gossip to hurt their reputation'. At the same time Layla herself engages in *badnam* when discussing young women who do not work, 'these uneducated girls, they are so hopeless'. Gossip and jealousy contributes to enforcing and reinforcing a patriarchal culture where young women are criticised for their public behaviour, whether they work or not.

Relationships and gift giving

Unlike Layla and Raya and their other working peers, the majority of young women, especially school-going young women, do not earn their own money. Rather, they obtain finances from different sources including family members and their boyfriends. Close and extended family provide large-scale consumption opportunities during holidays and festivals, while daily maintenance, a small allowance for *tiffin*, for example, is often provided by one's immediate family. Young women also have opportunities to participate in commodity consumption through relationships with their boyfriends. Young women both receive and ask for 'gifts' including food, clothing, accessories, entertainment and technology from their partners and prospective partners at various times in their relationship, and these gifts carry certain meanings. The sociological study of gift giving showcases the various cultural constructions of giving and receiving presents, and reveals how these actions can be underpinned by a range of meanings, from an altruistic sense of good will, to a contrived display of power which begs reciprocation. In the *bustees* a similar range of meanings is attributed to givers and recipients of gifts.

Kasum (18) for example, a participant in the 2012 *Nach Baliye* performance, is from an average *bustee* home near the research area. She is considered by all of her peers to be exceptionally beautiful and during her time in *Nach Baliye* the Organiser set her up with one of his friends Ali, who approached him to be set up with 'the most beautiful girl I knew'. From a very well-to-do family in Kolkata, Ali had recently returned from schooling overseas, 'at the time I just got back from college where I didn't have any time to take a girlfriend' (Ali, male, 25). The two began seeing each other in 2012 and at the time of writing, had married. Talking to Kasum about her relationship during the dating phase, she expressed a sense of good fortune, 'I will always remain grateful to (the Organiser) for setting us up. I'll remain indebted to him for the rest of my life, as never did I think I'll meet such a match.' She described to me in detail about first meeting Ali, their dates together and the various family support she received, 'my mom knew about him soon after he proposed [declaration to date exclusively]'. Her mother's support included taking social risks by covering for Kasum while she met with Ali. Underpinning Kasum's mother's risk taking was hope of a better life for her daughter, and gifts played an important role in encouraging risk taking.

Receiving 'good gifts' from Ali was important to both Kasum and her mother. Kasum recalled her excitement when bringing home a mobile phone he had presented her: 'he really cared about me and only brought me the best ... my new phone wasn't a *Chinese model* it was branded ... my mom was very pleased, she said "it is such an expensive gift".' Both Kasum and her mother inspected the gift closely and recognised it was a name brand phone (Samsung), a model which had 'lots of ads about it on TV' and not a cheap knock-off (*Chinese model*). Awareness of consumption literacy gained through popular culture enabled both Kasum and her mother to participate in consumption culture through Kasum's relationship with Ali.

Many young women I knew engaged in *badnam* when discussing Kasum, accusing her of sexual immorality, 'she uses her beauty to get what she wants' (Zeena, 15). Kasum's mother explained to me that she was initially upset about this *badnam*, but reflected on the complex relationship between men and women, class and poverty. 'I know what others say about (Kasum) but I think that they want to get out of this *bustee* too, and it's so hard because there are such few good boys.' Kasum's mother agreed that young women in this community have few avenues to gain upward mobility and marriage is the most realistic way they can leave the slums. These limited opportunities bred competition for a few good men, and this competition was stiff and created a culture of jealousy and gossip amongst young women. I do not wish to suggest that only material items and wealth were indicators of upward mobility. Ali's family were followers of the Salafi school, which is seen in this community as distinctly class-based, and these middle-class followers are understood to be following 'best practice' for Muslims. Ali himself did not mix different religious practices and was critical of superstitious practices. Being married to a 'proper, educated Muslim', was also another way this marriage benefits Kasum's desire for upward mobility.

Kasum and Ali's marriage was met with great relief and excitement by Kasum and her family. In contrast, Ali's family was not keen to have a daughter-in-law from the slums, 'it took a lot of convincing on my part for them to agree' (Ali). He later explained his perceived position in their relationship and how this influenced his commitment to marriage:

> She is very beautiful, but her family is not good. Her father does not have steady work, they live in (local *bustee*), so I will always be ahead of

her ... she will always be grateful for the things I buy her and I will always be able to dominate because I know where she comes from ... you can't say the same if she was from a good family.

(Ali, 25)

Ali understood that his gifts might not have been as well received if his girl-friend was upper class, presumably because she could afford them herself. While gifts were understood by Kasum to be proof of love, for Ali gifts reinforced his class position. Simplifying one's relationships along economic terms undercuts the realities of love, romance, passion and caring. I do not wish to discredit the real love that Ali and Kasum have in their relationship. My many conversations with Kasum and Ali reveal deep relief and happiness they both found in a caring and loving match. However, I give this example to highlight how in the *bustees* young women's access and participation in consumer culture is problematised by the context of their limited work opportunities, her relationships with parents and partners, and class and status.

Role models

Given that young women's ability to participate in consumer culture was dependent on various social, economic and mobility factors, their consumption role models must fit into *bustee* life. In the *bustees* young people draw their consumption inspiration from many role models including upper/middle-class youth, other young people in the slums, and Bollywood culture. Of the three role models, upper-class youth were the least accessible to young people. While there are middle-class families living side by side with poor families in the slums, encounters with upper-class peers are not that common. Middle-class youth have the luxury of using transport like auto rickshaws, and their peer groups were often of similar class and social status. *Nach Baliye* was certainly an exception, a chance for different members of society to meet, and a place to consume, for free, Bollywood dance culture. Thus unsurprisingly those who did participate gained cultural capital amongst their poor peers. Most young women interacted with higher-class peers almost always outside the slums, during excursions to shopping centres or parks. On my trips with young people to these spaces it was obvious that young women are very conscious of their low-class and low status positions and work hard to absorb higher-class and status clues from their higher-class peers.

Saldanha's (2002: 344) study of popular youth culture amongst the upper classes in Bangalore shows how young elite women demonstrate their class by articulating a fluency in global youth culture through deliberate and overt consumption of Western clothes (such as jeans, t-shirts), dance and alcohol 'for their poor worker audience'. He also describes how upper classes use the consumption of material goods and symbols to proclaim their class in public and private spaces. Saldanha (2002) found that young elites in Bangalore also:

feigned an indifference for the fascination they produced amongst the lower-classes ... they feigned, because they were thoroughly aware of the visibility of their Western fashion, music, behaviour and wealth.

(Saldanha 2002: 344)

Saldanha's study richly depicts how upper-class youth in India understand the importance of displaying their class status to poorer Indians. This display allows them to produce, re-produce and strengthen their class position, and in various spaces in Kolkata which young *bustee* women frequent, this performance does not go unnoticed. Young women in the slums eagerly watched upper/middle-class youth display their class knowledge and they discreetly, and often not so discreetly, view and comment on their upper-class peers as they pass them in passing cars, in shopping plazas and on the streets. Young women are discerning, and immerse themselves in class symbols and representations. I first noticed this during an outing when some of the young women came across a vendor selling earrings. It was Aysha (15) who first commented that a pair of feather earrings was similar to a pair worn by an upper-class girl whom we had briefly passed on the way to the plaza. Two of her friends disagreed, and the three of them proceeded to have a detailed discussion on colour, texture, length and style of the earrings. Although they had not viewed this 'other' girl for long, they were careful to gain, share and discuss their knowledge of upper-class style after this brief encounter.

We later had the opportunity to discuss the other girl's earrings in detail where young women contextualised the appropriateness of the earring in the slums:

> You couldn't wear those every day here, only on a special occasion. We do not live in good neighbourhoods, if we wear those earrings outside where we live people will talk. They'd tell my mother that I'm too concerned with fashion. She can wear them all the time because she lives in a good neighbourhood where good, educated people live and they don't make those comments.
>
> (Aysha, 15)

Like young people's perception of dance and romance culture, young women felt that upper-class youth live in more tolerant communities, where style was understood to be a reflection of good taste, rather than representing one's im/moral positioning. In contrast Donner (2008) stresses that in middle-class Kolkata women felt that the lower classes of the city were more free to make self-directed decisions about clothing, lovers and hobbies because they were less bounded by the expectations of *izzat* and notions of respectability.

In her interaction with the upper-class girl with the earrings Aysha stressed that more than just owning upper-class commodities, these commodities need to be read by one's peers as cool. Her quote moves beyond the importance of materialistic consumption by alluding to taste. For Bourdieu (1984: 99): 'taste in the sense of the faculty of immediately and intuitively judging aesthetic values is inseparable from taste in the sense of the capacity to discern the flavours of foods which implies preference for some of them'. Both are 'cultivated' even if they seem to imply some inherent quality. Aysha implies that refined taste comes from education and class. Religion is usually not a determining factor, as Aysha and her friends interact with middle-class Muslims in their own slum. Aysha later explained that 'only those who knew about fashion' would understand the high style of the earrings, suggesting that only people with sophisticated taste could appreciate them. General consensus amongst young women is that many *bustee* dwellers lack the knowledge and taste of high-quality fashion, which as I will show, can pose a risk to young women if they choose to adopt this fashion in the slums.

Of all the role models, the most valued source of consumption literacy is the media. To most young women material consumption displayed in Bollywood is the 'ideal'. Television programmes and advertisements tap into more regional specific consumption interests, which may or may not be imbued in the Hindi/Urdu language culture of Bollywood. Commodity consumption displayed in Bollywood can be over the top – for example taking a helicopter to work, going on continuous exotic holidays and eating out at nice restaurants for every meal. Films that portray an 'average' middle-class experience often depict lifestyles beyond the financial and social means of the young women I worked with. However, the lifestyle excesses shown in popular Bollywood films did not exclude marginalised young people from viewing and idealising consumption processes. Though certainly there were aspects of consumption culture that were off-putting, such as wasting food, most young people in the *bustees* tried to find ways to modify the consumption viewed on screen to fit their lives. Like dance and romance, young people 'adjusted' their consumption practices on the basis of their finances, mobility and temporal limitations, as Aliah explained:

> If you take clothing, for example, then they are all good role models: the stuff we see in Bollywood is the ultimate, but usually unrealistic for us too. Also what girls from good neighbourhoods wear might be a little too risky for us, but it is something that we can probably modify. And the girls from here, well it might not be as *hi-fi*, but it has its own good criteria and more likely we can get it.
>
> (Aliah, 16)

For Aliah the clothing displayed in Bollywood is seen as the ultimate fashion. In terms of these clothes being a modest and practical clothing choice for life in the *bustees*, however, they are not suitable. It is not only revealing and immodest, but also expensive. Moreover, as Wilkinson-Weber (2011) details, often a star's clothing is not available in mainstream shops in India and when it is it can be out of reach for modest budgets. For many young women including Aliah, 'girls from a good neighbourhood can wear more daring clothes', while local residents may 'see some girl in jeans and think that they can take advantage'. Moreover, upper-class role models do not represent a dependable source of inspiration, as their presence in the slums is limited. The most practical role models for young women are their fellow higher-status peers who live in the *bustees*. *Nach Baliye* provided many youth with the opportunity to participate in modern consumption experiences, and many young women were keen to have similar, and extended, experiences of Bollywood consumption practices as viewed/experienced in *Nach Baliye*:

> I went to (the 2007) *Nach Baliye* to watch the program, I loved it! The dances were so cool and the outfits were so stylish, just like in the films. They looked just like Bollywood stars ... I too want to get involved in the program next year.
>
> (Shireen, 14)

For Shireen dance knowledge and Western clothing were seen as valued cultural capital because they epitomised Bollywood 'cool'. Shireen, however, was quick to point out that although she admired the outfits of the dancers, they 'were not branded clothes, they got them stitched at the tailor'. Wilkinson-Weber's (2010, 2011) work on branding decisions in films and their relationship to clothing available for purchase throughout India, reveals both a symbiotic relationship between popular culture and fashion production, and a disconnect between what can be viewed on screen and what is actually available in the stores. Local girls as role models, and even higher status girls like *Nach Baliye* participants, can never hold the same position of cultural authenticity as upper-class girls who can buy ready-made garments from the shops, and Bollywood film stars who can display foreign clothing not available in India.

Im/modest clothing

In the *bustees*, clothing is the most important visible indicator of a young woman's cultural knowledge, marriage potential, social status and femininity. However, young women have limited possibilities for displaying their public identity through clothing. For almost all single young women their defining public outfit is the clean, ironed and starched school uniform, complete with two plaits and a shawl or *dupatta* covering the breasts, and a separate scarf covering their hair (*ghoomta/hijab*). For most school-going young women one's school outfit is the most recognisable uniform of the 'good girl' and an important visible indicator of her public identity as an unwed young person.

Saldanha's (2002: 343) observations amongst upper-class Bangaloreans show how the school uniform carries with it an intrinsic protectiveness, especially for male family members. He explains that this protectiveness wanes as young women replace the uniform with their college-going outfits. In the *bustees* a uniformed girl visually depicts someone who is innocent, chaste and unmarried. The morals and values of a 'good girl' are appended to the school uniform, thus when she is wearing it, she is expected to behave in a certain way. So strong are the expectations of the school uniform in the *bustees* that transgressing the norms of the good girl while wearing one's uniform is considered to be incredibly improper and offensive, as Layla described in 2012:

> We all knew (Raya) was going around with that married man. For one year – one year – she did not attend school. Every day she put on her school uniform and went straight to his shop ... she used to come to my house with her uniform too and I said, 'No! You can't come here with that uniform on'. It is one thing to sneak around with your boyfriend, but don't put everyone else at risk.
>
> (Layla, 20)

Layla's views align with larger society; in 2015 some of the bigger malls have banned entry of all unaccompanied school-uniform wearing students.

Layla later clarified that she did not have a problem with Raya wanting to have a boyfriend, rather it was Raya's overt transgression of the uniform that put other school-going young women at risk. 'Go [*sic*] have relations with your boyfriend, I don't care. Just don't forget other girls have to go to school too.' Layla reminds us that school attendance is still considered a privilege in spite of greater educational achievements by young women. School going has been a hard fought battle for many young women in their homes, and 'at any time they can be taken out, parents sometimes just wait for an excuse'. While many young women do use schooling time to develop relationships, most try to change out of their uniforms at or before their destination. Raya's overt transgression of the outfit can highlight to the community that the school uniform is a trope. This can jeopardise the educational mobilities of many young women. Young people, as well as the NGOs, were anxious about this. 'Uneducated girls like Raya are the reason why other girls have a hard time to actually want to make something better of themselves, to move up and stand on their own feet.' Layla (20) explains her commitment to community change, and reveals her own bias against young women who continue to impede the educational progress of young women in the slums. Layla's opinion of Raya, however, does not undercut young women's manipulation of the good girl in public; rather Layla reinforces that a successful way to pursue one's multiple desires and gain upward mobility without putting oneself and others at risk, was through the careful public presentation of purity. Thus Layla's advocacy for social change operates within a patriarchy where overt and public challenges to gendered norms are limited.

The other fixture in a young woman's wardrobe is the *salwar kameez*, a baggy pyjama pant with a loose tunic top, and a long scarf covering the breasts and hair. Young women are expected to continue to dress in the modest *salwar kameez* throughout marriage. Some young women might 'trade up' to the mature *sari*, which is the uniform for Bengali Muslims. In recent years the *sari* has become the subject of controversy, with many deeming the outfit as both immodest and distinctly Hindu (see Tarlo 2010; Osella and Osella 2007). These public discourses have seen the *sari* being pushed towards the realm of special occasion wear within some families. Outside of immodesty another reason the *salwar kameez* is preferred is related to domestic duties: 'if you wear a *salwar* suit you must wash it the next day and it takes little space to wash and dry and usually dries completely in the day. But you don't wash the *sari* everyday: it takes more water; more space to wash and dry; and hanging space is greater as well … and it is more difficult to work in, so sometimes *salawar* suit is better' (Aysha, 15). The link between domestic responsibilities, traditional gender roles and clothing choice is noteworthy; with limited access to water and the physicality of hand washing, the modest *salwar kameez* is the most popular choice of clothing for young women.

Modest clothing and Bollywood

Making steady inroads into the world of everyday fashion for young women in the *bustees* are Middle Eastern inspired modest Islamic wear. Global Islamic fashion trends, Tarlo reports (2005, 2007, 2010), have made a strong and fashionable impact on young women, particularly in relation to visible Islamic dress including the *niquab* and *burqa*. Traditionally associated with pious Islamic practice in the *bustees*, these robes cover women so as not to draw attention to the body, and allow women to uphold their modesty, especially in public. Both garments are an important means for young women to publicly display their Muslim identity, though these processes may be fraught with contention (Miller 2011; Hussain 2010; Rozario 2006). In the Bihari-dominated slums from where this book draws its material, the *niquab* and *burqa* are accepted modest garments for Muslim women, but they are seldom unfashionable garments.

I have been dress shopping with young women countless times, and it never ceases to amaze me the planning, coordination and effort it takes to systematically change this fundamentally modest outfit into a tailored and embroidered showpiece of one's Muslim identity. Their efforts to change the appearance of the garment have re-configured this traditional black synthetic robe into an adorned outfit in a range of colours and styles which is useful for coordinating to match the wearers' handbag. Bennett (2005a: 54) argues that calculated tailoring and modification of modest garments are ways young Muslim women enact a mode of 'sensual modesty', which enables young women to 'maximize their sexual desirability whilst protecting their sexual purity'. Similarly in the *bustees* by altering the garment in particular ways I understand young women are challenging the traditional interpretation of the robe as an unassuming garment, and publicly crafting a fashionable Muslim identity of their own direction.

In the *bustees* young women buy either ready-made robes or they tailor their own, fashioned from fabric they select themselves. When ready-made robes are sought, the handiwork on the robe is inspected with care. Young women who were on modest budgets can purchase fairly inexpensive plain ready-made robes and apply handiwork – *zardozi*, sequins, beading, and stone work – to the garment at home. Like ready-made jeans, ready-made robes introduce a particular style into the community. At the time of writing the short half-top over a longer robe and matching headscarf was at the height of modest fashion in Kolkata. Traditionally thought of as the cheaper option, tailoring one's own robe can be much more expensive, depending on the fabric, accessories and tailor one chooses. Tailoring an outfit allows young women to choose from a variety of colours, fabrics and textures, rather than the simple and 'boring' black synthetic piece. Darting throughout the back and sides of the robe gives the ordinary cloth shape and highlights a young woman's waist, transgressing the initial purpose of the gown, while buttons, sequins and hand embroidery add style elements to custom gowns.

Like *sari* styles and designs, young women turn to popular culture to inspire their public outfits, especially if they are tailoring their own robe:

> For the outfit I am wearing right now, I saw something similar on Preity Zinta and I really liked the combination, so I bought a similar fabric, and found gold and diamond buttons ... for my scarf I decided to go with this striped black and white fabric because I thought it complemented the buttons.
>
> (Layla, 20)

Layla describes one of her current spring robes, which draws inspiration from an outfit worn by a Bollywood star. In designing the robe she thinks of colour coordinating her headscarf, as the original inspiration did not have this detail. A few weeks after our conversation Layla showed me a tattered cutout from a cinema magazine. The image was of actress Preity Zinta in a tight dark pink top with three-quarter length sleeves and dark denim jeans, posing seductively with ample cleavage. This was the photo that inspired her current modest robe. Layla undertook multiple creative processes to design her outfit: she had to read the magazine; find an outfit she admired; and have the foresight to visualise the outfit as a modest Islamic dress, with a stylish headscarf. Layla laughs off such complexity after I commented on her design process: 'I liked the picture, so I made my *niquab* like that'. Rather than be excluded from the highly sexualised and immodest *filmi* styles, Layla actively participates in the glamorous world of Bollywood fashion by designing her own glamorous modest outfit, and crafting a stylish Muslim identity *through* a popular culture which can be immodest and exclude Muslims. Many of her peers, however, were thoroughly excluded from such fashion consumption. 'I asked my boyfriend if he can [*sic*] buy me jeans for my birthday he replied: "no need you wear *burqa* pants (*kameez*)". I said no one will see them, they will be for him only, but he said he wouldn't approve' (Rena, 17). While Rena was upset about this, she felt she argued her case as best as she could and chose not to jeopardise her relationship for her desire for popular clothing. Rena's example reminds us that there are a multitude of barriers – funding, moral, aesthetic and patriarchal barriers – that exist for girls when crafting a stylish and modern Muslim identity.

'Smart and modern': Western clothes

Bollywood also strongly influences and inspires young women's desire to wear Western clothes. For most young women the opportunity to publicly wear Western clothes is limited to their pre-pubescent girlhoods. Like dancing and singing in public, and socialising with members of the opposite sex, the wearing of Western clothes is acceptable when girls are young. As they start to physically develop they slowly start to discontinue dressing in pants, skirts and blouses in public. Most young women blamed the burden of the 'bad neighbourhood' for this change. Saldanha argues the limited exposure to Western wear for many lower-class people can result in the poor upholding the morals and values of traditional clothing:

> (Upper-class) girls in t-shirts and jeans on Indian streets often have to irritably acknowledge the androcentrism of India's puritan discourse as they defy the looks of the poorer and more traditional boys.
>
> (Saldanha 2002: 343)

The fear of eve-teasing, ever present in the discussion about young women's safety in the slums, enhanced the pressures to wear traditional and modest dress. Debates around clothing are intrinsic to discourses of female safety in India. In her study with youth in Bombay Banaji (2006b) discovered that both young men and women expressed concern over young women wearing *filmi* clothes. She found *filmi* clothes and Western clothes to be synonymous, and respondents in her study claimed that women who wear these clothes may be more prone to sexual violence (Banaji 2006b: 380). These viewpoints were evident in the reaction of the 2012 rape and murder of Nirbhaya in Delhi, with some politicians asking for the banning of skirts and other Western clothes, while other public commentaters questioned the clothing choice Nirbhaya had made that night in an effort to understand how she 'provoked' her assailants.

In the *bustees* young women saw Western clothes and *filmi* clothes as very similar. Indian-style clothing could be *filmi* clothes, but *filmi* ethnic clothes differed from everyday *salwar kameez* – which Raya saw as having 'no cutting and shape' – and did not flatter the body. For young women the ethnic outfits on screen are 'modern' ethnic outfits and in this way both Indian-style and Western-style *filmi* outfits can transgress the acceptable norms of modesty for the average *bustee* girl. 'You couldn't wear jeans here and it's not like you can wear a party *sari* outside to the shop, you'd have trouble either way' (Parveena). While *filmi* ethnic wear is contextually acceptable in the slums, to wear to a wedding, for example, Western clothes had limited public acceptability.

Although most young women in the *bustees* wear traditional clothes and school outfits in public, all of the young women I knew desired to wear trousers, jeans, T-shirts and blouses on a regular basis. In various parts of Asia scholars have shown that Western styles of clothing may be associated with loose sexual morals (Ong 1987; Beazley 2002; Marecek 2004). In particular Saldanha (2002: 343) explains: 'because of India's puritan identification of "vernacular" and "decent", casual and party clothing in Western style means, in itself, an eroticisation of the youthful body and a challenge to traditional authority'. All of the young people I worked with desired to wear Western clothes for a variety of reasons. One reason was that they felt these clothes were more comfortable, and did not require the effort of maintenance that ethnic outfits did. As Mumtaz explained to me, 'for *salawars* you always have to make sure the *dupatta* is in place, with pins. You constantly have to check on it.' The complaint that traditional clothes require a particular kind of upkeep in public was supported by Parveena (18) who added, 'not only do you have to always watch your *dupatta*, the fabric is light so it catches and rips. With jeans you don't have to worry about them tearing, or even washing everyday.'[2] Young women also long to wear Western outfits because they are seen as 'modern' clothing, and in direct contrast to their 'traditional' *salwar kameez*.

For young women in the *bustees* Western clothes are also seen as the public uniform of the upper classes. Thus to publicly wear jeans and a T-shirt in the *bustees* signifies a relational similarity with these class groups, and importantly, an implicit understanding of the language of modern style. As Wilkinson-Weber (2005: 138) comments, many young unmarried urban and upper-class people in India wear Western-style casual clothing as found in Bollywood, and their outfits are put together with careful consideration. It is not surprising that when young women in the *bustees* did have the chance to don Western clothing, they felt they embodied the characteristics of the upper class, as Aysha captions this photo taken of her, 'This is my favourite outfit'.

Sorting through a pile of photos she took, Aysha (15) points to this image with pride, 'I think it makes me look smart and modern. It is so comfortable and I wish I can wear it all the time.' In analysis of the photo Aysha explains that Western clothing presents a strong symbolic contrast to all things traditional, and thus by wearing this outfit she presents a modern identity. Close inspection of the image also highlights more than just a good sense of style: the jean's neat hems; a T-shirt brassiere underneath her top; and a self-confidence that develops from practising such style, all point to a network of support. Like dance and romance, young women receive various levels of private and public support to wear Western clothes in public. As it was with learning dance at *Nach Baliye,* many mothers and aunts are the most supportive of their daughters' clothing style, while fathers provide financial support for clothing. Aysha's mother, for example, provided her daughter with funding to buy a T-shirt after Aysha received a new pair of jeans from *Azeem*.

Figure 5.2 'This is my favourite outfit' (Photo of Aysha, female 15, taken by Layla, female 20)

Aysha's father did not approve of these immodest styles of clothing, with Aysha confessing to me that her father would 'skin her alive' if he ever caught her in such an outfit. However, unlike participation in dance and romance culture, many fathers and young men I knew backed young women's desire to wear Bollywood-inspired Western clothes, especially before marriage:

> We are Muslim ... (but) we have no problem with her wearing jeans, tops, jackets ... not all clothes are acceptable, no mini, no sleeveless, but modest Western wear is fine ... they are still modern but more conservative modern.
>
> (Shazana's father)

Although Shazana's father expressed his support for Western clothes, outfits that breach the norms of modesty did not receive his approval. Asking Shazana's father about the likelihood of young women wearing 'modest' jeans in the slums with less restriction, he is less confident, 'our *bustee* is no good, it is full of cheap minded people who say dirty things. Yes (Shazana) can wear jeans, but outside of the *bustee*. I cannot accept she wears it here, for her own safety.' Shazana's father reiterates that the onus of physical safety is on young women themselves, and clothing choices are important in keeping oneself safe. This mode of rationale puts little responsibility on young men, who continue to eve-tease as 'they cannot be controlled, we can only control our daughters' (Shazana's father).

The risks of physical harm and damage to *izzat* meant Western clothes exist in third spaces. For many it was with parental support that they obtained and wore Western clothes on special occasions with their families, 'far, far away from your *bustee* where we know we won't run into anyone from the *para* (neighbourhood)' (Shazana, 15). Thus the acceptability of Western clothing in the *bustees* is often hinged on who is viewing the Western clothing rather than the article itself.

Viewing a young woman's body is also contextual; for example, many of the parents approved of the sequin-pant and matching short blouse that girls wore during their *Nach Baliye* performance 'when my father saw me in the outfit he said that he didn't even recognise me because I looked foreign' (Shirzad). Shirzad's father related modern Western clothes with a non-Indian identity. He did not encourage her to wear the same clothes in the house or in public, even when away from the *bustees*; '(the pants) were for a special occasion, it was appropriate for that time only' (Shirzad's father). Giving young women temporary permission to wear jeans and blouses allowed adults to support limited transgressions of youth, without backing long-term change that challenges the norms of the community. On the flipside, married Abia received little support to wear alternative clothes. Discourses of 'mistake making' and limited transgressions from the 'good girl' were privileged for young people during the youth period of their lives, and support (within families, and publicly) often ended at marriage.

Western clothes and Bollywood-inspired identities also have strong public supporters, especially within *Azeem*. The NGO sought, and received, clothing donations – especially Western women's clothes – from foreign agencies and sponsors. Upon receiving these donations Layla and Heera sort through the items, picking out clothing for themselves before dividing up the remaining clothes to give to the many NFE centres in operation. These clothes are distributed to young women, and often become treasured items by the entire family, as Aysha's mother explained, 'I told her to keep the jeans nicely inside the *almirah*, so they stay in good shape for when she wears them on our next trip'. By extension, supporting their children's modern fashion also allows some parents to craft a modern identity for themselves – that of the supportive, less conservative and fashion-savvy parent – when outside of the slums.

Clothing and *Nach Baliye*

The process of shifting identities from the good girl to a modern fashion diva is further complicated by time spent on the *Nach Baliye* roof. Upon arriving at the Choreographer's home young women first made their way to the Choreographer's bedroom located on the third floor. Here they changed out of their school uniforms or regular *salwar kameez* into their rehearsal clothes. They also brushed their hair and applied make-up, taking care to look good for their friends and potential partners while rehearsing. In addition to impressing their peers, young people recognised they had limited time to play with fashion, thus it is not surprising that each day new hairstyles, new outfits and new make-up techniques were practised seriously. After rehearsals all of the young women systematically went back into the Choreographer's room and carefully removed their clothes, make-up and accessories, ensuring that not a trace of Bollywood remained on their bodies.

The outfits young people brought for rehearsals varied; some young women had their own Western clothes – jeans and T-shirts – which they kept in their school bags. These items would show up at the rehearsals every day, sometimes unwashed from the previous day, 'I used to bring the same jeans for weeks because I couldn't find a way to wash and dry them for the next day' (Tazeema, 15). Some young women borrowed jeans and T-shirts from friends or family members; these items did not appear regularly as they depended on the permission of the lender. Many younger brothers or cousins lent girls their jeans and tops, an example of male support for young women's alternative identities. Other braver young women 'borrowed' clothes from their brothers or siblings without their permission, careful to return these articles each day. All 'good' Western clothes are precious personal items in the slums. Lending clothes to sisters, friends and relatives, then, is symbolic of the rich level of assistance young women received from their supporters. The fact that no older boys lent their clothes aligns with the expectations of a dominant masculinity where older males should control the behaviours of young women in their families. Asking Tazeema about this she explains, 'yes, well maybe you have to ask (a little brother) if he would give his jeans to us in 5 years, because he probably wouldn't, then it is a question of protecting (his sister's) *izzat* and saving his own face'.

Some young women did not have or did not bring their own Western clothes. Instead they carried a spare *salwar kameez* to practise in, as practising in one's school uniform was considered highly unfashionable, highly transgressive and would require daily washing. Though divisions between young women – those with access to Western clothes and those with no access – could have created tension, young women avoided divisions in the group by circulating clothing and adjusting for various body types by accessorising with belts and clips. Young women used familiar communal social structures to negotiate the use of Western clothing and efficiently administer an informal clothing schedule so that everyone had a chance to wear whatever was available. By changing into outfits before rehearsing young people confirmed with one another their intention to wear a specific outfit, with other women placing informal requests for subsequent rehearsals.

Sharing items in this way is an example of group-imposed social levelling, and a way that 'internal differentiation in status or income that might diminish the community's solidarity *vis-à-vis* the outside world' (Scott 1990: 132) is reduced. Beazley's work with street children also shows how social levelling helps to build subcultural identity (Beazley 2002, 2003). Participation in what eventually turned into a fashion parade on the rehearsal roof also separates young women with *Nach Baliye* experience from those without. Tania explained to me that she was 'more confident walking in jeans than girls who can't come here'. Her experience with Western clothes and the cultural capital gained from the roof divides modern young women from their traditional *salwar kameez*-wearing peers. Through this practice many young women also felt they were gaining critical knowledge about the middle class, 'Yeah I think me and the Choreographer are becoming closer because she always wants to dress me up and style my outfits ... yes it feels good' (Mumtaz, 15).

Young women also recognised that these Bollywood-inspired fashion plays were limited to third spaces. Thus the *Nach Baliye* group made use of their limited freedom to wear 'every kind of modern dress that was available' (Raya, 16), and even crafted their own Western-style fashions including creating tops with their *dupattas*. Like Layla's *niquab* creation inspired by a Bollywood actress, young women on the roof manipulated the original meaning of many modest fashions to support a more *filmi* style. For example, by tying a *dupatta* into a short crop top, *Nach Baliye* girls also shifted the possibilities of the scarf from a symbol of modesty to risqué fashion. Another more extreme example is Mumtaz spending several weeks on the roof pretending she was 'Poo', a popular character in the film *Kabhie Kushi Kabhie Gham* (2001) played by the glamorous Kareena Kapoor. Conversations with Mumtaz (15) revealed that although she had seen this film on television years ago, she always remembered 'Poo's red crop top that she wore in *"you are my sonia"* (song) at the *disc* in the scene with Hritik ... and I know this is my only time to actually wear something like that'. With the help of the Choreographer she fashioned a bandeau-style top similar to Poo's, using a few red *dupatta* scarves, and confidently wore it to rehearse her mixed-sex dance routine. She also mimicked the dance steps that Poo performed at the *disc* in the film, and urged her peers to cheer her on, as Poo did in the famed nightclub scene.

Mumtaz's self-confidence, however, was crafted over a period of time. In the early stages of the rehearsals young women spent significant time tugging at their shirts and frequently adjusting their clothes. Though Mumtaz described to me how she always desired to wear modern clothes and dance in a Bolly-wood style, when given the chance she was initially overwhelmed by the opportunity. Negotiating dancing, mixed-sex interactions and Western clothes was hard in the beginning. 'I first said "ok I'll do this in *salawar*" because it was hard enough to learn dancing with boys'. Mumtaz (15) describes how wearing Western fashion and learning to be modern took time; she first needed to gain confidence with her dance identity before revealing her fashion desires. In contrast to many young women's dominant view of Western clothes being 'the most comfortable', many young women chose to initially wear the comfortable and familiar *salwar kameez* to perfect their dance steps, before graduating to different styles of Western clothes. The separate social space and group support helped young women gain self-confidence to display and draw attention to their bodies. Thus it is not surprising that over time the clothing became tighter and more fitting, and the last week of the rehearsals saw two female participants wearing crop-tops on the roof.

Clothing and local Islam

Initially wearing the *salwar kameez* on the roof allowed young women to perform by the rules of modesty, whilst overtly transgressing the good girl through dance and romance. Like manipulating the serving of food and practising *purdah* on the roof, picking and choosing some 'traditional' clothes allow young women to construct a hybrid identity which emerges out of the third space. This process, however, was full of self-doubt and contradictions. Parveena (18) explains how she struggled with her desire to wear Western clothes and with her understanding of Islam:

> A good girl wears the *burqa* and practices *purdah* strictly at all times … I know I should want to wear the *burqa*, I know that is the right thing to want to wear, but I am not ready for it right now. When I am older I will take the *burqa* seriously … and become a better Muslim … when I become a wife and mother. But now I am young and I want to try things … now I want to wear jeans, does this make me a bad Muslim?
>
> (Parveena, 18)

Here Parveena explains that a good Muslim girl should wear the *burqa*, and modesty is an important way a young woman achieves her Muslim identity.

She explains that the *burqa* protects a young woman's modesty in public and that it signifies to others that she is a 'strict Muslim' and that boys should not be bothered to be interested in her. It is a garment that Parveena understands is easier to wear when older, when the temptations of youth have been fulfilled or averted. The garment is also worn by young women for projecting a chaste identity in public, which is handy for many young women to win the freedom and mobility that contravene the fundamental purpose of the robe. Like Layla (and Muskan in the previous chapter), Parveena also articulates that the *burqa* is a great 'disguise' for many young women. 'No one will bother you in the *burqa*, so you can wear jeans underneath. No one will suspect.' As I have described in the previous two chapters, modest dress helps young women gain access to sexual encounters and win time to learn dance. For Parveena herself the *burqa* carries with it moral, religious and social expectations.

For Parveena, wearing the *burqa* is an ideological decision that places the wearer into a contract (Rozario 2006). It is a serious ideological decision and once she takes the *burqa*, she generally must wear it in public and continue to do so after marriage. For Parveena wearing a *burqa* is to practise Islam correctly, and she sometimes struggled with how her Western-dress-wearing identity fits into her *burqa*-wearing identity. By choosing to wear Western dress Parveena experiences a personal risk. Asking her what this means for her Muslim identity on the roof she proposes a strategy – she is committed to 'do things when I'm young' so her relationship with *haram* clothing and identities was temporary. She would absolve herself from these sins by taking the *burqa* seriously when married and practise an Islamic way of life with more sincerity.

But not all participants experienced these internal risks. On the 2005 *Nach Baliye* roof Raya (16), the female dance captain, felt that modest clothing was a choice and 'you can be a good Muslim even if you don't wear it (*burqa*)'. Rather Raya experienced internal pressure to wear Western clothing, 'Western clothes are better to dance in because you then feel the part, so I have to wear it, I have no choice'. Raya explains that her identity as a dancer within the third space is only complete when she wears Western clothes. Raya's awareness of her 'fundamental incompleteness of the self' (Beck 1992) was obvious to her when she felt something was preventing her from becoming a complete dancer. For Raya to live out her Bollywood-inspired self she had to move, dress and look the part – every aspect of her character had to be in place in order for her to be true to her dancing identity on the roof.

In between Parveena's sense of guilt for wearing jeans and Raya's commitment to Western dress, was Aysha's mixing and matching of fashion styles:

> I did like that skirt and top outfit that Preity (Zinta, an actress) wore, but I won't wear that here. No, I won't wear sleeveless or miniskirts because I do not feel comfortable like that … If I grew up with this, then yes, but I am just not used to it.
>
> (Aysha, 15)

Aysha explained that while she admired the aesthetics of many Western clothes she herself was not comfortable with exposing her upper arms and legs. Within the safe space of the roof Aysha donned jeans, tight-fitting T-shirts and on a few occasions a long skirt. She chose not to wear sleeveless tops and short skirts while her friends and the Choreographer did. 'I guess I wanted to keep some of my modesty, but I did also enjoy showing off all my clothes.' This example shows how the roof was not a competitive space in the sense that the most 'modern' look was most admired. Rather it was a creative space where girls were able to practise, up to their comfort level, a Bollywood fashion sensibility.

The roof is also a space where young people negotiated financial resources. As mentioned, young people's modern fashion and accessories were prized possessions, but by dancing and sweating in the clothes they were effectively sullying them. Most young people were willing to ruin their 'best clothes' and/or face punishment for devaluing someone else's best clothes, because it was important to look their best in this space and take advantage of this freedom. Young people's acceptance that they would ruin their best clothes shows a confidence that they could easily replace them; young men were especially confident about this. My conversations with young men revealed that during the six-month *Nach Baliye* rehearsal period in 2005 (and the subsequent rehearsals in 2007 and 2012 which were about 3 months) almost all of them took up extra weekend shifts at work and purchased new Western clothes and accessories to wear on the roof. Young women were a lot more careful with their clothes because their access to money was more constrained. They took care to keep items of clothing in good condition, placing them in plastic bags when not in use and washing them when they had a chance. They stressed over ruining clothing that did not belong to them, as replacing it was not as easy. Many young women also explained to me that they asked for Western clothes and accessories from their boyfriends as gifts during this time.

Food and independence

Third spaces are also areas where young people can play with their alternative food desires and use food to craft more self-perceived modern identities. For young women in the *bustees* food is one of the most accessible avenues of consumption, and an important aspect of their identity. As Valentine (1999: 491) notes, 'food is perhaps one of the most mundane and taken for granted parts of our everyday life, yet the ways we think about shopping, cooking and eating are actually intensively reflexive'. In India, food consumption is an important visual marker of class, caste and religious identity. The Hindu upper class, especially those belonging to the priestly Brahman caste, are known to be piscatarian (in West Bengal), while other classes and regional groups are known for their consumption of meat. Particular types of food, like pork, are also important cultural dishes for tribal people, Indo-Chinese and Anglo-Indian populations in Kolkata and this food serves to demarcate cultural areas of the city. One could argue that the public availability of beef in spaces like Beck Bagan and Kidderpore reinforces these localities as 'Muslim areas' of Kolkata. Unlike many cities in India, the slaughter and consumption of beef is permissible in Kolkata, with the public selling of beef evident in various 'Muslim neighbourhoods'. Beef consumption is one of the accepted visible markers of Muslim identity in West Bengal, and as Donner (2008) observes, in a multicultural space like Kolkata eating beef helps to reinforce communal divisions, thus food in the city 'is closely tied to the moral and social status of individuals and groups and is never medically or morally neutral' (Appadurai 1988: 10).

Most young women in the *bustees* were able to make limited independent food choices during school. School-going young women bought traditional snacks like *jalmuri* and *achar* during school breaks at stalls set up in front of their school. These consumption opportunities allowed young women to participate in the ritual of eating and sharing with friends. Like sharing clothes, young women shared all their food during snack time and if a young woman did not have spending money she could usually depend on her friends for snacks. In contrast a young woman who did not share her food developed a reputation for being 'cheap' or a 'snob' and could face rejection by the group. Unlike the label of 'poor', these cheap and snobbish young women were considered selfish because they do not play by the rules of friendship. Like the fun and frolic young women experience together in dance and during courtship, sharing and participation in group processes ensures that friendships are sustained.

The consumption choices that young women make at school are limited by the stalls that are available, but even within this restricted environment, young people make conscious food choices. Most young women talked about 'variety' in their snacks, and how they tried their best not to eat the same snack several days in a row. Young women in the *bustees* associated their cheap school snacks as being food for the poor. Upon asking some young women what they would buy if they had unlimited funds for food at school Sakina responded, 'oh, then we would get all the food that kids from good neighbourhoods get, like *biryani* and ice cream ... the stuff we usually have at weddings ... and *chowmein* and patties too'. Sakina felt that upper-class girls ate different snacks at school. Rather than *jalmuri* they have what is considered in this neighbourhood to be 'proper food', *biryani* and meat dishes. Proper meals in a social context also mean meals that are eaten together as a family and are often the main meals of the day (Valentine 1999: 492). Another perceived part of the upper-class food repertoire is what many young women described as 'modern fast food' – foods such as burgers and sandwiches, and food from other nations. Appadurai (1988: 9; 2004) would agree with young women's observations that the exploration of 'new cuisine' is being practised, transmitted and learned in the homes and restaurants of the new middle class.

Changing foodscapes

The last two decades have seen a steady rise in the availability of multi-ethnic and international foods, which has changed the face of public and private food consumption for many people across the nation (Jackson 2004), especially in urban areas. A globalising India has certainly been affected by transnational food movements. Mukhopadhyay argues that while 'the Chinese have lived in Calcutta for about two centuries [the] elevation of fried greasy noodles (*chowmein*) to street-food is a recent phenomenon and has to do with the vogue of South-East Asian food' (Mukhopadhyay 2004: 39).

The changing environment of food selection and consumption in Kolkata has helped to include new and different kinds of food in writing identities for the rich and poor. As Appadurai (1988: 9) notes, 'public eating places in modern India still seek to maintain boundaries among castes, regions, and food preferences'. In particular, street 'junk food' (*habijabi/bhaji*) sold from carts has the distinction of being lower-class food – which Donner (2008) argues has to do with production processes dominated by the lower class – and/or the snacks of school children. Of *habijabi/bhaji*, Mukhopadhyay (2004: 37–38) reflects:

> Like most middle-aged Bengali *bhadraloks*, street-food is an absolute no-no for me...even if I had the robust stomach of a Bengali peasant from Burdwan who can digest even iron (as the Bengali proverb goes), it is doubtful if I would ever venture out of my bland *jhol-bhat* regimen. It is not befitting of a man of my age and class to fall for the lure of street-food. It is not 'respectable'.

For young Muslim women and their families – many of whom operate small food stalls or make snacks for the market in their homes – street junk foods are ordinary snacks that are consumed during afternoon tea and are a part of the everyday food choices available in the *bustees*. Within the home, food experimentation is limited, unlike Donner's (2008) observations in middle-class Kolkata of mothers preparing multi-ethnic and modern cuisine in the home to prevent their children from eating outside and falling ill.

Pizzas and burgers are not cooked within *bustee* homes for a multitude of reasons including the cost of these ingredients, lack of infrastructure and unusual taste combinations. There are rules to be followed in the *bustees* that relate to illness and stomach upset. These rules are similar to those across the state and include no cold or sour foods at night, as these create a sore throat, and no mixing of milk products and vegetable products, as this causes 'acid'. Unlike many of the Muslim diaspora in Europe and America, the consumption of certified *halal* foods, in particular food outside of the home, is not a concern amongst poor people in the slums. In India food certification is a contemporary product of globalisation and is prominent in fast-food culture and packaged meals in the city. Such certification plays little role in young women's consumption of these, or any other, food items. For young women in this community *halal* concerns exist only in relation to pork; places which serve pork are *haram* and are to be avoided. At a focus group at McDonalds in 2011 Maisoon (15) comments, 'as long as there is no pork, it's okay. But pork, yes, I wouldn't come here if they have that, it's a problem for me.' The production of meat and symbols of *halal* meat slaughter is not looked for, as most young women are unaware of this symbol. By 2013 some young people were more exposed to *halal* certification, and even then non-certified (but non-pork-serving) spaces are acceptable because they are a temporary treat, 'and we have our whole lives to buy *halal* from *qusab* (from butchers in the *bustee*)' (Maisoon).

Food and the party

Throughout India relationship to food helps to reinforce gender roles, especially within the home (Donner 2008). In Aliah's house a good girl has a duty to serve all meals. Aliah believes that one day she will take the place of 'main cook' in her married home, which means she would be in charge of preparing and serving meals, and would be the last to eat. For Aliah it is a privilege to eat last, and a good girl should never complain about this:

> A good girl helps her mother prepare meals; she serves everyone food and is always the last one to eat. This is showing her love and commitment to her family. If there is not enough food after the meal, she will fry an egg and some *paapar* (lentil crisps) to eat with rice, it's no big deal. A good girl would never complain.
>
> (Aliah, 16)

Women and girls face nutritional discrimination in India in part due to the practice of women eating last. Aliah is clearly aware of these disadvantages, she explained of her photo, which is of her older sister resting after her meal, and her aunty eating last.

Serving food also played an important role during all three *Nach Baliye* performances I attended. For each show the Organising Committee set aside funds each day to purchase snacks for the dance participants, who were often famished after hours of practice. During a break in practice, young people decided what foods to have and as with school snacks, variety was important and different treats made an appearance on the roof each day. A few young men would go down to the street to buy and carry the food back onto the roof, and young women would then serve the food. Participants enjoyed a variety of savoury snacks – *phuchkha, ghoogni,* and *patties.*[3] A single cake and soda were the only foods to make a consistent daily appearance on the roof.

During my first attendance on the roof in 2005 I initially saw the cake's daily regularity as a group preference for ending a meal with something sweet. Further discussions with young people, however, revealed that cake and

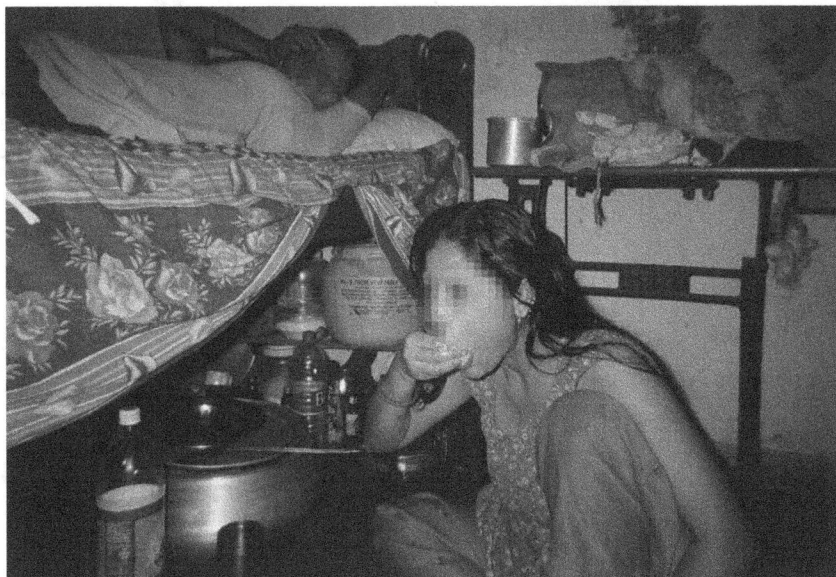

Figure 5.3 'A good girl helps out around the house'

drinks were purposefully served to create a 'party' atmosphere. 'This is a party everyone, don't just sit there!' exclaimed Mumtaz (15) one day in the early days of the rehearsals when the parties were in their infancy. Subsequent months saw parties becoming bigger affairs, with friends from outside *Nach Baliye* trying to secure invitations to the event. Cake and soda was brought onto the roof to purposefully create an imagined party which many young people thought was a regular occurrence among upper-class Indians. Candles also decorated the cake on certain days when youth were able to secure them. The Choreographer and the young women explained to me that they were inspired by Bollywood films, where the hero/heroine and their friends had parties with cake (and candles) and international beverages like Pepsi.

Young people used their time on the roof to create the party, and asked for savoury snacks, cake, soda, as well as a music system, to re-create the standard party sequence in Bollywood films. While celebrating birthdays with sweets and gifts is common, birthday parties with music and dance and a specialised venue are unheard of in the slums, but a growing phenomenon in middle-class Kolkata where restaurants offer party day packages for a limited number of guests. Speaking about her time on the roof, Fiza (19) revealed that it was the first time she attended a party. 'That was my first party ... we had cake and got to listen to music and sing and have fun...the party (on the roof) was really great'. Getting a coveted invite to the party was also exciting for non-*Nach Baliye* participants. Zaria (female, 16) who was a friend of Fiza's, also said, 'Fiza told me about this party, so I brought a change of clothes ... it is my first party too'. Attending parties in 2007 and 2012 showed a greater frequency of Western branded foods, but other than that the excitement and prestige remained.

The daily party allowed youth to experiment with interesting food, and this was an enviable situation, in line with middle-class lifestyles that value eating out and displaying one's wealth (Fernandes 2006). More importantly attending a party bursting with drinks, food and dancing is of critical importance to Bollywood-inspired depictions of a global youth culture. Young women's multi-cuisine experience helped them gain status amongst their peers, and continued to separate the 'cool youth', who participated in *Nach Baliye*, from their lower-status peers with no 'party' experience. I observed young women displaying their higher status at tuition by explaining party images in books and films, and describing taste combinations unknown to many *bustee* girls.

While eating new food was not especially risky, consuming food with young men was definitely a risk. Donner (2008) describes how in middle-class Kolkata intimacy and hierarchies are reinforced through serving, sharing and eating food. Food was certainly used on the roof by both young women and men to emit messages of love, lust and anger as well as to elucidate social hierarchies. On the roof a young man interested in a young woman could express romantic interest by waiting for her to drink her soda before enjoying his own, or even more risky, by feeding her a piece of cake. Developing intimacy through food is a culturally appropriate way to create romance.

Gendered divisions of labour were also reconstructed on the roof using food, with young men responsible for public shopping and monetary negotiations, while young women were responsible for serving food and maintaining the cleanliness of the space. As described in the dance chapter, some young women reinforced the norms of the good girl by taking charge of the food preparation and serving processes. Young women like Tazeema (15) scolded others during food serving, which allowed her to perform a commitment to gender norms. Many young women were annoyed by this performance, 'yeah she's really busy playing housewife on the roof' Zafreen once commented to me. For Zafreen (17) the food-related tasks on the roof were different to those at home. 'Sometimes the boys would help and that was fine, and sometimes they didn't and that was fine too ... we all choose to do different things and I had my chores and they had their chores'. Zafreen felt that within the home serving snacks would be a girl's 'duty', while on the roof it was her 'choice'. She did not feel pressured to enact the self-sacrificing server but instead saw serving as a task to which she was assigned. Zafreen also never waited for the boys to finish their snacks; rather she ate with them at the same time. Tazeema's performance annoyed Zafreen who saw her showboating with the intention of keeping a partner and making other women seem less committed to normative expectations of femininity, but Zafreen conceded that keeping in line with patriarchal standards may impress the boys on the roof, 'but I guess she has to because she wants to impress Waqar'.

Food around the city

Shopping malls and parks where planned excursions occurred are also places where young women make independent food choices and use food to challenge their lower status. Indeed around the world shopping malls are a critical geography for youth culture to flourish. Young women used their time in these third spaces to consume Bollywood-inspired food, clothing and technology. During dates and trips to malls and parks young people have a wider selection of food to choose from compared to school and the *Nach Baliye* roof. Shopping malls in particular offer the opportunity to try 'other cuisine' such as popular international food like pizzas, burgers and fries in food courts within shopping complexes – key edible features of youth culture the world over. This greater food repertoire also comes with increased risk. Outside of the obvious financial risks, food pavilions increase risks because of the sheer number of choices offered. Giddens (1991: 82) notes that overall lifestyle patterns are less diverse than the plurality of choices available in the day-to-day globalised world. To negotiate this landscape of choice, young women turned to Bollywood and peer role models for insight into how to correctly behave in these modern spaces.

For example, Shirzad was taken to a food court for the first time by a boy that she liked. She described how she was confronted by all the choices available to her:

> I wanted to try everything it seemed! But I knew I had to pick one and I was watching the price as well … but everything like burgers and pizzas and sandwiches is all something I wanted to get, I just couldn't make up my mind!
>
> (Shirzad, 16)

The foods that she had to select from were mostly international foods, and she confessed that she had never had the chance before this date 'to actually eat "what is called a burger or pizza"', although she viewed these foods countless times in Bollywood culture. Greatly influenced by Bollywood she used this experience to actually consume the foods she had so long been hearing about. Though she could have chosen regional food, Shirzad felt that in this middle-class youth-dominated public space, with a boy she wanted to impress, she wanted to take on an identity that appreciated international foods, and more importantly, understood international foods. Thus on a date she was keen on exhibiting a more modern identity and used her selection to make a statement.

Here it is helpful to heed food sociologist Falk (1994: 40), who suggests that food as a commodity is consumed not just for nutrition or to stave off hunger, but because of the cultural values that surround it, and the persona that is presented when consuming. On the date Shirzad finally decided on a chicken burger, which had been modified with chilli sauce and lots of onions. She later admitted to me that the burger lacked flavour, and 'could have used more chilli sauce'. But she did not regret her decision, commenting that the experience of being in a food court and choosing from the neat rows of indoor food stalls 'just like the films' was more important than the food she ate. Shirzad's sentiment that the experience was more important than the food aligns with Lupton's (1996: 23) understanding that 'when food is consumed symbolically, its taste is often of relatively little importance; it is the image around the food product that is the most important'.

Food also helps to build intimacy and for most young people dates often revolve around the sharing of a meal. The act of using the same straw or fork during a date is laden with meanings of closeness, especially in a culture where *jutha khana/pina* – the rules of sharing of food and utensils – is often limited to very close relationships. *Jutha* rules are rooted in a Hindu culture where caste contamination is a concern, and where more recently sharing utensils is considered unhygienic. While some families actively do not observe *jutha* rules in direct opposition to this Hindu-rooted practice, in Muslim families I worked with, utensils, glasses and water bottles are only shared in close relationships, such as between siblings. Thus for many young people publicly sharing foods and accompanying utensils implicates young people in a romantic relationship. For example Raya (16) recalled a time she was recognised in the city by her uncle, sharing a straw with her then-boyfriend at a juice stall. When she got home her mother had already received the news. While she was furious that she was out with a young man, she was particularly angry that Raya was caught sharing a straw because this act made it obvious they were girlfriend and boyfriend, or as Raya's mother shouted to her 'now everyone knows what you are doing'.

While food-sharing rules may be an added risk, food courts and restaurants are a safer date venue than other locales such as parks and movie theatres. Accusations of impropriety are more difficult to avoid if caught in spaces that have the potential to be secluded. In the very public food court, filled with men, women and children, one can claim they 'bumped into a brother of a friend'. Skipping school and wearing inappropriate clothing would be more problematic to explain if caught. Thus for many young women using the *burqa* during these outings can help with winning space. While many young women would remove the *burqa* at some time during the date, it is not uncommon for many to keep their gowns on unless totally privacy is guaranteed. This was especially true of women who have been caught in the past. Participation of visibly Muslim young women in these middle-class and globalised spaces is met with pride by many in the slums, as a member of the 2012 *Nach Baliye* Organising Committee describes:

> There is a sense of pride in their acheivements (*sic*) and now you will find that both liberal, and moderate muslim girls in Burkhas are frequenting places like KFC and McDonalds.
>
> (Email correspondence, *Nach Baliye* Organising
> Committee member, male)

This committee member is proud that some seemingly conservative young Muslim women are making their way into these other public spaces and participating in globalised arenas which have normally been thought of as off-limits. Greater participation in globalised spaces in India is linked to middle-class consumption practices and employment. The possibilities for this participation, and the pride they feel when participating, is something many youth like Parveena, Layla and Aysha, share. These young women hope Bollywood-inspired consumption, public employment and greater education will allow them to challenge the dominant discourses of 'poor' Muslim youth.

Conclusion

Scholars researching middle-class youth cultures in India (Banaji 2006a, 2006b; Fernandes 2006; Lukose 2009; Nakassis 2013) argue that although the state encourages participation in the free market across classes, the avenues for participation are not equally supported. While many young women in the *bustees* are trying hard to manage middle-class participation and a higher status we see their limited scope for meaningful paid employment and their dependence on working men, as barriers to fulfilling class and status mobility. As Wilkinson-Weber observes with youth fashion trends in India:

> Advantages in employment and opportunity accrue to those who follow global fashion trends through magazines and television, attend fashion shows and shoots, or browse the internet, particularly against the backdrop of a lack of training programs, poor worker organisation and enduring exclusionary, class-based practices that are reflective of Indian society more generally.
>
> (Wilkinson-Weber 2010: 6)

Barriers that limit *bustee* young women from gaining upward mobility are multiple. One such barrier to full participation is middle- and upper-class youth in Kolkata. In one memorable discussion, while waiting in a cinema hall queue with an elite member of youth society, my acquaintance commented on how she could spot all the lower-class youth at the shopping mall:

> Don't you notice how hard they try? They get dressed up like Rani in a wedding shot and come to the mall (laughs). It's just a mall ... but I guess for them it's a big deal.
>
> (Elite acquaintance)

In this quote we can see how going to the mall and participating in contemporary youth culture is implied to be 'ordinary' for upper-class young people. In contrast for poor youth, the mall is a special place and they use this space for carnivalesque displays of higher status and modern identities. Going to the mall becomes an event, where lower-class youth need to dress up (like film stars, such as Rani Mukerjee) and perform in a particular way.

Entering modern youth spaces in India requires special preparation for poor youth. Moreover, it was their inability to access other exclusive arenas of youth culture, including nightclubs and English films, music and gaming culture, that 'kept' *bustee* youth in their low-class positions. This elite acquaintance is clearly mistaken as most youth across class groups who go to the mall often put in an effort to look good, but the point being made here is that upper, class youth in Kolkata see their participation in a globalising India and their knowledge and membership of a 'cool' youth culture as inherent. For middle- and upper-class youth it is precisely *bustee* youth's *dependence* on Bollywood culture and their self-conscious awareness of their own class position that continues to position them as 'low class' and not indigenous members of a globalising youth culture in India.

In this chapter I examined how young women try to participate in growing and changing arenas of consumption culture in India. Intrinsic to this discussion is young women's relationship between *purdah* and paid employment, and how consumption access is related to societal expectations, self-identity and risk taking. I have shown that third spaces provide an opportunity for young women to experiment with various clothing and food styles and live identities that are inspired by Bollywood. Participation and consumption of certain foods, clothes and spaces give some women cultural capital over their peers and this is used to create more upwardly mobile and higher status identities in the face of many poor young women who have never had the chance to wear jeans or go to a food court. These opportunities for most youth are temporal, and indeed transcience is the hallmark of youth participation in transgressions. Most young people recognise and accept the limited time and space they have to experiment with their identities, before rooting themselves as adults (through marriage). While young women use this time and consumption to subvert the dominant discourses of poor *bustee* youth, they face road blocks in their quest to gain enviable youth cultural capital and related status, not only from within their own class, but from upper classes as well. Many find themselves transitioning into adulthood with few shifts to status. While not completely satisfied with the outcome, many young women are happy to have had their experience of youthful fun, which they can reminisce about fondly when they are older.

Notes

1 The roots of this shift are complex and multifaceted (Jeffrey, Jeffery and Jeffery 2004, 2008; Jeffrey 2010, 2011).
2 The link between domestic responsibilities, traditional gender roles and clothing choice is noteworthy; as Miller (2011) reports, denim jeans are possibly the preferred outfit of Muslim men and not women because men have not met the burden of hand-washing such heavy fabric.
3 *Phuchkha* are puffed crispy shells with a spicy pea and potato mash (also *pani puri* in other parts of India), *ghoogni* is a spicy pea curry and *patties* are puffed pastries with a variety of vegetarian and non-vegetarian fillings.

Conclusion

Young Muslim women in the *bustees* of Kolkata negotiate considerable risks to live more self-directed lives and participate in a Bollywood-inspired youth culture. This book reveals their risky struggles for self-determination in a globalising India, where traditional resources for identity formation are not straightforward and are rapidly changing (Buckingham 2008). Examples of both external and internal risk, and how young women navigate through them have been detailed. In Chapter 3 we see young women negotiate physical violence to participate in a key element of perceived global youth culture – Bollywood dance. We see this participation was temporary and highly restricted. In Chapter 4 young women participate in *haram* premarital relationships, without confirmed prospects for marriage. Chapter 5 shows young women opportunistically indulging in middle-class consumption culture with boyfriends and friends. Throughout the book we see youth making choices about how to live their lives, and the backdrop here is a pan-Indian youth culture where middle-class aspirations, higher education and higher status, are read by many *bustee* youth as 'cool' and desirable.

The experiences of the young women in this book speak to theories of risk, identity and individualisation. Beck (1992: 87) argues that within a risk society risks occur when there is 'a social surge of individualisation [and] at the same time the relations of inequality remain stable'. When young women pursue transgressive identities they challenge the norms of the slums. They are expected to behave in a particular way and place themselves in danger by breaching these normative expectations. Examples of the risks they face include physical violence, slander, forced withdrawal from school, forced marriages and disownment. On the flipside, by not participating in transgressive acts young women risk not keeping up with the *bindaas* youth culture of their middle- and upper-class peers, whose lives they view through Bollywood. They risk being mocked as 'uneducated' by some upwardly mobile peers who are able to gain support for long-term schooling plans and public work opportunities. While participating in consumption, education and work opportunities in a globalising nation are a way for young people to gain status and class mobility in the slums, we see aligning with more middle-class faith-based practices which disapprove of Sufi and Shia traditions as also another way to be a 'modern' youth.

We see throughout this book that changing social norms challenge traditional sources of knowledge, such as community elders, who are often unable to maintain their capacity for guidance. Beck (1992) and Giddens (1991) argue that within changing social systems new 'experts' emerge who challenge the norms and values of traditional culture. In the slums Bollywood popular culture is the most important emerging guide for youth. Bollywood influences young women's participation in different aspects of a globalising nation, including new public and private spaces such as shopping centres and private dance venues.

Bollywood and a modern India

More than just fantasy or entertainment, Bollywood culture helps young women understand what it means to be 'modern' in India. It is an important educational tool for young women particularly in *bustees* where sex education is not standardised, work opportunities are poor and mixed-sex interactions are curbed. Throughout the book we see examples of young women turning to Bollywood to educate themselves through new experiences. Shirzad, for example, relied on knowledge gained from Bollywood to make appropriate food decisions at a shopping centre, while Heera learned from Bollywood how to go on a public date with a local young man. While Bollywood has always been an important guide into all things 'cool', this book has shown how Bollywood is used by young women in the slums to consider a wider range of possible lives than they did before. Thus following Appadurai I show that for young women in the slums Bollywood 'presents a rich, ever-changing store of possible lives'. It is through Bollywood that young women 'see their lives through the prisms of the possible lives offered by mass media ... [thus] fantasy is now a social practice; it enters, in a host of ways, into the fabrication of social lives' (Appadurai 1996: 54).

While Bollywood sets the framework for alternative identities and is eagerly studied by young women, it does not always provide accurate information. After watching films Heera struggled to understand how sexual intercourse occurred, and relying on Bollywood direction for courtship can propagate unequal power relationships. While popular culture is an important role model for youth across India, young women only discuss the power of this role model in certain aspects of their lives. It is *bindaas*, for example, to say one copied their fashion and dance moves from a particular film, but it is embarrassing to say that Bollywood dialogue influenced romantic discussions with one's boyfriend. Many of the young women in this study want to be seen as discerning followers of Bollywood culture and indeed they are influenced by a multitude of literacies – including popular culture, a globalising Islam, family and friends, and community leaders – in their pursuit of more self-directed lives. While multiple literacies help some young women write more 'modern' identities, it is clear that Bollywood significantly shapes young women's understandings of modernity in India. The book thus supports Nandy's (1998: 7) claim that it is 'through' Hindi cinema that poor Indians participate in, understand and explore a modernising India and a globalising world.

Bollywood as an expert intersects with other new and existing authorities including community elders and Islamic teachings. These intersections can create tensions. We see, for example, young women struggling with their commitments to Islamic modesty when dancing on the *Nach Baliye* roof. Many vacillate back and forth between finding ways to accommodate their dance desires as Muslim girls. They use the attitude of *meri marzi* (my choice) to navigate through tricky situations where Bollywood literacies conflict with family and religious expectations. For example, Parveena struggled to explain how dancing with boys was not wrong in Islam. Rather than withdraw from *Nach Baliye* she decided that it was *meri marzi* to dance, and she knew that *Allah* would forgive her. In this example Parveena's *izzat* was not displayed in her actions. Rather, by keeping faith and honour in her heart, by thinking good thoughts and being a good girl in other ways such as by helping with family chores, observing *azan* on the roof and trying to keep up with her studies, she was able to pursue her dance identity without compromising her identity as a 'good Muslim girl'.

Risk, individualisation and youth

While young women are certainly actively negotiating risks to live out transgressive desires and identities, what this research clearly shows is that there is no social shift towards individualisation within slum youth culture. Beck, Giddens and Lash (1994: 128) suggests that individualisation is a key occurrence in a globalising world. They argue that for societal shifts towards individualisation to occur one must be removed from historically prescribed social forms and commitments, experience a loss of traditional security with respect to practical knowledge, faith and guiding norms, and finally be re-embedded in a new type of social commitment. We see throughout the book that 'third spaces' (Bhabha 1994, 1996) like the roof, the shopping plaza, and other geographies of resistance can make room for young women to remove themselves from historically prescribed roles. In these spaces some may experience a 'loss of traditional security' with respect to faith or gender norms. For example, young women challenge aspects of normative femininity and religious understandings on the roof and at the mall.

Identity negotiations within these third spaces reveal calculated and fragmented times for resistance, with a finite beginning and end. The ability to transgress and accept the finite nature of transgressions and re-embed themselves into the *bustees* with modern experiences and some cultural capital, is one way young women understand what it means to be a 'modern' young woman in the slums. This latter point is an important departure from dominant

Euro-centric ideas of risk and individualisation (Beck 1992; Giddens 1992) where shifts to societal structures are the goal.

Another point of departure from Euro-centric ideas of risk and individualisation is the importance of communal risk taking and identity building. In the communal *bustees* young women experience individualised lives *together*. It is through group risk taking that young women are writing individualised identities. Rather than wanting to fulfil all desires all of the time, compromise and selective risk taking guide young women to seek out more self-directed life courses, particularly in third spaces. Success in fulfilling alternative identities in these spaces is greatly dependent on corporate risks. We see throughout the book that young women cooperate with each other in order to pursue alternative identities that align with a Bollywood-inspired youth culture. They depend on their female friends to create cover stories about their whereabouts. Friends provide romantic advice and support during difficult periods; friends and family share clothes, food and accessories, and lend money. Community leaders help fund events and support young people's desires for romance, dance and consumption opportunities.

Young women seldom build their transgressive identities without thinking about having 'fun with friends'. Group dating and group intimacy are examples of how the collective pursuit of transgressive and self-directed identities is both strategic and enjoyable. The book also reveals other support systems in young women's risk taking, and these include both private and public supporters. Elder females are anchors of support; mothers and aunts make excuses for young women to be out of the house and provide crucial emotional and material support. Men can also play an important supporting role, with some boyfriends, cousins and younger brothers providing crucial material support. There are also examples of fathers supporting their daughters' dance identities by allowing them to make 'mistakes' and in the case of Raya, fathers even advocating for their daughter's public dance opportunities.

Importantly we have seen how family support hinges on a temporal acceptance of transgressions to be contained within the period of 'youth'. Rather than being a linear progression based on age or through biology alone, periods of childhood, youth and adulthood are constructed through love and marriage, consumption and by risk taking. Twenty-year-old Layla, an unmarried working 'girl', has a greater ability to participate in transgressive Bollywood dance culture than 16-year-old Abia, her married working peer. Layla's participation hinges on her 'immaturity' because she is a child who is not married and is attending college. Meanwhile Abia is propelled into adulthood because of her early marriage, withdrawal from school, her home-based employment and domestic responsibilities. Layla's transgressions are forgiven and written off as a youthful experience. Abia's inability to participate in Bollywood dance culture is tied to her public reputation as a married responsible woman. Participating in dance would see not only community elders, but her own peers, engage in gossip and violence because Abia would be occupying safe spaces for youth, and engaging in behaviours not appropriate for adults. The book thus shows the importance of the social and cultural constructions of categories of 'youth', 'child' and 'adult' and how these categories are not fixed on biological or developmental realities, as often understood in Western youth studies scholarship.

Another important ally in women's pursuit of more self-directed life courses has been civil society. The formidable impact of non-governmental organisations (NGOs) and community-based organisations (CBOs) in the lives of urban poor youth makes contemporary youth culture very different than one generation ago. Often using language of both 'rights' and 'needs', NGOs and CBOs are helping to shape young women's higher education and paid employment goals. The NGO *Azeem* uses its own funding to organise dance practice spaces, hire cars to chauffeur young people on trips, and put on large public shows. NGO workers like the Organiser took many risks to put on a Bollywood show, and faced a strong backlash from the community. He used his class and social status as a middle-class man from an influential family to stave off long-term harm. His actions show public support for young women's alternative identities. Like parental support, NGOs in the *bustees* see temporary transgressions as an important experience youth should undertake to have fun in their lives, but that long-term transgressions which challenge social expectations – such as the imperative to marry, have children and engage in joint family living – are not appropriate.

Throughout this book we also see how support for young women is not consistent. Parents are quick to use violence against young women to deal with any perceived loss of *izzat*. They also pull their daughters out of school to punish them for their behaviours. Young women fear the topsy-turvy boyfriend who supports them during courtship, but uses his patriarchal power in marriage. Raya, for example, was pleased with her loving and supportive boyfriend during the courtship phase; now married and selling toys on the pavement, she worries about the faithfulness of her husband and is afraid he will take on a second wife. Friendship support is also inconsistent. Young women can be their own worst enemies as gossip and slander are used by female peers to highlight their own good moral standings, and to 'prevent other young women from making something of themselves' (Aysha). For example Abia spreads gossip about Layla being of loose morals; she jealously accuses the college-educated Layla of being unfaithful during her out-of-town work trips. Gossiping in this way allows Abia to write her own chaste-identity despite having poor educational qualifications and marrying early. Abia's strategy to write a chaste and morally superior identity is at odds with Layla's interpretation of her 'backwards' peers who practise early marriage and school truancy. These competitive attitudes damage the possibility of reliable solidarity between young women.

We have seen throughout the book how some young women create social hierarchies through transgressive biographies that include dance, education and paid work. Young women like Layla write their own modern identities in contrast to other young women like Sheena and Abia who have married young and dropped out of school. It is important to note, however, that competition for status and class is grounded in patriarchy. Even if a self-identifying modern young woman like Heera works to obtain higher education and learns to dance, she is limited to what she can do post-marriage in a community where marriage is still the only real way of securing a stable future for oneself.

Thus while the youth period can see young people taking great social risks which challenge gender norms, adulthood must not incorporate values of individualisation and risk, and should not transgress *bustee* norms of young women being married, a mother and living in a joint family. While pursuing more self-directed lives in the *bustees* is a risk-laden project, young women do not desire to free themselves from the influence of family – a key outcome of the individualisation project as conceptualised by Beck (1992). Nor has agency become more important than social structure (including societal rules and resources) as Giddens (1994) suggests. Young women's risk negotiations in the slums take place both externally and internally. Physical violence, slander, gossip and developing bad reputations are some examples of external risks that young women have to navigate. Strategies employed in dealing with these external risks include deliberate performances of the good girl, collaborative risk taking with friends, support from family and community elders and using romantic (boyfriend) and familial relationships (*bhai* relationships, siblings/cousins) to gain certain protection.

Internal negotiations of risks see young women debating within themselves the kind of Muslim girls they wish to be. We see throughout the book that many young women perceive a commitment to Islamic gender norms such as taking the *burqa* full-time and romantic restraint as aspects of life they are committed to pursue when older. The community also supports this; we are reminded of Shirzad who is beaten by her father for dancing with boys but is later forgiven as he appreciates that 'small children make mistakes'. The youth period can accommodate certain transgressions, including transgressions which challenge piety, as long as they are contained to a finite period occurring within the social and culturally constructed period of childhood and youth.

Young women in the *bustees* are not deterred by the temporal limitations of risky identities and desires. Indeed permanence is *not* the goal; an individualised lifestyle is *not* what young women are aiming to achieve, and a permanent break from normative femininities is *not* always desired. Those who do permanently transgress social norms relinquish the kinship support needed to live comfortable lives in the slums. Nargis, for example, struggled with loneliness in her small nuclear family, while Raya worried that her early love-marriage would result in her husband taking a second wife.

Contemporary theories on risk and individualisation have not considered that to be 'modern' means different things to youth in India. Kaur (2002) suggests that ideas of modern behaviours are adjusted for what she calls 'moral advantage' in India. In the slums this adjustment sees young people participating in consumption, dance and love through reflexive consideration of culture and faith. In the *bustees* for example young women do not rush into mixed-sex dance but instead consider Islam's view on such interactions and decide how to appropriately approach Bollywood dance in a culturally sensitive way. Many young women accept that learning and performing mixed-sex dance is a one-time occurrence. They accept that the Western clothes worn when dancing are 'special clothes'. While many desire that their dance identities be performed every day, accepting limited clothing and dance participation allows young women be 'good girls' in the slums.

There is no doubt, however, that compromise and adjustment intersect within a cultural context where there is violence against women, where men and family members beat and harass young women, and where young women use slander and gossip to demean other women. Adjusting and compromising keeps young women safe, but we cannot dismiss how many adjust to participating in dance, romance and consumption culture to hold onto their cultural advantage. As Layla explains:

> Even if I was taken to Canada to do whatever I want, I will always think of my parents and what Islam says about my behaviour and what I am comfortable with. I don't want to shame myself ...I'm an Indian I have to keep some of my modesty.
>
> (Layla, 20)

Layla's viewpoint reminds us that for youth in the *bustees* some aspects of modernity are equated with an imagined Western or upper-class lifestyle. While young women desire class mobility within the slums there are some behaviours, such as *zina*, that most do not wish to engage in. It is a negotiated participation in a globalising India and a Bollywood-inspired youth culture that is the hallmark of what it means to be a 'good' young modern woman in the slums. To be modern in the *bustees* demands calculated risk taking and requires adjusting, compromising and veiling (literally and figuratively) one's transgressive identities for performance during the period of youth, not adulthood.

This book adds to knowledge about what it means to be a young person within a patriarchy by depicting everyday interactions with violence and gendered restrictions. I have shown how young Muslim women in the *bustees* struggle in a patriarchal society and are often excluded from employment, education and other social possibilities. Violence, poverty and inequality are a common part of their lives, but this is not their only reality. Young women carve out spaces of resistance and challenge dominant discourses by winning time and space to learn dance, have romances and participate in consumer culture. Risk management underpins their lived experiences, creating new and different lifestyle possibilities, very different from a decade ago. We see how popular culture is an important role model and how, by turning to Bollywood to guide them, young women challenge dominant opinions within India, and indeed popular global discourses, that young Muslim women in poor slum communities are too reserved to socialise with boys; that they are too submissive to participate in higher education and paid work; that they are victims of patriarchy; and that they live highly controlled and limited lives. While they do face some of these challenges, their skilled negotiation of risk, their savvy identity performances, and their behaviour and consumption patterns, particularly during leisure time, challenge the dominant rhetoric and representations of who they are and what they should be.

Glossary

Achar   Any type of spiced pickle.

adda   To sit and chat (often with snacks and tea) about philosophical/political/religious/economic or other intellectual discourse.

Adjust   A term used in India meaning 'to compromise'.

Almirah   A wardrobe.

Azan   The Muslim call to prayer.

bacha   a small child.

Badnam   Literally translates to 'bad name', and often used in the context of reputation or honour.

Baraat   A large wedding party where guests sing and dance while entering the wedding venue.

Baul   A term to describe both a mystic sect, and a musical style. Prominent in West Bengal and Bangladesh.

bechari   poor darling (affectionate or with concern), someone who is helpless.

bekar   someone who is unemployed, or doing nothing. Can be used as a pejorative term.

Bhai   Brother (can be older or younger).

Bhai-behen   Literally brother-sister.

Bhangra   A traditional Punjabi folk dance.

Bhaji   Fried food. Also used to mean junk food or street food.

Bharata Natyam   A classical Indian dance originating from South India.

Bindaas   To be cool/something cool (a noun and a verb).

Biryani   A traditional meat and rice dish, with a strong Muslim history.

BJP   Bharatiya Janata Party, an Indian political party (Hindu-based party).

Bollywood   The Hindi/Urdu language popular cinema of India. Films often are musicals, having both singing and dancing.

Burqa   A long, loose flowing robe with a loose head-covering, shielding the entire face.

Bustee(s)   An umbrella term used to define both urban and rural slum communities, refugee camps and squatter settlements.

CEO   Chief Executive Officer.

Changra   A person, usually male, who is an idler and has little goals in life. Could also be used to mean a boy who does drugs or a 'loser'. Derogatory.

Chinese Model   A cheap knockoff mobile phone, made in China.

Chowmein   An Indian-Chinese (sometimes referred to as Manchurian or Hakka) dish of fried noodles and Indian spices.

CPI(M)   Communist Party of India, Marxist.

Crore   10 million.

Day of Ashura   The tenth day of Muharram is when Shia Muslims observe the death of Imam Hussein.

Deobandi   An Islamic school of thought, originating in India.

Didi   Older sister.

Disc   A disco venue or nightclub.

Dupatta   A Punjabi term meaning a long scarf. One of the three parts to the *Salwar Kameez* outfit.

Eve-teasing   The sexual harassment of females, usually in public.

Ferengi   A foreigner, can be both male and female.

Filmi   A descriptive term meaning 'inspired by Bollywood'.

Gana   A Hindi/Urdu term meaning song.

Ghar   A house, or a room within a house.

ghatiya   someone who is cheap-minded.

Ghoomta   A headscarf, same as hijab or jilbab in other parts of the Muslim world.

Ghoogni   A spicy lentil snack.

Ghram   A village.

GOI   Government of India.

Goli   A Bengali term meaning a narrow alleyway.

Goonda   A Bengali word meaning thug, perhaps with links to the underworld. Can also be used to mean a person who has committed a crime, or more generally, a 'bad' person. Gunday is the Hindi term.

Habijabi   A Bengali slang term to mean snacks, street food or junk-food.

Halal   Literally means 'acceptable' in accordance with Islam. Often used in the West to denote foods prepared by acceptable Islamic standards.

Haram   An Arabic term, literally translating to 'forbidden'. Specifically used in reference to acts that are forbidden within Islamic texts.

Hero   Literally a male film star, but colloquially used in India to mean a 'cool' male or male friend.

Hi-fi   A slang term meaning top quality. Can be used when referring to a branded item.

Hijab   A scarf used to cover the hair of a female, an Arabic term. Similar to Ghoomta.

Hindutva   Hindu nationalist movement (political).

Housefull   A sold out cinema hall show.

INGO   International Non-Government Organisation.

Inshallah   An Arabic term meaning God-willing. In India it is used mostly by Muslims.

imam   An Islamic leader. May be the spiritual leader of the masjid.

Ishstyle   Style inspired by Bollywood.

Izzat   An Urdu term meaning honour (of a person or a family).

Jalmuri   A type of snack, made of puffed rice, boiled potatoes, fried lentils, chilli, cucumber, onion and mustard oil.

Jhatak/Matak   The hip-shake and pelvic thrusting action found in popular Indian dance.

Jhol-bhat   A Bengali term literally translating to 'gravy and rice'. A euphemism for traditional Bengali food, specifically fish curry and rice.

Jhupris   An unestablished slum settlement; a squatter settlement.

Jodi   A pairing, a couple.

Jutha khana/pina   Food or drink which has been eaten or tasted by someone else. Jutha items are seen as contaminated or polluted in Hindu culture especially.

Kaam se kaam rakhne   An Urdu/Hindi expression meaning to mind your own business.

Kathak   A form of classical Indian dance from North India. This form has a strong Muslim history, and was important during the Mughal period.

Kharaab   Bad or poor.

Kismet   Fate.

Lac   One hundred thousand (100,000).

Loafer   An unemployed or useless person.

Lungi   A sarong, generally worn by men.

Maahaul   A Hindi/Urdu term meaning neighbourhood.

Madraasa   An Islamic school.

Masala   Usually a mixture of five types of spices. Is also used in India as a descriptive term to mean something that is hip and trendy, or inspired by Bollywood culture.

Masjid   An Urdu term meaning mosque.

Mazar   A tomb or mausoleum, can be symbolic, or indeed hold the body of a revered person.

mendhi   A natural dye, applied in different contexts. At weddings it is used to decorate brides and grooms hands, and this is increasingly common across all religious groups in West Bengal.

Meri Marzi   A Hindi/Urdu term that literally translates to 'my choice'.

MLA   Member of the Legislative Assembly, Indian Government.

Muharram   Is the first month of the Islamic calendar, and for Shia Muslims it is an important time to mourn the death of Imam Hussein.

Mulla   An Islamic religious leader.

Nach   Dance (or to dance).

Nach Baliye   Literally translates to 'everyone dance' in Punjabi. The name of both a popular song from the film *Bunty Aur Babli* (2005), and a popular television dance programme. It is also the title of the competitive dance programme that was observed in this research.

Namaz   An Urdu term, referring to the Islamic ritual of praying five times a day

Natak   Drama.

NFE   Non-formal education.

NGO   Non-governmental organisation.

Nikah   An Islamic marriage ceremony.

Niquab   A long, loose flowing robe, usually worn with a hijab. Not a full covering modest dress.

NRI   Non-resident Indian.

Paapar   A thin crispy snack made out of lentils. Also referred to as Papadum or Papad.

Para   A Bengali term meaning local neighbourhood.

Patties   A puffed pastry with an often curried or savoury filling.

phataphat   To do something quickly. Colloquial .

Phuckha   A street snack food of a small puffed crisp, filled with a spicy mash and sour tamarind water. Also known as pani puri or gol gappa in other parts of India.

Pir   A wise Sufi person who is well learned or saint-like. They can be thought to be powerful or mystical with immense knowledge or healing powers.

Proposing   To ask someone to be their girlfriend/boyfriend or to express interest in someone with the intent for romance.

Pukka   Ripe (fruit); well planned or constructed (building); well developed.

Purdah   The separation of men and women in both public and private spaces. Both a Hindu and Islamic term. Can also mean curtain.

Qawwali   Sufi devotional music.

Rabindra Sangeet   Classical Bengali music, inspired by the poetry of Rabindranath Tagore; considered a national musical form in West Bengal.

Rakhi   A thread tied to a brother-figure during the rakshabandhan festival. In Kolkata rakhi-tying is predominantly secular, and symbolically used to cement a brother-sister relationship across religious groups.

Ramzan   An Urdu term, meaning the holy month of fasting. Also referred to as Ramazan or Ramadan in Arabic.

Randi   A 'slut' or a prostitute.

Salam   A Muslim welcome greeting.

Salwar Kameez   A long tunic (shalawar) worn over loose pyjama pants (kameez).

salwar kameez   Baggy pants and a tunic top.

sangeet   A music show, formal or informal, where there may be singing and musical instruments and dancing. A sangeet celebration day is also a part of many wedding customs in India.

Sawm   An Arabic term, meaning 'to fast'. Used in the context of fasting during specific religious events.

Shaadi   A Hindi term, literally meaning a wedding, but often used to describe both a wedding ceremony and reception.

sharam   To feel shame.

Shar'ia   Islamic law text.

Showpiece   A small trinket that one usually displays in the home.

Talaq   A verbal articulation of divorce used by men in Muslim communities. When said three times in succession by a man, he is religiously divorced from his partner.

Tiffin   A term to describe a light lunch or meal. Currently this term is used in India to describe a light lunch or a snack – not a 'proper' larger meal.

Timepass   An Indian-English term used to mean passing the time, an activity that kills time, usually in response to boredom, but also as entertainment or in response to unemployment.

VIP   Executive guests.

Zardosi   Hand embroidery, often done with silver or gold metallic thread.

Zina   An Arabic term meaning illegal sex which includes premarital sex.

Bibliography

Abbas, T. 2011. Honour Related Violence Towards South Asian Muslim Women in the UK: A Crisis of Masculinity and Cultural Relativism in the Context of Islamophobia and the War on Terror. In M.M. Idriss and T. Abbas (eds) *Honour, Violence, Women and Islam*. London: Routledge, pp. 16–28.

Abraham, L. 2001. 'Redrawing the Lakshman Rekha: Gender Differences and Cultural Constructions in Youth Sexuality in Urban India'. *South Asia* xxiv: 133–156.

Abraham, L. 2002. 'Bhai-Behen, True Love, Time Pass: Friendships and Sexual Partnerships among Youth in an Indian Metropolis'. *Culture, Health & Sexuality* 4(3): 337–353.

Abraham, L. 2003. "Risk Behaviour and Misperceptions among Low-Income College Students of Mumbai". In S. Bott, I. Jejeebhoy, I. Shah and C. Puri (eds) *Towards Adulthood: Exploring the Sexual and Reproductive Health of Adolescents in South Asia*. Geneva: World Health Organization, pp. 73–77.

Abraham, Y. 2010. "Boys' Love Thrives in Conservative Indonesia". In A. Levi, M. McHarry and D. Pagliassotti (eds) *Boys' Love Manga: Essays on the Sexual Ambiguity and Cross-Cultural Fandom of the Genre*. Jefferson, NC: McFarland, pp. 44–57.

Ahmed, S. 2004. *The Cultural Politics of Emotion*. London: Routledge.

Akhtar, N. and M. Narula. 2010. 'The Role of Indian Madrasahs in Providing Access to Mainstream Education for Muslim Minority Students: A West Bengal Experience'. *Journal of International Migration and Integration* 11(1): 91–107.

Alexander, M., L. Garda, S. Kanade, S. Jejeebhoy and B. Ganatra. 2006. 'Romance and Sex: Pre-Marital Partnership Formation Among Young Women and Men, Pune District, India'. *Reproductive Health Matters* 14(28): 144–155.

Amin, S. 1997. 'The Poverty-Purdah Trap in Rural Bangladesh: Implications for Women's Roles in the Family'. *Development and Change* 28(2): 213–233.

Appadurai, A. 1988. 'How to Make a National Cuisine: Cookbooks in Contemporary India'. *Comparative Studies in Society and History* 30(1): 3–24.

Appadurai, A. 1996. *Modernity at Large*. Minneapolis, MN: University of Minnesota Press.

Asadullah, N.M. and N. Chaudhury 2009. 'Reverse Gender Gap in Schooling in Bangladesh: Insights From Urban and Rural Households'. *Journal of Development Studies* 45(8): 1360–1380.

Balagopalan, S. 2014. *Inhabiting 'Childhood': Children, Labour and Schooling in Postcolonial India*. Basingstoke: Palgrave Macmillan.

Banaji, S. 2005. 'Intimate Deceptions'. *South Asian Popular Culture* 3(2): 177–192.

Banaji, S. 2006a. *Reading Bollywood: The Young Audience and Hindi Films*. London: Palgrave-MacMillan.

Banaji, S. 2006b. 'Loving with Irony: Young Bombay Viewers Discuss Clothing, Sex and their Encounters with Media'. *Sex Education* 6(4): 377–391.

Bansal, P. 2013. *Youth in Contemporary India: Images of Identity and Social Change.* New Delhi: Springer.

Beazley, H. 2002. 'Vagrants Wearing Makeup: Negotiating Spaces on the Streets of Yogyakarta, Indonesia'. *Urban Studies* 39(9): 1665–1683.

Beazley, H. 2003. 'Voices From the Margins: Street Children's Subcultures in Indonesia'. *Children's Geographies* 1(2): 181–200.

Beazley, H. 2008. "The Geographies and Identities of Street Girls in Indonesia". In M. Gutman and N. Coninck-Smith (eds) *Designing Modern Childhoods: History, Space, and the Material Culture of Children*. New Brunswick, NJ: Rutgers University Press, pp. 233–249.

Beazley, H., S. Bessell, J. Ennew and R. Waterson. 2009. 'The Right to be Properly Researched: Research with Children in a Messy, Real World'. *Children's Geographies* 7(4): 365–378.

Beazley, H., S. Bessell, J. Ennew and R. Waterson. 2011. "How are the Human Rights of Children Related to Research Methodology?" In A. Invernizzi and J. Williams (eds) *The Human Rights of Children: From Visions to Implementation*. Aldershot: Ashgate, pp. 159–177.

Beck, U. 1992. *Risk Society: Towards a New Modernity*. London: Sage.

Beck, U., A. Giddens and S. Lash. 1994. *Reflexive Modernization: Politics, Tradition and Aesthetics in the Modern Social Order*. Cambridge: Polity Press.

Beck, U. and E. Beck-Gernsheim. 1995. *The Normal Chaos of Love*. Cambridge: Polity Press.

Bennett, L.R. 2005a. *Women, Islam and Modernity: Single Women, Sexuality and Reproductive Health in Contemporary Indonesia*. London and New York: Routledge and Curzon.

Bennett, L.R. 2005b. 'Patterns of Resistance and Transgression in Eastern Indonesia: Single Women's Practices of Clandestine Courtship and Cohabitation'. *Culture, Health and Sexuality* 6(4): 6–12.

Bennett, L.R. 2007. 'Zina and the Enigma of Sex Education for Indonesian Muslim Youth'. *Sex Education* 7(4): 371–386.

Bennett, L.R., S. Andajani-Sutjahjo and N. Idrus. 2011. 'Domestic Violence in Nusa Tenggara Barat, Indonesia: Married Women's Definitions and Experiences of Violence in the Home'. *The Asia Pacific Journal of Anthropology* 12(2): 146–163.

Bernal, V. and I. Grewal. 2014. *Theorizing NGOs: States, Feminisms, and Neoliberalism*. Durham, NC: Duke University Press.

Bhabha, H. 1994. *The Location of Culture*. London: Routledge.

Bhabha, H. 1996. *Cultures in Between: Questions of Cultural Identity*. London: Sage.

Bhatia, M., S. Verma and O.P. Murty. 2006. 'Suicide Notes: Psychological and Clinical Profile'. *The International Journal of Psychiatry in Medicine* 36(2): 163–170.

Bhattacharya, N. 2004. 'A "Basement" Cinephilia: Indian Diaspora Women Watch Bollywood'. *South Asian Popular Culture* 2(2): 161–183.

Bijoy, A.K. 2005. 'Star One Terms Nach Baliye a "Universal Success" on Indian-television.com'. Accessed at: www.indiantelevision.org.in/headlines/y2k5/dec/dec 271.htm.

Bourdieu, P. 1984. *Distinction: A Social Critique of the Judgment of Taste* (R. Rice, trans). Cambridge, MA: Harvard University Press.

Buckingham, D. 2008. "Introducing Identity". In D. Buckingham (ed.) *Youth, Identity, and Digital Media*. Cambridge, MA: The MIT Press, pp. 1–24.

Butcher, M. 2003. *Transnational Television, Cultural Identity and Change: When STAR Came to India*. New Delhi: Sage.

The Blank Noise Project. 2007. *Interventions and Techniques of the Project*. Accessed at: http://blog.blanknoise.org/2007/09/interventions-and-techniques.html

Chakravarty, S. 1993. *National Identity in Indian Popular Cinema, 1947–1987*. Austin, TX: University of Texas Press.

Chakrabarty, D. 2002. *Habitations of Modernity: Essays in the Wake of Subaltern Studies*. Delhi: Permanent Black.

Chakraborty, K. 2009. "'The Good Muslim Girl'": 'Conducting Qualitative Participatory Research to Understand the Lives of Young Muslim Women in the bustees of Kolkata'. *Children's Geographies* 7(4): 421–434. Special issue '20 years since the United Nations Convention on the Rights of the Child'.

Chakraborty, K. 2010a. 'The Sexual Lives of Muslim Girls in the bustees of Kolkata, India'. *Sex Education* 10(1): 1–21.

Chakraborty, K. 2010b. 'Unmarried Muslim Youth and Sex Education in the bustees of Kolkata'. *South Asian History and Culture* 1(2): 268–281. Special issue 'Health, Culture and Religion: Critical Perspectives'.

Chakraborty, K. 2012a. 'Young Married Muslim Couples Negotiating their Sexual Lives in the Urban Slums of Kolkata'. *Intersections: Gender and Sexuality in Asia and the Pacific. Issue* 28. Accessed at: www.intersections.anu.edu.au/issue28_contents.htm.

Chakraborty, K. 2012b. 'Virtual Mate-Seeking in the Urban Slums of Kolkata, India'. *South Asian Popular Culture* 10(2): 197–216.

Chakraborty, K., B. Nansen, L. Gibbs and C. MacDougall. 2012. 'Ethical Negotiations: Committees, Methods and Research With Children'. *International Journal of Children's Rights* 20(2): 541–533.

Ciecko, A. 2001. 'Superhit Hunk Heroes for Sale: Globalisation and Bollywood's Gender Politics'. *Asian Journal of Communication* 11(2): 121–143.

Dasgupta, S. 1996. 'Feminist Consciousness in Woman Centred Hindi Films'. *Journal of Popular Culture* 30(1): 173–189.

David, A.R. 2007a. 'Beyond the Silver Screen: Bollywood and Filmi Dance in the UK'. *South Asia Research* 27(1): 5–24.

David, A.R. 2007b. 'Religious Dogma or Political Agenda? Bharatanatyam and its Re-emergence in British Tamil Temples'. *Journal for the Anthropological Study of Human Movement* 14(4). Accessed at: http://jashm.press.illinois.edu/14.4/david.html.

David, A.R. 2010. 'Dancing the Diasporic Dream? Embodied Desires and the Changing Audience for Bollywood Film Dance'. *Participations: Journal of Audience and Reception Studies* 7(2). Accessed at: www.participations.org/Volume%207/Issue%202/special/david.htm.

Davis, M. 2007. *Planet of Slums*. New York: Verso.

Deacon, R. 2014. 'Doing No Harm? Rethinking Vulnerability in Sexuality Research With Young People in the Eastern Cape, South Africa'. *Global Studies of Childhood* 4(4): 264–275.

Derne, S. 1994. "Arranging Marriages: How Fathers' Concerns Limit Women's Educational Achievements". In C. Mukhopadhyay and S. Seymour (eds) *Women, Education, & Family Structure in India*. Boulder, CO: Westview, pp. 83–102.

Derne, S. 2000. *Movies, Masculinity and Modernity: An Ethnography of Men's Filmgoing in India*. Westport, CT: Greenwood Press.

Derne, S. 2005. 'The (Limited) Effect of Cultural Globalization in India: Implications for Culture Theory'. *Poetics* 33: 33–47.

Derne, S. 2008. *Globalization on the Ground*. New Delhi: Sage.

Desai, J. 2004. *Beyond Bollywood: The Cultural Politics of South Asian Diasporic Film*. London: Routledge.

Desai, J., R.K. Dudrah and A. Rai. 2005. 'Bollywood Audiences Editorial'. *South Asian Popular Culture*, 3(2): 79–82.

Deshpande, S. 2005. "The Consumable Hero of Globalized India". In R. Kaur and A. Sinha (eds) *Bollyworld: Popular Indian Cinema through a Transnational Lens*. New Delhi: Sage, pp. 186–203.

Dickey, S. 1993. *Cinema and the Urban Poor in South India*. Cambridge: Cambridge University Press.

Donner, H. 2002. 'One's Own Marriage: Love Marriage in a Calcutta Neighbourhood'. *South Asia Research* 22(1): 79–94.

Donner, H. 2008. *Domestic Goddesses: Maternity, Globalization and Middle Class Identity in Contemporary India*. London: Ashgate.

Donner, H. 2011. *Being Middle Class in India: A Way of Life*. Abingdon: Routledge.

Dudrah, R.K. 2002. 'Zee TV-Europe and the Construction of a pan-European South Asian Identity'. *Contemporary South Asia* 11(2): 163–181.

Dudrah, R. 2005. 'Zee TV: Diasporic Non-terrestrial Television in Europe'. *South Asian Popular Culture* 3(1): 33–47.

Dudrah, R.K. 2006. *Bollywood. Sociology Goes to the Movies*. New Delhi: Sage.

Dudrah, R.K. 2008. "Queer as Desis. Secret Politics of Gender and Sexuality in Bollywood Films in Diasporic Urban Ethnoscapes". In Sangita Gopal and Sujata Moorti (eds) *Global Bollywood. Travels of Hindi Song and Dance*. Minneapolis, MN: University of Minnesota Press, pp. 288–307.

Dudrah, R.K. 2012. *Bollywood Travels: Culture, Diaspora and Border Crossings in Popular Hindi Cinema*. London: Routledge.

Dwyer, R. 2000. *All You Want is Money, All You Need is Love: Sex and Romance in Modern India*. London: Cassell.

Dwyer, R. 2010. 'Bollywood's India: Hindi Cinema as a Guide to Modern India'. *Asian Affairs* 41(3): 381–398.

Dwyer, R. and D. Patel. 2002. *Cinema India: The Visual Culture of Hindi Film*. London: Reaktion.

Dyson, J. 2014. *Working Childhoods: Youth, Agency and Environment in India*. Cambridge: Cambridge University Press.

Eddleston, M. and M. Phillips. 2004. 'Self-poisoning With Pesticides'. *BMJ* 328: 42–44.

Engle, Y. and T. Kasser. 2005. 'Why do Adolescent Girls Idolize Male Celebrities?' *Journal of Adolescent Research* 20(2): 263–283.

Ennew, J. 2010. *The Right to be Properly Researched: How to do Rights-based scientific Research with Children*. Kuala Lumpur: Knowing Children.

Falk, P. 1994. *The Consuming Body*. London: Sage.

Feldman, S. and F. McCarthy. 1983. 'Purdah and Changing Patterns of Social Control among Rural Women in Bangladesh'. *Journal of Marriage and the Family* 45(4): 949–959.

Fernandes, L. 2000a. 'Nationalizing the Global: Media Images, Cultural Politics and the Middle Class in India'. *Media Culture & Society* 22(5): 611–628.

Fernandes, L. 2000b. 'Restructuring the New Middle Class in Liberalizing India'. *Comparative Studies of South Asia, Africa and the Middle East* XX(1&2): 88–112.

Fernandes, L. 2006. *India's New Middle Class: Democratic Politics in an Era of Economic Reform*. Minneapolis, MN: University of Minnesota Press.

Fuller, C. and H. Narasimhan. 2007. 'Information Technology Professionals and the New-Rich Middle Class in Chennai (Madras)'. *Modern Asian Studies* 41(1): 121–150.

Ganguly-Scrase, R. and T. Scrase. 2009. *Globalization and the Middle Classes in India: The Social and Cultural Impact of Neoliberal Reforms*. London: Routledge.

Ganti, T. 2004. *Bollywood: A Guide Book to Popular Hindi Cinema*. New York and London: Routledge.

Ganti, T. 2012. *Producing Bollywood: Inside the Contemporary Hindi Film Industry*. Durham: Duke University Press.

George, A. 2006. 'Reinventing Honourable Masculinity: Discourses From a Working Class Indian Community'. *Men and Masculinities* 9(1): 35–52.

Giddens, A. 1991. *Modernity and Self-Identity. Self and Society in the Late Modern Age*. Cambridge: Polity Press.

Giddens, A. 1992. *The Transformation of Intimacy: Sexuality, Love and Eroticism in Modern Societies*. Cambridge: Polity Press.

Giddens, A. 1994. "Living in a Post-traditional Society". In Ulrich, Beck, Anthony Giddens and Scott Lash (eds) *Reflexive Modernization. Politics, Tradition and Aesthetics in the Modern Social Order*. Cambridge: Polity Press, pp. 56–109.

Gill, A. and A. Brah. 2014. 'Interrogating Cultural Narratives about Honour-based Violence'. *European Journal of Women's Studies* 21(1): 79–93.

GOI 2011. *Government of India, Ministry of Statistics, Census 2011*. Accessed at: http://mospi.nic.in/Mospi_New/site/home.aspx.

Gopal, S. and S. Moorti. 2008. 'Introduction: Travels of Hindi Song and Dance'. In S. Gopal and S. Moorti (eds) *Global Bollywood: Travels of Hindi Song and Dance*. Minneapolis, MN: University of Minnesota Press, pp. 1–62.

Gopinath, G. 2000. 'Queering Bollywood: Alternative Sexualities in Popular Indian Cinema'. *Journal of Homosexuality* 39(3–4): 283–297.

Gopinath, G. 2005. *Impossible Desires: Queer Diasporas and South Asian Public Cultures*. Durham, NC: Duke University Press.

Gosh, D. 2011. 'Eve-teasing: The Role of the Patriarchal System of the Society'. *Journal of the Indian Academy of Applied Psychology* 37 (Special Issue): 100–107.

Grover, S. 2009. 'Lived Experiences: Marriage, Notions of Love, and Kinship Support Amongst Poor Women in Delhi'. *Contributions to Indian Sociology* 43(1): 1–33.

Grover, S. 2010. *Marriage, Love, Caste and Kinship Support: Lived Experiences of the Urban Poor in India*. New York: Social Science Press.

Hennink, M., R. Imran and R. Iqbal. 2005. 'Knowledge of Personal and Sexual Development Amongst Young People in Pakistan'. *Culture, Health & Sexuality* 7(4): 319–332.

Hindustan Times 2007. *Where were the police when Rizwanur died?* October 5. Accessed at: www.hindustantimes.com/comment/edits/where-were-the-police-when-rizwanur-died/article1-251327.aspx.

Husain, Z. 2005. 'Analysing Demand for Primary Education: Muslim Slum Dwellers in Kolkata'. *Economic and Political Weekly* January 8.

Hussain, N.A. 2010. 'Religion and Modernity: Gender and Identity Politics in Bangladesh'. *Women's Studies International Forum* 33(4): 325–333.

Hutnyk, J. 1996. *The Rumour of Calcutta: Tourism, Charity, and the Poverty of Representation*. New York: Zed Books.

ILT. 2004. *Indian Listenership Track Media Research User's Council's Radio Audience Measurement Study With AC Nielsen ORG-Marg*. Accessed at: www.indiantelevi sion.com/special/y2k4/radio.htm.

Jackson, P. 2004. 'Local Consumption Cultures in a Globalizing World'. *Transactions of the Institute of British Geographers* 29(2): 165–178.

Jackson, P. and B. Holbrook. 1995. 'Multiple Meanings: Shopping and the Cultural Politics of Identity'. *Environment and Planning A*,27(12): 1913–1930.

James, A., C. Jenks and A. Prout. 1998. *Theorizing Childhood*. Cambridge: Polity Press.

Jeffrey, C. 2010. *Timepass: Youth, Class and the Politics of Waiting*. Stanford, CA: Stanford University Press.

Jeffrey, C. 2011. "Great Expectations: Youth in Contemporary India". In I. Clark-Decès (ed.) *A Companion to the Anthropology of India*. Oxford: Wiley-Blackwell. doi: 10.1002/9781444390599.ch3.

Jeffrey, C., P. Jeffery and R. Jeffery. 2004. '"A Useless Thing!" or "Nectar of the Gods?" The Cultural Production of Education and Young Men's Struggles for Respect in Liberalizing North India'. *Annals of the Association of American Geographers* 94(4): 961–981.

Jeffery, P., R. Jeffery and C. Jeffrey. 2004. '"View article on Modern Asian Studies website" Islamisation, Gentrification and Domestication: "A Girls' Islamic Course" and Rural Muslims in Western Uttar Pradesh'. *Modern Asian Studies* 38(1): 1–52.

Jeffrey, C., R. Jeffery and P. Jeffery. 2005. 'When Schooling Fails: Young Men, Education and Low Caste Politics in North India'. *Contributions to Indian Sociology*, 39(1): 1–38.

Jeffrey, C., Jeffery, P. and R. Jeffery. 2008. *Degrees Without Freedom? Education, Masculinities and Unemployment in North India*. Stanford, CA: Stanford University Press.

Jeffery, P. and R. Jeffery. 2012. "South Asia: Intimacy and Identities, Politics and Poverty". In R. Fardon, J. Gledhill, O. Harris, T.H.J. Marchand, M. Nuttall, C. Shore, V. Strang and R.A. Wilson (eds) *Sage Handbook of Social Anthropology*. London: Sage, pp. 295–311.

Jejeebhoy, S. 1995. *Women's Education, Autonomy and Reproductive Behaviour*. Oxford: Clarendon Press.

Jejeebhoy, S. and Z. Sathar. 2001. 'Women's Autonomy in India and Pakistan: The Influence of Religion and Region'. *Population and Development Review* 27(4): 687–712.

Kabeer, N. 1994. *Reversed Realities: Gender Hierarchies in Development Thought*. London: Verso.

Kabeer, N. 2013. *Grief and rage in India: Making Violence Against Women History? 50:50 Open Democracy*. Accessed at: www.opendemocracy.net/5050/naila-kabeer/ grief-and-rage-in-india-making-violence-against-women-history (26 November 2015).

Kapur, C.C. 2010. 'Rethinking Courtship, Marriage and Divorce in an Indian Call Centre'. In D. Mines and S. Lamb (eds) *Everyday Life in South Asia*. Bloomington, IN: Indiana University Press, pp. 50–61.

Kaur, R. 2002. 'Viewing the West Through Bollywood: A Celluloid Occident in the Making'. *Contemporary South Asia* 11(2): 199–209.

Kazmi, N. 1998. *The Dream Merchants of Bollywood*. New Delhi: UBS Publishers' Distributors.

Kibria, N. 1995. 'Culture, Social Class, and Income Control in the Lives of Women Garment Workers in Bangladesh'. *Gender & Society* 9(3): 289–309.

Kilby, P. 2011. *NGOs in India: The Challenges of Women's Empowerment and Accountability*. Abingdon: Routledge.

Kohli-Kandhekar, V. 2010. *The Indian Media Business* (3rd edition). Thousand Oaks, CA: Sage.

Kripalani, C. 2007. 'Trendsetting and Product Placement in Bollywood Film: Consumerism through Consumption'. *New Cinemas: Journal of Contemporary Film* 4(3): 197–215.

Kumar, S. 2006. *Gandhi Meets Primetime: Globalization and Nationalism in Indian Television*. Urbana, IL: University of Illinois Press.

Kundu, N. 2003. "Summary of City Case Studies: The Case of Kolkata". In *UN-Habitat Global Report on Human Settlements 2003, The Challenge of Slums*. London: Earthscan, pp. 195–228.

Lamb, S. 2000. *White Saris and Sweet Mangoes: Ageing, Gender and the Body in North India*. Berkeley, CA: University of California Press.

Lukose, R. 2005. 'Consuming Globalization: Youth and Gender in Kerala, India'. *Journal of Social History* 38(4): 915–935.

Lukose, R. 2009. *Liberalization's Children: Gender, Youth and Consumer Citizenship in Globalizing India*. Durham, NC: Duke University Press.

Lupton, D. 1996. *Food, the Body and the Self*. London: Sage Publications.

Madan-Bahel, A. 2007. *Sexual Health and Bollywood Films: A Culturally Based Program for South Asian Teenage Girls*. Amherst: Cambria Press.

Mahmood, S. 2005. *Politics of Piety: The Islamic Revival and the Feminist Subject*. Princeton, NJ: Princeton University Press.

Malhotra, S. and T. Alagh. 2004. 'Dreaming the Nation: Domestic Dramas in Hindi Films post-1990'. *South Asian Popular Culture* 2(1): 19–27.

Mankekar, P. 1999. *Screening Culture, Viewing Politics: An Ethnography of Television, Womanhood, and Nation in Postcolonial India*. Durham, NC: Duke University Press.

Marecek, J. 2004. 'Gender Goes Global: Women's Lives in Transnational Perspective'. *Reviews in Anthropology* 33(3): 281–297.

Maslak, M. and G. Singhal. 2008. 'The Identity of Educated Women in India: Confluence or Divergence?' *Gender & Education* 20(5): 481–493.

Matthews, H., M. Limb and M. Taylor 1998. 'The Geography of Children: Some Ethical and Methodological Considerations'. *Journal of Geography in Higher Education* 22(3): 311–324.

Mazumdar, R. 2000. "From Subjectification to Schizophrenia: The "Angry Man" and the "Psychotic" Hero of Bombay Cinema". In R. Vasudevan (ed.) *Making Meaning in Indian Cinema*. New Delhi: Oxford University Press, pp. 238–264.

Mazzarella, W. 2003. *Shoveling Smoke: Advertising and Globalization in Contemporary India*. Durham, NC: Duke University Press.

McDougall, J., J. Edmeades and S. Krishnan. 2011. '(Not) Talking About Sex: Couple Reports of Sexual Discussion and Expression in Bangalore, India'. *Culture, Health and Sexuality* 13(2): 141–156.

McRobbieA. 2000. *Feminism and Youth Culture* (3rd edition). Basingstoke: Palgrave Macmillan.

Medora, N. 2003. "Mate Selection in Contemporary India: Love Marriages Versus Arranged Marriages". In R. Hamon and B. Ingoldsby (eds) *Mate Selection across Cultures*. Thousand Oaks, CA: Sage, pp. 209–231.

Mehra, S., R. Savithri and L. Coutinho. 2002. 'Sexual Behaviour Among Unmarried Adolescents in Delhi, India: Opportunities Despite Parental Controls'. Paper presented at the IUSSP Regional. Population Conference, Bangkok, June. Accessed at: http://iussp.org/Bangkok2002/S30Mehra.pdf.

Mehta, R. and R. Pandhairpande. 2011. *Bollywood and Globalisation: Indian Popular Cinema, Nation and Diaspora.* New York: Anthem Press.

Mehta, S. 2004. 'Bollywood Confidential'. *New York Times Sunday Magazine,* November 14. Accessed at: www.suketumehta.com/nytm.html (December 2010).

Miller, D. 2011. "The Limits of Jeans in Kannaur, Kerala". In D. Miller and S. Woodward (eds) *Global Denim.* New York: Berg, pp. 87–102.

Mishra, V. 2002. *Bollywood Cinema: Temples of Desire.* New York: Routledge.

Mody, P. 2006. "Kidnapping, Elopement and Abduction: An Ethnography of Love-marriage in Delhi". In Francesca Orsini (ed.) *Love in South Asia.* Cambridge: University of Cambridge Oriental Publications, pp. 207–221.

Mody, P. 2008. *The Intimate State: Love Marriage and the Law in Delhi.* London: Routledge.

Moorti, S. 2005. 'Uses of the Diaspora'. *South Asian Popular Culture* 3(1): 49–62.

Morcom, A. 2013. *Elicit Worlds of Indian Dance: Cultures of Exclusion.* Oxford: Oxford University Press.

Moxon, M. 1998. *Mark Moxon's Travel Writing: Calcutta – India.* Accessed at: www.moxon.net/india/calcutta.html.

Mukhopadhyay, B. 2004. 'Between Elite Hysteria and Subaltern Carnivalesque: the Politics of Street-Food in the City of Calcutta'. *South Asia Research* 24(1): 37–50.

Munshi, S. 2010. *Prime Time Soap Operas on Indian Television.* Delhi: Routledge.

Nakassis, C. 2013. 'Youth Masculinity, "Style" and the Peer Group in Tamil Nadu, India'. *Contributions to Indian Sociology* 47(2): 245–269.

Nandy, A. 1998. *The Secret Politics of Our Desires.* New Delhi: Oxford.

Nandy, A. 2003. 'Notes Towards an Agenda for the Next Generation of Film Theorists'. *South Asian Popular Culture* 1(1): 79–84.

Nandy, A. 2007. 'What Fuels Indian Nationalism?' *Tehelka Online Magazine.* Accessed at: www.tehelka.com/story_main.asp?filename=Fe021404fuels.asp.

Netting, N. 2010. 'Marital Ideoscapes in 21st-Century India: Creative Combinations of Love and Responsibility'. *Journal of Family Issues* 31(6): 707–726.

Nieuwenhuys, O. 2009. 'Is There an Indian Childhood?' *Childhood* 16(2), 147–153.

Nijhawan, A. 2009. 'Excusing the Female Dancer: Tradition and Transgression in Bollywood Dancing'. *South Asian Popular Culture* 7(2): 99–112.

Nilan, P., M. Howson and M. Donaldson. 2007. 'Indonesian Muslim Masculinities in Australia'. *Asian Social Science* 3(9). Accessed at: www.ccsenet.org/ass.htm.

Ninan, S. 1995. *Through the Magic Window: Television and Change in India.* Delhi: Penguin Books Ltd. India.

NYP National Youth Policy. 2014. *Ministry of Youth Affairs and Sports, Government of India. New Delhi, India.* Accessed at: http://yas.nic.in/sites/default/files/NYP%20Brochure.pdf.

Ong, A. 1987. *Spirits of Resistance and Capitalist Discipline: Factory Women in Malaysia.* Albany, NY: State University of New York Press.

Orsini, F. 2006. "Introduction". In F. Orsini (ed.) *Love in South Asia: A Cultural History.* Cambridge: Cambridge University Press, pp. 1–42.

Osella, C. 2012. 'Desires Under Reform: Contemporary Reconfigurations of Family, Marriage, Love and Gendering in a Transnational South Indian Matrilineal Muslim Community'. *Culture and Religion* 13(2): 241–264.

Osella, C. and F. Osella. 2000. *Social Mobility in Kerala: Modernity and Identity in Conflict*. Sterling, VA: Pluto Press.

Osella, C. and F. Osella. 2006. *Men and Masculinities in South India*. London: Anthem Press.

Osella, C. and F. Osella. 2007. 'Muslim Style in South India'. *Fashion Theory: The Journal of Dress, Body & Culture*, 11(2–3): 233–252.

Osella, C. and F. Osella. 2008. 'Islamism and Social Reform in Kerala, South India'. *Modern Asian Studies* 42(2–3): 317–346.

Oza, R. 2001. 'Showcasing India: Gender, Geography, and Globalization'. *Signs* 26(4): 1067–1095.

Oza, R. 2006. *The Making of Neo-Liberal India*. New York: Routledge.

Pande, R., T. Falle, S. Rathod, J. Edmeades and S. Kirshnan. 2011. 'If Your Husband Calls, You Have to Go: Understanding Sexual Agency Among Young Married Women in Urban South India'. *Sexual Health* 8(1): 102–109.

Patel, R. 2010. *Working the Night Shift: Women in India's Call Center Industry*. Stanford, CA: University Press.

Phadke, S., S. Khan and S. Ranade. 2011. *Why Loiter?: Women and Risk on Mumbai Streets*. New Delhi: Penguin.

Prout, A. 2005. *The Future of Childhood*. London: Routledge.

Punathambekar, A. 2005. 'Bollywood in the Indian–American Diaspora'. *International Journal of Cultural Studies* 8(2): 151–173.

Punch, S. 2002. 'Research With Children: The Same or Different From Research With Adults?' *Childhood* 9(3): 321–341.

Raheja, D. and J. Kotari 2004. *Indian Cinema: The Bollywood Saga*. New Delhi: Roli Books.

Rajadhyaksha, A. 2003. 'The "Bollywoodization" of the Indian Cinema: Cultural Nationalism in a Global Arena'. *Inter-Asia Cultural Studies* 4(1): 25–39.

Rajagopal, A. 2001. *Politics after Television: Hindu Nationalism and the Reshaping of the Public in India*. Cambridge: Cambridge University Press.

Rajan, D., D. Dhanraj and K. Lalita. 2011. '"Bahar Nikalna": Muslim Women Negotiate Post-conflict Life in Gujrat'. *Inter-Asia Cultural Studies*, 12(2): 213–224.

Ram, K. 2000. 'Dancing the Past into Life: The Rasa, Nrtta and Raga of Immigrant Existence'. *The Australian Journal of Anthropology* 11(3): 261–273.

Ramasubramanian, S. and M.B. Beth Oliver. 2003. 'Portrayals of Sexual Violence in Popular Hindi Films, 1997–1999'. *Sex Roles* 48(7/8): 327–336.

Rao, S. 2007. 'The Globalization of Bollywood: An Ethnography of Non-Elite Audiences in India'. *The Communication Review* 10(1): 57–76.

Rao, S. 2010. '"I Need an Indian Touch": Globalization and Bollywood Films'. *Journal of International and Intercultural Communication* 3(1): 1–19.

Roohi, S. 2007. Unbecoming Citizens: Muslim Women in Calcutta. Mahanirban Calcutta Research Group. Research Paper. Accessed at: www.mcrg.ac.in/.

Rosario, S. 1992. *Purity and Communal Boundaries: Women and Social Change in a Bangladeshi Village*.London: Zed.

Rosario, S. 2006. 'The New Burqa in Bangladesh: Empowerment or Violation of Women's Rights'. *Women's Studies International Forum* 29(4): 368–380.

Rushdie, S. 1995. *The Moor's Last Sigh*. London: Jonathan Cape.

Sachar Committee. 2006. *Sachar Committee on Social, Economic and Educational Status of the Muslim Community*. (Chairman: Justice Rajinder Sachar), Prime Minister's High Level Committee, Cabinet Secretariat, New Delhi, Government of India.

Salamah, S.A. 2007. 'Dancing, What is Aallowed and What is Not. *Islam online*. Accessed at: www.islamonline.net/servlet/Satellite?pagename=Islamonline-English-Ask_Scholar/FatwaE/FatwaE&cid=1119503545778 (May 2010).

Saldanha, A. 2002. 'Music, Space, Identity: Geographies of Youth Culture in Bangalore'. *Cultural Studies* 16(3): 337–350.

Schielke, S. 2009. 'Being Good in Ramadan: Ambivalence, Fragmentation and the Moral Self in the Lives of Young Egyptians'. *Journal of the Royal Anthropological Institute* 15(1): S24–S40.

Schinder, N. and F. Titzmann. *Introduction. 2015. Youth, Media, and Gender in Post-Liberalization India: Focus on and Beyond the Delhi Gang Rape*. Berlin: Frank & Timme, pp. 9–16.

Scott, J.C. 1990. *Domination and the Arts of Resistance: Hidden Transcripts*. New Haven, CT: Yale University Press.

Sengupta, U. 2010. 'The Hindered Self-help: Housing Policies, Politics and Poverty in Kolkata, India'. *Habitat International* 34(3): 323–331.

Sharma, P., M.K. Unnikrishnan and A. Sharma. 2014. 'Sexual Violence in India: Addressing Gaps between Policy and Implementation'. *Health Policy and Planning*. March doi:10.1093/heapol/czu015.

Shresthova, S. 2004. 'Swaying to an Indian Beat: Dola Goes My Diasporic Heart'. *Dance Research Journal* 36(2): 91–102.

Shresthova, S. 2010. 'Under India's Big Umbrella? Bollywood Dance in Nepal'. *South Asian Popular Culture* 8(3): 309–323.

Simpson, E. 2008. 'The Changing Perspectives of Three Muslim Men on the Question of Saint Worship Over a 10-Year Period in Gujarat, Western India'. *Modern Asian Studies* 42(2–3): 377–403.

Sleightholme, C. and I. Sinha. 1996. *Guilty Without Trial: Women in the Sex Trade in Calcutta*. Kolkata: Stree.

Soares, B. 2005. *Islam and the Prayer Economy: History and Authority in a Malian Town*. Edinburgh: Edinburgh University Press.

Sodhi, G. and M. Verma. 2003. 'Sexual Coercion Amongst Unmarried Adolescents of an Urban Slum in India'. In S. Bott, S. Jejeebhoy and I. Shah (eds) *Towards Adulthood: Exploring the Sexual and Reproductive Health of Adolescents in South Asia*. Geneva: World Health Organization, pp. 91–94.

Srinivas, Lakshmi. 2002. 'The Active Audience: Spectatorship, Social Relations and the Experience of Cinema in India'. *Media, Culture and Society* 24: 155–173.

Srinivas, L. 2005. 'Communicating Globalization in Bombay Cinema: Everyday Life, Imagination and the Persistence of the Local.' *Comparative American Studies* 3(3): 319–344.

Srivastava, S. 2007. *Passionate Modernity, Sexuality, Consumption, and Class in India*. New Delhi: Routledge.

Srivastava, S. 2009. 'Urban Spaces, and Moral middle classes in Delhi'. *Economic and Political Weekly* 44(26): 338–345.

Still, C. 2011. 'Spoiled Brides and the Fear of Education: Honour and Social Mobility Among Dalit in South India'. *Modern Asian Studies* 45(5): 1119–1146.

Svanemyr, J., V. Chandra-Mouli, C. Christiansen and M. Mbizvo. 2012. 'Preventing Child Marriages: First International Day of the Girl Child "My Life, My Right, End Child Marriage'. *Reproductive Health* 9(31). Accessed at: www.biomedcentral. com/content/pdf/1742-4755-9-31.pdf.

Swami, P. 2008. 'The Well-Tempered Jihad: The Politics and Practice of Post-2002 Islamist Terrorism in India'. *Contemporary South Asia* 16(3): 303–322.

Tarlo, E. 2005. 'Reconsidering Stereotypes: Anthropological Reflections on the Jilbab Controversy'. *Anthropology Today* 21(6): 13–17.

Tarlo, E. 2007. 'Hijab in London: Metamorphosis, Resonance and Effects'. *Journal of Material Culture* 12(2): 131–156.

Tarlo, E. 2010. *Visibly Muslim: Fashion, Politics, Faith.* Oxford: Berg.

Trivedi, I. 2014. *Love in India: Marriage and Sexuality in the 21st Century.* New Delhi: Aleph (Rupa Publications).

Uberoi, P. 1998. 'The Diaspora Comes Home: Disciplining Desire in DDLJ'. *Contributions to Indian Sociology* 32(2): 305–336.

Uberoi, P. 2006. *Freedom and Destiny: Gender, Family, and Popular Culture in India.* New Delhi: Oxford University Press.

UNCRC. 1989. 'United Nations Convention on the Rights of the Child', G.A. res. 44/25, annex, 44 U.N. GAOR Supp. (No. 49) at 167, U.N. Doc. A/44/49 (1989), entered into force September 2 1990. /C/93/Add.5 of 16 July 2003.

UNHABITAT. 2003. *The Challenge of Slums – Global Report on Human Settlements 2003.* London: Earthscan.

Valentine, G. 1999. 'Eating in: Home, Consumption and Identity'. *The Sociological Review* 47(3): 491–524.

Vasudevan, R. 2000. *In Making Meaning in Indian Cinema.* New Delhi: Oxford University Press.

Verma, G. 2002. *Slumming India: A Chronicle of Slums and their Saviours.* New Delhi: Penguin.

Verma, P.K. 2007. *The Great Indian Middle Class.* New Delhi: Penguin.

Wang, C. and M.A. Burris. 1997. 'Photovoice; Concept, Methodology and Use for Participatory Needs Assessment'. *Health and Behaviour* 24(3): 369–387.

Wilkinson-Weber, C. 2005. 'Tailoring Expectations'. *South Asian Popular Culture* 3(2): 135–159.

Wilkinson-Weber, C. 2010. 'From Commodity to Costume Productive Consumption in the Making of Bollywood Film Looks.' *Journal of Material Culture* 15(1): 3–29.

Wilkinson-Weber, C. 2011. "Diverting Denim: Screening Jeans in Bollywood". In D. Miller and S. Woodward (eds) *Global Denim.* New York: Berg, pp. 87–102.

Films Cited

2 States (2014)
Production: Dharma Productions and Nadiadwala Grandson Entertainment
Director: Abhishek Varman

Aashiqui 2 (2013)
Production: Super Cassettes Industries Limited (T-Series) and Vishesh Films
Director: Mohit Suri

Aitraaz (2004)
Production: Mukta Arts
Director: Abbas-Mustan

Band Baaja Baaraat (2010)
Production: Yash Raj Films
Director: Maneesh Sharma

Basic Instinct (1992)
Production: Carolco Pictures and Canal +
Director: Paul Verhoeven

Border (1997)
Production: JP Flims
Director: JP Dutta

Bunty Aur Babli (2005)
Production: Yash Raj Films
Director: Shaad Ali (Saigal)

Dabangg (2010)
Production: Arbaaz Khan Productions and Shree Ashtavinayak Cine Vision
Director: Abhinav Singh Kashyap

Dilwale Dulhania Le Jayenge (1995)
Production: Yash Raj Films
Director: Aditya Chopra

Gangs of Wasseypur, Part 1 (2012)
Production: Anurag Kashyap Films and Jar Pictures
Director: Anurag Kashyap

Hum Saath Saath Hain (1999)
Production: Rajshri Productions
Director: Sooraj Barjatya

Kabhie Kushi Kabhie Gham (2001)
Production: Dharma Productions
Director: Karan Johar

Krazzy 4 (2008)
Production: Filmcraft Productions
Director: Jaideep Sen

Lage Raho Munna Bhai (2006)
Production: Vinod Chopra Productions
Director: Raj Kumar Hirani

My Name is Khan (2010)
Production: Dharma Productions
Director: Karan Johar

Neal and Nikki (2005)
Production: Yash Raj Films
Director: Arjun Sablok

Raanjhanaa (2013)
Production: Colour Yellow Pictures and Eros International
Director: Aanand Rai

Rab Ne Bana De Jodi (2008)
Production: Yash Raj Films
Director: Aditya Chopra

Raja Hindustani (1996)
Production: Cineyugg Entertainment and Tips Films
Director: Darmesh Darshan

Slumdog Millionaire (2008)
Production: Warner Brothers, Celador Films, Film4 and Pathé Pictures International
Director: Danny Boyle and Loveleen Tandan

Yeh Jawaani Hai Deewani (2013)
Director: Ayan Mukherjee
Production: Dharma Productions

Television Shows Cited

Boogie Woogie (Sony Pictures Television, 1996–2014)

Dance India Dance (ZeeTV, 2009–present)

Dance India Dance Li'l Masters (ZeeTV, 2012–present)

Dil Dosti Dance (Channel V, 2011–present)

India's Dancing Superstar (STARPlus, 2013–present)

Kyunki Saas Bhi Kabhi Bahu Thi (STARPlus, 2000–2008)

Sasural Simar Ka (Colors, 2011–present)

Index

For Product Safety Concerns and Information please contact our EU
representative GPSR@taylorandfrancis.com
Taylor & Francis Verlag GmbH, Kaufingerstraße 24, 80331 München, Germany

www.ingramcontent.com/pod-product-compliance
Lightning Source LLC
Chambersburg PA
CBHW050440280326
41932CB00013BA/2186